## INTERNETWORKING LANs AND WANs
### Concepts, Techniques and Methods

Internetworking is one of the fastest growing markets in the field of computer communications. However, the interconnection of LANs and WANs tends to cause significant technological and administrative difficulties. This book provides valuable guidance, enabling the reader to avoid the pitfalls and achieve successful connection.
**1993   0  471  93568  9**

## THE MULTIPLEXER REFERENCE MANUAL

Designed to provide the reader with a detailed insight into the operation, utilization and networking of six distinct types of multiplexers, this book will appeal to practising electrical, electronic and communications engineers, students in electronics, network analysts and designers.
**1993  0  471  93484  4**

## PRACTICAL NETWORK DESIGN TECHNIQUES

Many network design problems are addressed and solved in this informative volume. Gil Held confronts a range of issues including through-put problems, line facilities, economic trade-offs and multiplexers. Readers are also shown how to determine the numbers of ports, dial-in lines and channels to install on communications equipment in order to provide a defined level of service
**1991  0  471  93007  5  (Book)**
       **0  471  92942  5  (Disk)**
       **0  471  92938  7  (Set)**

## NETWORK MANAGEMENT
### Techniques, Tools and Systems

Techniques, tools and systems form the basis of network management. Exploring and evaluating these three key areas, this book shows the reader how to operate an effective network.
**1992  0  471  92781  3**

*Please refer to the inside-back cover for further details*

Network management involves many complex problems. Here's a new source of solutions . . .

## International Journal of **Network Management**

Editor-in-Chief
Gilbert Held
4-Degree Consulting
Macon, Georgia, USA

This Journal is dedicated to the dissemination of practical information which enables readers to manage, operate and maintain communications networks.

Articles and columns for the journal are selected to help the reader's evaluation of equipment and systems, to provide a detailed understanding of performance issues, and to discuss the advantages and disadvantages of a variety of networking approaches that can be used to satisfy an organization's communications requirements.

### The Journal:

- examines a variety of internetworking problems and their solutions

- investigates LAN connectivity methods, including performance constraints and implementation issues

- probes the operation and utilization of performance analyzers, monitors and other types of communications test equipment

- provides in-depth coverage of network management systems that operate on mainframes, minicomputers and microcomputers

If you would like to increase the effectiveness of your organization, and keep yourself abreast of the latest advances in network management, then send for further information on the **International Journal of Network Management** today.

## INTERNATIONAL JOURNAL OF NETWORK MANAGEMENT

☐ Please send me subscription details for the International Journal of Network Management

☐ Please send me a free sample copy

**Name** (PLEASE PRINT) ...........................................................................................................................

**Position** ...................................................................................................................................................

**Address** ..................................................................................................................................................

....................................................................................................................................................................

....................................................................................................................................................................

**Date** ........................................................................................................................................................

HELD/TRN
8.93

Dept AC, John Wiley & Sons Ltd
Baffins Lane
Chichester
West Sussex PO19 1UD
UK

# TOKEN-RING
# NETWORKS

# TOKEN-RING NETWORKS

## CHARACTERISTICS, OPERATION, CONSTRUCTION AND MANAGEMENT

**Gilbert Held**
*4-Degree Consulting*
*Macon, GA, USA*

JOHN WILEY & SONS

Chichester · New York · Brisbane · Toronto · Singapore

*Other Wiley Editorial Offices*

John Wiley & Sons, Inc., 605 Third Avenue,
New York, NY 10158-0012, USA

Jacaranda Wiley Ltd, G.P.O. Box 859, Brisbane,
Queensland 4001, Australia

John Wiley & Sons (Canada) Ltd, 22 Worcester Road,
Rexdale, Ontario M9W 1L1, Canada

John Wiley & Sons (SEA) Pte Ltd, 37 Jalan Pemimpin #05-04,
Block B, Union Industrial Building, Singapore 2057

**Library of Congress Cataloging-in-Publication Data**

Held, Gilbert, 1943–
    Token-ring networks : characteristics, operation, construction,
  and management / Gilbert Held.
      p.    cm.
    Includes index.
    ISBN 0 471 94041 0
    1. IBM Token-Ring Network (Local area network system)   I. Title.
  TK5105.8.I2H45    1994
  004.6′8—dc20                                        93–13740
                                                        CIP

**British Library Cataloguing in Publication Data**

A catalogue record for this book is available from the British Library

ISBN 0 471 94041 0

Typeset in $10\frac{1}{2}/12\frac{1}{2}$pt Bookman from author's disks by Text Processing Department,
John Wiley & Sons Ltd, Chichester
Printed and bound in Great Britain by Bookcraft (Bath) Ltd

# CONTENTS

## 2    Network Standards   41

## 9     Managing the Network     275

### Index     303

# PREFACE

The pioneering efforts of an individual many times results in the proverbial 'arrow' imbedded in his or her back. Other times, the work of an individual can have a profound effect upon an industry. In the communications industry, we are indebted to the foresight and efforts of Olof Soderblom, whose pioneering work and patent resulted in the development of token-ring networks—the subject of this book.

This book was written in recognition of the requirement of many persons in small and large organizations, government agencies, and academia to obtain a comprehensive reference to the operation and utilization of token-ring networks. The networks covered in detail in this book include the IBM 4- and 16-Mbps Token-Ring networks and the 100-Mbps Fiber Distributed Data Interface (FDDI) network. In actuality, IBM Token-Ring networks are defined by the IEEE 802.5 standard and are commonly referred to as 802.5 networks. However, several features of the 16-Mbps network, including its operating rate and a feature known as early token release, were not standardized at the time this book was written. In comparison, a significant portion of FDDI was standardized at the time this book was written; however, the standardization process was performed by the American National Standards Institute. Thus, we will refer to both IBM networks collectively as Token-Ring networks and the 100-Mbps network as FDDI in this book to avoid confusion that might otherwise occur if we strictly referenced the networks by their standard, partial standard, or simply referenced them as token-rings.

In developing this book, I attempted to strike a balance between theory and practicality. Thus, I included information on such topics as signal encoding techniques, since knowledge of those techniques provides readers with an insight to determining error conditions and understanding coding efficiencies that affect network performance. Since I like to view myself as a real world author who gets involved in constructing and interconnecting networks, I have included a significant amount of information in this book concerning the operation and utilization of different local and wide area networking devices, such as repeaters, bridges, routers, and gateways. This information is not always applicable to a token-ring network standard; however, this information provides you with an insight into how rings are linked to other rings and different types of computers connected to those rings.

As a professional author, I attach a significant value to reader comments as you are the audience whose requirements for knowledge I am attempting to satisfy. Thus, I sincerely welcome your comments which may assist me in developing future editions to better satisfy your quest for communications information. You can either write to me directly or through my publisher whose address is on this book.

**Gilbert Held**
*Macon, GA*

# ACKNOWLEDGEMENTS

In our modern society, a visit to a bookstore or perusal of a mail order catalog exposes us to hundreds or thousands of books. While it is quite convenient to obtain a book that meets our reading requirements, the process involved in producing that book is literally another story. From the origination of an idea to the reading of a manuscript, preparation of artwork, cover design, typesetting, printing, binding, marketing, and advertising, a large number of persons are directly responsible for putting those books onto the shelf of a bookstore or into the pages of a mail order catalog. Thus, I would be remiss if I did not acknowledge and thank a few of the persons involved in this process.

First, and most important if I wish to go home, I must thank my family. Writing a book requires long weekends and numerous late evenings when my presence is conspicuous by my absence.

The publication of a book requires the backing of a publisher that recognizes an author's idea and its potential to satisfy reader information requirements. To Laura Denny and Ann-Marie Halligan, let me express my thanks in a true international manner. Cheers!

Once I start writing, I do it the old-fashioned way—by hand! I'm not averse to using a laptop or notebook—it's just that creating a technical manuscript with numerous illustrations for me works better when I write and draw on paper. However, the process of taking those author notes and drawings and correctly converting them into an electronic manuscript is an extensive process. Once again, I am indebted to Mrs Carol Ferrell for her fine efforts.

The proofing of the electronic manuscript, its conversion into galley pages, the generation of an appropriate cover, and all those hundreds of 'minor' items are critical for the production of a book. To Mr Stuart Gale, who again has guided one of my books through the production process, I am deeply indebted.

# 1

# INTRODUCTION TO NETWORKING CONCEPTS

One of the most logical assumptions an author can make is that readers will have diverse backgrounds of knowledge and experience. To make this book as valuable as possible to persons with different backgrounds requires an introductory chapter that covers basic networking concepts. Unfortunately, basic concepts for one person may not be similar to the concepts required by another person, which presents an interesting challenge for an author. To meet this challenge, two courses of action were taken. First, this book assumes that some readers will have limited knowledge concerning different types of communications systems available for transporting information, the relationship between wide area networks (WANs) and local area networks (LANs), and the relationship between different types of local area networks. Thus, this introductory chapter was written to provide those readers with a common level of knowledge concerning those important topics. Secondly, since readers have diverse levels of knowledge and experience, it was felt that many persons will have a requirement to immediately become familiar with portions of this book rather than the entire book. To satisfy those readers, each chapter was written to be as independent as possible from preceding and succeeding chapters. Thus, readers who are familiar with wide and local area networking concepts, as well as the technical characteristics of LANs, may elect to skim or bypass this chapter. For other readers, information contained in this chapter will provide a level of knowledge that will make succeeding chapters more meaningful.

In this introductory chapter, we will first focus our attention upon the key concepts behind the construction of wide area networks and local area networks. In doing so we will examine each type of network to obtain an understanding of its primary design goal. Next, we will compare and contrast their operation and utilization to obtain an appreciation for the rationale behind the use of different types of local area networks.

Although this book is about Token-Ring networks, there are other types of local area networks that provide a viable data transportation highway for millions of users. By reviewing the technological characteristics of different types of LANs, we will obtain an appreciation for the governing characteristics behind the use of different local area networks. In addition, to paraphrase a famous quotation, we can safely say few LANs are an island, alluding to the fact that many local area networks will be connected to other LANs and WANs. Due to this, we will conclude this chapter by focusing upon the technological characteristics of local area networks that will form a foundation for discussing a variety of Token-Ring internetworking issues in succeeding chapters in this book.

## 1.1 WIDE AREA NETWORKS

The evolution of wide area networks can be considered to have had its origination in the mid- to late 1950s, commensurate with the development of the first generation of computers. Based upon the use of vacuum tube technology, the first generation computers were physically relatively large, power-hungry devices whose placement resulted in a focal point for data processing and the coining of the term 'data center.'

### Computer-communications evolution

Originally, access to the computational capability of first generation computers was through the use of punched cards. After an employee of the organization used a keypunch to create a deck of cards, that card deck was submitted to a window in the data center, typically labeled input/output (I/O) control. An employee behind the window would accept the card deck and complete a form which contained instructions for running the submitted job. The card deck and instructions would then be sent to a person in production control who would schedule the job and turn it over to operations for execution at a predefined time. Once the job was completed, the card deck and any resulting output would be sent back to I/O control, enabling the job originator to return to the window in the data center to retrieve his or her card deck and the resulting output. With a little bit of luck, programmers might see the results of their efforts on the same day that they submitted their job.

Since the computer represented a considerable financial investment for most organizations, it was understandable that they would be receptive to methods that would enable an extension of access to its computational capability. By the mid-1960s, several computer manufacturers had added remote access capabilities to one or more of their computers.

## Remote batch transmission

One method of providing remote access was obtained by the installation of a batch terminal at a remote location. That terminal was connected via a telephone company supplied analog leased line and a pair of modems to the computer in the corporate data center.

The first type of batch terminal developed to communicate with a data center computer contained a card reader, printer, serial communications adapter, and hard-wired logic in one common housing. The serial communications adapter converted the parallel bits of each internal byte read from the card reader into a serial data stream for transmission. Similarly, the adapter performed a reverse conversion process by converting a sequence of received serial bits into an appropriate number of parallel bits to represent a character internally within the batch terminal. Since the batch terminal was located remotely from the data center, it was often referred to as a remote batch terminal, while the process of transmitting data was referred to as remote batch transmission. In addition, the use of a remote terminal as a mechanism to group a number of card decks representing individual jobs to be executed at the remote data center resulted in the term 'remote job entry terminal' being used as a synonym to reference this device.

Figure 1.1 illustrates in schematic form the relationship between a batch terminal, transmission line, modems, and the data center computer. Since the transmission line connected a

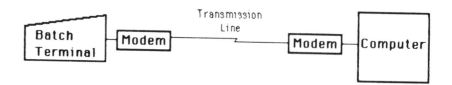

**Figure 1.1** Remote batch transmission. The transmission of data from a remote batch terminal represents one of the first examples of wide area data communications networks.

remote batch terminal in one geographic area to a computer located in a different geographic area, Figure 1.1 represents one of the earliest types of wide area data communications networks.

Paralleling the introduction of remote batch terminals was the development of a series of terminal devices, control units, and specialized communications equipment which resulted in the rapid expansion of interactive computer applications. One of the most prominent collections of products was introduced by the IBM Corporation under the trade name 3270 Information Display System.

## IBM 3270 Information Display System

The IBM 3270 Information Display System was a term used to originally describe a collection of products ranging from interactive terminals, referred to as display stations that communicate with a computer, through several types of control units and communications controllers. Later, through the introduction of additional communications products from IBM and numerous third party vendors and the replacement of previously introduced products, the IBM 3270 Information Display System became more of a networking architecture and strategy rather than a simple collection of products.

First introduced in 1971, the IBM 3270 Information Display System was designed to extend the processing power of the data center computer to remote locations. Since the data center computer typically represented the organization's main or primary computer, the term 'mainframe' was coined to reference a computer with a large processing capability. As the mainframe was primarily designed for data processing, its utilization for supporting communications degraded its performance.

*Communications controller*

To offload communications functions from the mainframe, IBM and other computer manufacturers developed hardware whose primary function was to sample communications lines for incoming bits, group bits into bytes, and pass a group of bytes to the mainframe for processing as well as performing a reverse function for data destined from the mainframe to remote devices. When first introduced, such hardware was designed using fixed logic circuitry and the resulting device was referred to as a communications controller. Later, minicomputers were developed to execute communications programs, with the ability to change the functionality of communications support by the modification of software; a considerable enhancement to the capabilities of this series of products. Because both hard-wired communications controllers and programmed minicomputers performing communications offloaded communications processing from the mainframe, the term 'front-end processor' evolved to reference this category of communications equipment. Although most vendors reference a minicomputer used to offload communications processing from the mainframe as a front-end processor, IBM has retained the term 'communications controller,' even though their fixed logic hardware products were replaced over 20 years ago by programmable minicomputers.

*Control units*

To reduce the number of controller ports required to support terminals as well as the cabling between controller ports and terminals, IBM developed 'poll and select' software to support its 3270 Information Display System. Doing so enabled the communications controller to transmit from one port messages that could be destined to one or more terminals in a predefined group of devices. To share the communications controller port IBM developed a product called a control unit which acts as an interface between the communications controller and a group of terminals.

In general terms, the communications controller transmits a message to the control unit. The control unit examines the terminal address and retransmits the message to the appropriate terminal connected to the control unit. Thus, control units can be considered as devices which economize on the number of lines required to link display stations to mainframe computers. Both local and remote control units are available, with the key difference between the two primarily pertaining to the method of attachment to the mainframe computer and the use of intermediate devices between the control unit and the mainframe.

Local control units are usually attached to a channel on the mainframe, whereas remote control units are connected to the mainframe's front-end processor, which is also known as a communications controller in the IBM environment. Since a local control unit is within a limited distance of the mainframe, no intermediate communications devices, such as modems, are required to connect a local control unit to the mainframe. In comparison, a remote control unit can be located in another building or in a different city and normally requires the utilization of intermediate communications devices, such as a pair of modems, for communications to occur between the control unit and the communications controller. The relationship of local and remote control units to display stations, mainframes, and a communications controller is illustrated in Figure 1.2.

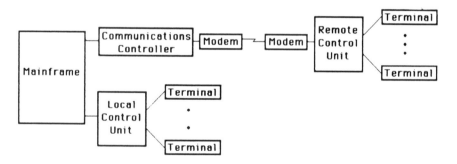

**Figure 1.2**  Relationship of 3270 Information Display System products.

## Network construction

To provide batch and interactive access to the corporate mainframe from remote locations, organizations began to build sophisticated networks. At first, communications equipment such as modems and transmission lines was only obtainable from AT&T and other telephone companies. Commencing in

1974 in the United States with the well-known Carterphone decision, competitive non-telephone company sources for the supply of communications equipment became available. The divestiture of AT&T during the 1980s and the emergence of many local and long-distance communications carriers paved the way for networking personnel being able to select from among two to hundreds of vendors for transmission lines and communications equipment.

As organizations began to link additional remote locations to their mainframes, the cost of providing communications began to escalate rapidly. This in turn provided the rationale for the development of a series of line sharing products referred to as multiplexers and concentrators. Although most organizations operated separate data and voice networks, beginning in the mid-1980s communications carriers began to make available for commercial use high-capacity circuits known as T1 in North America and E1 in Europe. Through the development of T1 and E1 multiplexers, voice, data, and video transmission can share the use of common high-speed circuits. Since the interconnection of corporate offices via the use of communications equipment and facilities normally covers a wide geographical area outside the boundary of one metropolitan area, the resulting network is known as a wide area network.

Figure 1.3 illustrates an example of a wide area network spanning the continental United States. In this example, regional offices in San Francisco and New York are connected with the corporate headquarters located in Atlanta via the use of T1 multiplexers and T1 transmission lines operating at 1.544 Mbps. Assuming each T1 multiplexer is capable of supporting the direct attachment of a private branch exchange (PBX), both voice and data are carried by the T1 circuits between the two regional offices and corporate headquarters. The three T1 circuits can be considered as the primary data highway or backbone of the corporate network.

In addition to the three major corporate sites that require the ability to route voice calls and data between locations, let us assume the corporation also has three smaller area offices located in Sacramento, CA, Macon, GA, and New Haven, CT. If those locations only require data terminals to access the corporate network for routing to the computers located in San Francisco and New York, one possible mechanism to provide network support is through the installation of tail circuits. Those tail circuits could be used to connect a statistical time

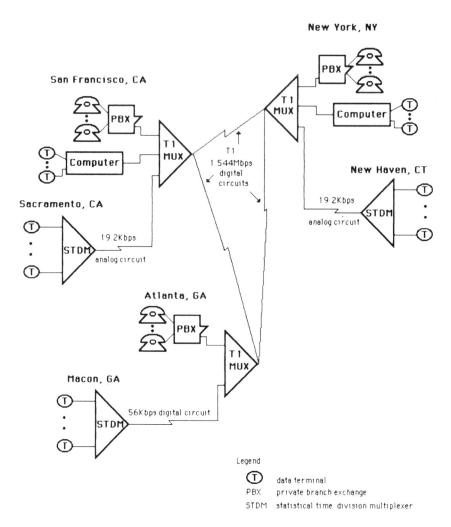

**Figure 1.3** Wide area network example. A wide area network uses telecommunications lines obtained from one or more communications carriers to interconnect geographically dispersed locations.

division multiplexer (STDM) in each area office serving a group of data terminals to the nearest T1 multiplexer, using either analog or digital circuits. The T1 multiplexer would then be configured to route data terminal traffic over the corporate backbone portion of the network to its destination.

## Network characteristics

There are certain characteristics we can associate with wide area networks. First, the WAN is typically designed to interconnect two or more geographically dispersed areas. This interconnection is accomplished by the lease of transmission facilities from one or more communications vendors. Secondly, most WAN transmission occurs at or under a data rate of 1.544 Mbps or 2.048 Mbps, which are the operating rates of T1 and E1 transmission facilities.

A third characteristic of WANs concerns the regulation of transmission facilities used for their construction. Most, if not all, transmission facilities marketed by communications carriers are subject to a degree of regulation at the federal, state, and possibly at the local government level. Even though we now live in an era of deregulation, carriers must seek approval for many offerings prior to making new facilities available for use. In addition, although many of the regulatory controls governing the pricing of services were removed, the communications market is still not a truly free market. Thus, regulatory agencies at the federal, state, and local level still maintain a degree of control over both the offering of new services as well as the pricing of existing and new services.

## 1.2 LOCAL AREA NETWORKS

The origin of local area networks can be traced, in part, to IBM terminal equipment introduced during 1974. At that time, IBM introduced a series of terminal devices designed for use in transaction processing applications for banking and retailing. What was unique about those terminals was their method of connection, with a common cable that formed a loop being used to provide a communications path within a localized geographical area. Unfortunately, limitations in the data transfer rate, incompatibility between each IBM loop system, and other problems precluded the widespread adoption of this method of networking. The economics of media sharing and the ability to provide common access to a centralized resource were, however, key advantages that resulted in IBM and other vendors investigating the use of different techniques to provide a localized communications capability between different devices. In 1977, Datapoint Corporation began selling its Attached Resource Computer Network (Arcnet), considered by most persons to be the first commercial local area networking product to be marketed. Since then, hundreds of companies have developed local area networking products, and the installed base of terminal devices connected to such networks has exponentially increased until they now number in the tens of millions.

## Comparison to WANs

Local area networks can be distinguished from wide area networks by geographic area of coverage, data transmission and error rates, ownership, government regulation, and data routing, and, in many instances, by the type of information transmitted over the network.

*Geographic area*

Concerning the geographic area of coverage, the name of each network provides a general indication of the scope of the area in which they can support the interconnection of devices. As its name implies, a LAN is a communications network which covers a relatively small local area. This small local area can range in scope from a department located on a portion of a floor in a single office building to the corporate staff located on several floors in the building, or to several buildings on the campus of a university.

Regardless of the LAN's area of coverage, its geographic boundary will be primarily restricted by the physical transmission limitations of the local area network. Those limitations are primarily in the area of cable distance between devices connected to the LAN and the total length of the LAN cable. In comparison, a wide area network can provide communications support to an area ranging in size from a town or city to a state, country, or even a good portion of the entire world. Here the major factor governing transmission is the availability of communications facilities at different geographic areas that can be interconnected to route data from one location to another.

To better grasp the differences between LANs and WANs, we can view the LAN as being analogous to our local telephone or cable TV company, while the WAN can be considered to be the long-distance communications carrier. Then, communications support in different cities is provided by the local telephone company in each city. However, for calls between cities, the local telephone companies must interconnect to the long-distance carrier. Similarly, we can have separate LANs in different cities or within different buildings in the same city; however, to interconnect those LANs we would normally require the use of a wide area network.

*Data transmission and error rates*

Two additional areas that both differentiate LANs from WANs, as well as explain the physical limitation of the LAN geographic area of coverage, are the data transmission rate and error rate for each type of network. LANs normally operate at the low megabit-per-second rate, typically ranging from 4 Mbps to 16 Mbps, with one recently standardized fiber optic-based LAN operating at 100 Mbps. In comparison, the communications facilities used to construct a major portion of most WANs provide a data transmission rate at or under the T1 and E1 data rates of 1.544 Mbps and 2.048 Mbps.

Since LAN cabling is primarily within a building or extends over a small geographical area, it is less susceptible to the impairments of nature, such as thunderstorms, lightning, and other acts of God. This in turn enables transmission at a relatively high data rate resulting in a relatively low error rate. In comparison, since wide area networks are based upon the use of communications facilities that are much more distant in length and always exposed to the elements, they have a much higher probability of being disturbed by changes in the weather, or by electronic emissions generated by equipment, as well as such unforeseen problems as construction workers tearing up a street or paving a highway and accidentally causing harm to a communications cable. It is due to the greater exposure to the elements, the higher probability of accidents affecting circuits, and the greater chance of electrical interference that the error rate on WANs is considerably higher than the rate experienced on LANs. On most WANs you can expect to experience an error rate of between 1 in a million and 1 in 10 million ($1 \times 10^6$ to $1 \times 10^7$) bits. In comparison, the error rate on a typical LAN may exceed that range by one or more orders of magnitude, resulting in an error rate of between 1 in 10 million and 1 in 100 million bits.

*Ownership*

> The construction of a wide area network requires the leasing of transmission facilities from one or more communications carriers. Although your organization can elect to purchase or lease communications equipment, the transmission facilities used to connect diverse geographical locations are owned by the communications carrier. In comparison, an organization which installs a local area network normally owns all of the components used to form the network, including the cabling used to form the transmission path between devices.

*Regulation*

> Since wide area networks require transmission facilities that may cross local, state, and national boundaries, they may be subject to a number of governmental regulations at the local, state, and national level. Most of those regulations will govern the services communications carriers can provide to customers and the rates they can charge for those services, with the latter referred to as a tariff. In comparison, regulations affecting local area networks are primarily in the areas of building codes. Such codes regulate the type of wiring that can be installed in a building and whether or not the wiring must run in a conduit.

*Data routing and topology*

> In a local area network, data is routed along a path which defines the network. That path is normally a bus, ring, tree, or star structure and data always flows on that structure. The topology of a wide area network can be much more complex than the network structure of a local area network. In fact, many wide area networks may resemble a mesh structure, with equipment used to reroute data in the event of the failure of a particular communications circuit or equipment, or when too much traffic flows between two locations. Thus, the data flow on a wide area network can dynamically change, while the data flow on a local area network primarily follows the same basic route.

*Type of information carried*

> The last major difference between local and wide area networks concerns the type of information carried by each network. Many

wide area networks support the simultaneous transmission of voice, data, and video information. In comparison, most local area networks are currently limited to carrying data. In addition, although all wide area networks can be expanded to transport voice, data, and video, many local area networks are restricted by design to the transportation of data. Table 1.1 summarizes the similarities and differences between local and wide area networks.

**Table 1.1**   Comparing LANs and WANs.

| Characteristic | Local Area Network | Wide Area Network |
|---|---|---|
| Geographic area of coverage | Localized to a building, group of buildings, or campus | Can span an area ranging in size from a city to the globe |
| Data transmission rate | Typically 4 Mbps to 16Mbps, with fiber optic-based networks operating at 100 Mbps | Normally operate at or below T1 and E1 transmission rates of 1.544 Mbps and 2.048 Mbps |
| Error rate | 1 in $10^7$ to 1 in $10^8$ | 1 in $10^6$ to 1 in $10^7$ |
| Ownership | Usually with the implementor | Communications carrier retains ownership of line facilities |
| Data routing | Normally follows fixed route | Switching capability of network allows dynamic alteration of data flow |
| Topology | Usually limited to bus, ring, tree, and star | Virtually unlimited design capability |
| Type of information carried | Primarily data | Voice, data, and video commonly integrated |

*Utilization benefits*

In its simplest form, a local area network can be considered a cable that provides an electronic highway for the transportation of information to and from different devices connected to the network. By providing the capability to route data between devices connected to a common network within a relatively limited distance, numerous benefits can accrue to users of the network. Such benefits can include the ability for sharing the use of peripheral devices, obtaining common access to data files and programs, the ability to communicate with other people on the LAN by electronic mail, and obtaining access to the larger processing capability of mainframes or minicomputers through common gateways that link a local area network to larger computer systems. Here the gateway can be directly cabled to the mainframe or minicomputer if they reside at the same location or it may be connected remotely via the use of the corporate wide area network.

Peripheral sharing allows network users to access laser printers, CD-ROM systems, and other devices whose utilization may only be required a small portion of the time a workstation is in operation. Thus, users of a LAN can obtain access to resources that would probably be too expensive to justify for each individual workstation user.

The ability to commonly access data files and programs can substantially reduce the cost of software. In addition, shared access to database information allows network users to obtain access to updated files on a real-time basis.

One popular type of application program used on LANs enables users to transfer messages electronically. Commonly referred to as electronic mail, this type of application program can be used to supplement and, in many cases, eliminate the need for paper memorandums.

For organizations with mainframe or minicomputers, a local area network gateway can provide a common method of access to those computers. In comparison, without the use of a LAN gateway, each personal computer requiring access to a mainframe or minicomputer would require a separate method of access. This might increase both the complexity of providing access as well as the cost of providing access.

## Technological characteristics

Although a local area network is a limited-distance transmission system the variety of options available for constructing such networks is anything but limited. Many of the options available for the construction of local area networks are based upon the technological characteristics which govern their operation. Those characteristics include different topologies, signaling methods, transmission media, access methods used to transmit data on the network and the hardware and software required to make the network operate.

*Topology*

The topology of a local area network means the structure or geometric layout of the cable used to interconnect work stations on the network. Unlike conventional data communications networks that can be configured in a variety of ways by the addition of hardware and software, most local area networks are designed to operate based upon the interconnection of stations that follow a specific topology. The most common topologies used in LANs include the loop, bus, ring, star, and tree as illustrated in Figure 1.4.

**Loop**

As previously mentioned in this chapter, IBM introduced a series of transaction processing terminals in 1974 that communicated through the use of a common controller on a cable formed into a loop. This type of topology is illustrated at the top of Figure 1.4.

Since the controller employed a poll and select access method, terminal devices connected to the loop required a minimum of intelligence. Although this reduced the cost of terminals connected to the loop, the controller lacked enough intelligence to distribute the data flow evenly among terminals. A lengthy exchange between two terminal devices or between the controller and a terminal would thus tend to bog down this type of network structure. A second problem associated with this network structure was the centralized placement of network control in the controller. If the controller failed, the entire network became inoperative. Due to these problems, the use of loop systems is restricted to several niche areas and is essentially considered as a derivative of a local area network.

**Bus**

In a bus topology structure, a cable is usually laid out as one long branch onto which branches are used to interconnect each

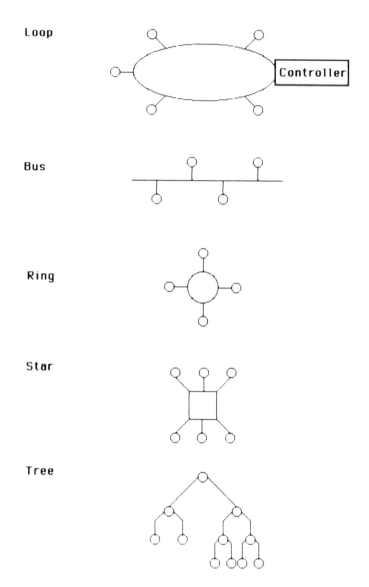

**Figure 1.4** LAN topology. The five most common geometric layouts of local area network cabling form a loop, bus, ring, star, or tree structure.

station on the network to the main data highway. Although this type of structure permits any station on the network to talk to another station, rules are required to govern the action necessary to recover from situations such as when two stations attempt to communicate at the same time. Later in this chapter, we will examine the relationship between the network topology, the method employed to access the network and the transmission medium employed in building the network.

### Ring

In a ring topology, a single cable that forms the main data highway is shaped into a ring. Similar to the bus topology, branches are used to interconnect stations to one another via the ring. A ring topology can thus be considered to be a looped bus. Typically, the access method employed in a ring topology requires data to circulate around the ring, with a special set of rules governing when each station connected to the network can transmit data.

### Star

The fourth major local area network topology is the star structure illustrated in the lower portion of Figure 1.4. In a star network, each station on the network is connected to a network controller. Then, access from any one station on the network to another station can be accomplished through the network controller. Here the network controller can be viewed as functioning similarly to a telephone switchboard, since access from one station to another station on the network can occur only through the central device.

### Tree

A tree network structure can be considered to represent a complex bus. In this topology the common point of communications at the top of the structure is known as the headend. From that location feeder cables radiate outward to nodes, which in turn provide workstations access to the network or provide a feeder cable route to additional nodes from which workstations gain access to the network.

### Mixed Topologies

Some networks, from a topology perspective, are a mixture of topologies. For example, as previously discussed, a tree structure can be considered as a series of interconnected buses. Another example of the mixture of topologies is the IBM Token-Ring network. That network can actually be considered to be a 'star–ring' topology, since up to 8 to 16 devices known as stations are first connected to a common device known as a multistation access unit or MAU, which in turn is connected in a ring topology to other MAUs.

*Comparison of topologies*

Although there is a close relationship between the topology of the network, its transmission media, and the method used to access the network, we can examine topology as a separate entity and make several generalized observations. First, in a star network the failure of the network controller will render the entire network inoperative. This results from the fact that all data flow on the network must pass through the network controller. On the positive side, the star topology is normally in existence within most buildings in the form of telephone wires that are routed to a switchboard. This means that a local area network that can use in-place twisted-pair telephone wires is normally simple to implement and usually very economical.

In a ring network, the failure of any node connected to the ring normally inhibits data flow around the ring. Due to the fact that data travels in a circular path on a ring network, any cable break has the same effect as the failure of the network controller in a star-structured network. Since each network station is connected to the next network station, it is usually easier to install the cable for a ring network. In comparison, if existing telephone wires are not available you would have to cable each station in a star network to the network controller, which could result in the installation of very long cable runs.

In a bus-structured network, data is normally transmitted from one station to all stations located on the network, with a destination address appended to each transmitted data block. As part of the access protocol only the station with the destination address in the transmitted data block will respond to the data. This transmission concept means that a break in the bus may affect only network stations on one side of the break that wish to communicate with stations on the other side of the break. Thus, unless a network station functioning as the primary network storage device becomes inoperative, a failure in a bus-structured network is usually less serious than if a failure occurs in a ring network. While the preceding statement is true, Token-Ring and FDDI networks were designed to overcome the effect of certain types of cable failures. Token-Ring networks include a backup path whose manual placement into operation may be able to overcome the effect of a cable failure between MAUs. In an FDDI network, a second ring can be activated automatically as part of a self-healing process to overcome the effect of a cable break.

A tree-structured network is similar to a star-structured network in that all signals flow through a common point. In the tree-structured network the common signal point is the headend. In addition to the failure of the headend rendering the network inoperative, this network structure requires the transmission of information between some stations to traverse relatively long distances. For example, communications between two stations located at the most distant ends of the network would require a signal to propagate twice the length of the longest network segment. Due to the propagation delay associated with the transmission of any signal the use of a tree structure may result in a degree of response time delay when transmission occurs between two stations located at the most distant node or pair of nodes from the headend.

*Signaling methods*

The signaling method used by a local area network references both how data is encoded for transmission and the use of the frequency spectrum of the media. To a large degree the signaling method is related to the use of the frequency spectrum of the media.

**Broadband versus Baseband**

Two signaling methods used by LANs are broadband and baseband. In broadband signaling the bandwidth of the transmission medium is subdivided by frequency to form two or more subchannels, with each subchannel permitting data transfer to occur independently of data transfer on another subchannel. In baseband signaling only one signal is transmitted on the medium at any point in time.

In comparison to baseband signaling, broadband is more complex. Broadband signaling requires information to be transmitted via the modulation of a carrier signal, requiring the use of special types of modems discussed later in this chapter.

Figure 1.5 illustrates the difference between baseband and broadband signaling with respect to channel capacity. It should be noted that although a twisted-pair wire system can be used to transmit both voice and data, the data transmission is baseband since only one channel is normally used for data. In comparison, a broadband system on coaxial cable can be designed to carry voice and several subchannels of data as well as facsimile and video transmission.

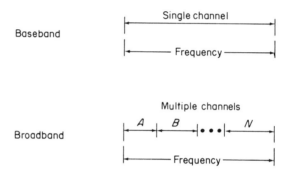

**Figure 1.5** Baseband versus broadband signaling. In baseband signaling the entire frequency bandwidth is used for one channel. In comparison, in broadband signaling the channel is subdivided by frequency in many subchannels.

*Broadband signaling*

A broadband local area network uses analog technology in which high frequency (HF) modems operating at or above 4 kHz place carrier signals onto the transmission medium. The carrier signals are then modified—a process known as modulation, which impresses information onto the carrier. Other modems connected to a broadband LAN reconvert the analog signal block into its original digital format—a process known as demodulation.

Figure 1.6 illustrates the three primary methods of data encoding used by broadband analog systems—amplitude, frequency and phase modulation. The most common modulation method used on broadband LANs is frequency shift keying (FSK), in which two different frequencies are used, one to represent a binary 1 and another frequency to represent a binary 0.

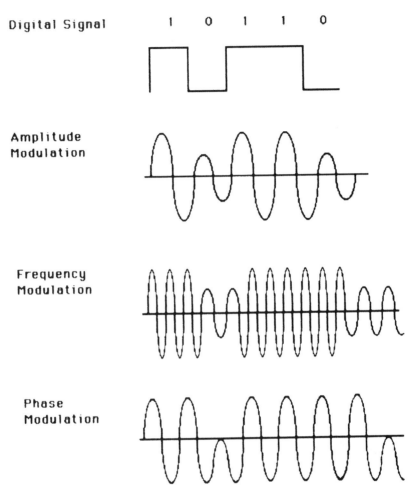

**Figure 1.6** Modulation methods. Baseband signaling uses amplitude, frequency or phase modulation, or a combination of modulation techniques to represent digital information.

Another popular modulation method uses a combination of amplitude and phase shift changes to represent pairs of bits. Referred to as amplitude modulation phase shift keying (AM PSK), this method of analog signaling is also known as duobinary signaling as each analog signal represents a pair of digital bits.

As it is not economically feasible to design amplifiers that boost signal strength to operate in both directions broadband LANs are unidirectional. To provide a bidirectional information transfer capability a broadband LAN will use one channel for inbound traffic and another channel for outbound traffic. These channels can be derived by frequency or obtained from the use of a dual cable.

*Baseband signaling*

In comparison to broadband local area networks that use analog signaling, baseband LANs use digital signaling to convey information.

To understand the digital signaling methods used by most baseband LANs let us first review the method of digital signaling used by computers and terminal devices. In that signaling method a positive voltage is used to represent a binary 1, while the absence of voltage (0 volts) is used to represent a binary 0. If two successive 1 bits occur, two successive bit positions then have a similar positive voltage level or a similar zero voltage level. Since the signal goes from 0 to some positive voltage and does not return to 0 between successive binary 1s it is referred to as a unipolar non-return to zero signal (NRZ). This signaling technique is illustrated at the top of Figure 1.7.

Although unipolar non-return to zero signaling is easy to implement, its use for transmission has several disadvantages. One of the major disadvantages associated with this signaling method involves determining where one bit ends and another begins. To overcome this problem would require synchronization between a transmitter and receiver by the use of clocking circuitry, which can be relatively expensive.

To overcome the need for clocking, baseband LANs use Manchester or Differential Manchester encoding. In Manchester encoding a timing transition always occurs in the middle of each bit while an equal amount of positive and negative voltage is used to represent each bit. This coding technique provides a good timing signal for clock recovery from received data due to its timing transitions. In addition, since the Manchester code always maintains an equal amount of positive and negative voltage, it prevents direct current (CD) voltage buildup, enabling repeaters to be spaced further apart from one another.

The lower portion of Figure 1.7 illustrates an example of Manchester coding. Note that a low to high voltage transition represents a binary 1, while a high to low voltage transition represents a binary 0. Under Differential Manchester encoding the voltage transition is used only to provide clocking. The encoding of a binary 0 or 1 is represented by the presence or absence of a transition at the beginning of each bit period.

Unipolar non-return to zero

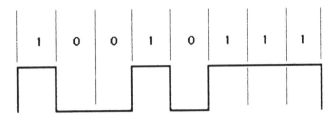

Manchester coding

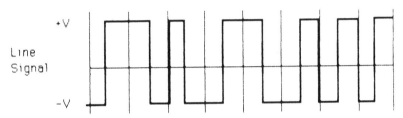

**Figure 1.7** Manchester coding. In Manchester coding, a timing transition occurs in the middle of each bit and the line code maintains an equal amount of positive and negative voltage.

Readers are referred to Chapter 4 for specific information concerning Differential Manchester encoding used for signaling on IBM Token-Ring networks.

Both Manchester and Differential Manchester encoding use two signal changes (2 baud) to represent each bit. While 8- and 32-Mbaud signaling components are reasonably priced and are incorporated into 4- and 16-Mbps Token-Ring networks, the 100-Mbps operating rate of FDDI would require a 200-Mbaud signaling rate if either coding technique were used. Due to the expense associated with building components to provide that signaling rate, FDDI uses a different coding technique known as 4B/5B encoding. Under 4B/5B encoding every group of four bits is encoded using a five-bit pattern. This signaling technique only requires a signaling rate of 125 Mbaud to obtain a 100-Mbps operating rate.

*Transmission medium*

The transmission medium used in a local area network can range in scope from 'twisted-pair' wire, such as is used in conventional telephone lines, to coaxial cable, fiber optic cable and the atmosphere which is used by some transmission schemes, including FM radio and infrared. Each transmission medium has a number of advantages and disadvantages associated with its use in comparison to other mediums. The primary differences between media concern their cost and ease of installation, the bandwidth of the cable which may permit only one or several transmission sessions to occur simultaneously, the maximum speed of communications permitted and the geographic scope of the network that the medium supports.

**Twisted-pair Wire**

In addition to being the most inexpensive medium available for LAN installations, twisted-pair wire is very easy to install. Since this wiring uses the RJ11 and RJ45 modular connectors used with the telephone system, once a wire is cut and a connector fastened the attachment of the connector to network devices is extremely simple. Normally, a screwdriver and perhaps a pocket knife are the only tools required for the installation of twisted-pair wire. Anyone who has hooked up a pair of speakers to a stereo set normally has the ability to install this transmission medium.

Although inexpensive and easy to install, unshielded twisted-pair (UTP) wire is very susceptible to noise generated by fluorescent light ballasts and electrical machinery. In addition, a length of twisted-pair wire acts as an antenna. Thus, the longer the wire length the greater the noise it gathers. At a certain length the received noise will obliterate the signal which attenuates or decreases in strength as it propagates along the length of the wire. This noise can affect the error rate of data transmitted on the network, although the utilization of lead-shielded twisted-pair (STP) cable can be employed to provide the cable with a high degree of immunity to the line noise and enable extended transmission distances.

Since the bandwidth of twisted-pair cable is considerably less than coaxial or fiber optic cable, normally only one signal is transmitted on this cable at any point in time. As previously explained, this signaling technique is known as baseband signaling and should be compared to the broadband signaling capability of coaxial and fiber optic cable.

It should be noted that, although a twisted-pair wire system can be used to transmit both voice and data, the data transmission is baseband since only one channel is normally used for data. In comparison, a broadband system on coaxial or fiber optic cable can be designed to carry voice and several subchannels of data as well as facsimile and video transmission. Another constraint of unshielded twisted-wire is the rate at which data can flow on the network and the distance it can flow. Although data rates up to 16 megabits per second (Mbps) can be achieved, normally local area networks employing unshielded twisted-pair wiring operate at a lower data rate. In addition, unshielded twisted-pair systems normally cover a limited distance measured in terms of several hundred to a few thousand feet, while coaxial and fiber optic cable-based systems may be limited in terms of miles. To extend transmission distances over twisted-pair wire requires the use of both shielded wire and the periodic insertion of repeaters into the cable. The repeater receives a digital signal and then regenerates it; hence, it is also known as a data regenerator.

### Coaxial Cable

Coaxial cable consists of a center conductor copper wire which is then covered by an insulator known as a dielectric. An overlapping woven copper mesh surrounds the dielectric and the mesh, in turn, is covered by a protective jacket which can consist of polyethylene or aluminum. Figure 1.8 illustrates the composition of a typical coaxial cable; however, it should be noted that over one hundred types of coaxial cable are currently marketed. The key differences between such cables involve the number of conductors contained in the cable, the dielectric employed and the type of protective jacket and material used to provide strength to the cable which allows it to be pulled through conduits without breaking.

Two basic types of coaxial cable are used in local area networks, with the type of cable based upon the transmission technique employed: baseband or broadband signaling. Both cable types are much more expensive than twisted-pair wire; however, the greater frequency bandwidth of coaxial cable permits higher data rates than you can obtain over twisted-pair wire.

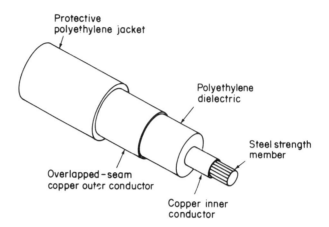

**Figure 1.8** Coaxial cable.

Normally, 50 ohm coaxial cable is used in baseband networks, while 75 ohm cable is used in broadband networks. The latter coaxial is identical to that used in cable television (CATV) applications, including the coaxial cable used in a home. Data rates on baseband networks using coaxial cable range upward to between 50 and 100 Mbps. With broadband transmissions, data rates up to and including 400 Mbps are obtainable.

A coaxial cable with a polyethylene jacket is normally used for baseband signaling. Data is transmitted from stations on the network to the baseband cable in a digital format and the connection from each station to the cable is accomplished by the use of a simple coaxial T-connector. Since data on a baseband network travels in a digital form, those signals can be easily regenerated by the use of a device known as a line driver or data regenerator. The line driver or data regenerator is a low-cost device that is constructed to look for a pulse rise and upon detecting the occurrence of the rise, it will disregard the entire pulse and regenerate an entirely new pulse. Thus, you can install low-cost line drivers into a baseband coaxial network to extend the distance transmission can occur on the cable. Typically, a coaxial cable baseband system can cover an area of several miles and may contain hundreds to thousands of stations on the network.

To obtain independent subchannels derived by frequency on coaxial cable broadband transmission requires a method to translate the digital signals from workstations into appropriate frequencies. This translation process is accomplished by the use of radio-frequency (RF) modems which modulate the digital data into analog signals and covert or demodulate received analog signals into digital signals. Since signals are transmitted at one frequency and received at a different frequency, a 'headend' or frequency translator is also required for broadband transmission on coaxial cable. This device is also known as a remodulator as it simply converts the signals from one subchannel to another subchannel.

The requirement for modems and frequency translators normally makes broadband transmission more expensive than baseband. Although the ability of broadband to support multiple channels provides it with an aggregate data transmission capacity that exceeds baseband, in general, baseband transmission permits a higher per-channel data flow. While this is an important consideration for mainframe-to-mainframe communications when massive amounts of data must be moved, for most personal computer interactive screen sessions and file transfer operations the speed of either baseband or broadband transmission should be sufficient. This fact may be better understood by comparing the typical transmission rates obtainable on baseband and broadband networks to drive a high-speed dot matrix printer and the differences between the time required to transmit data on the network and the time required to print the data.

Typical transmission speeds on commonly employed baseband and broadband networks range from 2 to 16 Mbps. In comparison, a high-speed dot matrix printer operating at 120 cps would require approximately 200 seconds to print 1 second's worth of data transmitted at 2 Mbps and 1600 seconds to print 1 second's worth of data transmitted at 16 Mbps.

**Fiber Optic Cable**

Fiber optic cable is a transmission medium for light energy and as such provides a very high bandwidth, permitting data rates ranging up to billions of bits per second. The fiber optic cable consists of a thin core of glass or plastic which is surrounded by a protective shield. Several shielded fibers in turn are bundled in a jacket with a central member of aluminum or steel employed for tensile strength.

Digital data represented by electrical energy must be converted into light energy for transmission on a fiber optic cable. This is normally accomplished by a low-power laser or through the use of a light emitting diode and appropriate circuitry. At the receiver, light energy must be reconverted into electrical energy. Normally, a device known as a photo detector, as well as appropriate circuitry to regenerate the digital pulses and an amplifier, are used to convert the received light energy into its original digital format.

In addition to the high bandwidth of fiber optic cables, they offer users several additional advantages in comparison to conventional transmission mediums. Since data travels in the form of light, it is immune to electrical interference and to building codes that may require expensive conduits to be installed for conventional cables through which electricity flows are usually unnecessary. Similarly, fiber optic cable can be installed through areas where the flow of electricity could be dangerous since only light flows through such cables.

Since most fibers provide only a single, unidirectional transmission path a minimum of two cables is normally required to connect all transmitters to all receivers on a network built using fiber optic cable. Due to the higher cost of fiber optic cable than coaxial or twisted-pair, the dual cable requirement of fiber cables can make them relatively expensive in comparison to other types of cable. In addition, until recently it was very difficult to splice such cable, which usually required sophisticated equipment and skilled installers to implement a fiber optic-based network. Similarly, once this type of network was installed, until recently it was difficult to modify the network.

Currently, the cost of the cable, a degree of difficulty of installation and of modification make the utilization of fiber optic-based local area networks impractical for many commercial applications. Today, the primary use of fiber optic cable is to extend the distance between stations on a network or to connect two distant networks to one another. The device used to connect a length of fiber optic cable into the LAN or between LANs is a fiber optic repeater. The repeater converts the electrical energy of signals flowing on the LAN into light energy for transmission on the fiber optic cable. At the end of the fiber optic cable, a second repeater converts light energy back into electrical energy. Another common use of fiber optic cable occurs in constructing FDDI networks. Such networks are now primarily used to function as a 'backbone' data highway, interconnecting two or more lower operating rate local area networks. Although a few organizations have extended fiber to the desktop, its cost as well as the cost of FDDI components currently precludes its widespread adoption as a replacement for other types of local area networks. With the cost of the fiber optic cable and fiber optic components declining and improvements that simplify the installation and modification of networks using this type of cable continuing to be introduced, the next few years may witness a profound movement toward the utilization of this transmission medium throughout local area networks.

*Access method*

If the topology of a local area network can be compared to a data highway, then the access method might be viewed as the set of rules that enable data from one workstation to successfully reach its destination via the data highway. Without such rules, it is quite possible for two messages sent by two different workstations to the same or a different address to collide, with the result that neither message reaches its destination. The three access methods primarily employed in local area networks are Carrier-Sense Multiple Access/Collision Detection (CSMA/CD), Carrier-Sense Multiple Access/Collision Avoidance (CSMA/CA) and token passing. Each of these access methods is uniquely structured to address the previously mentioned collision and data destination problems.

Prior to discussing how access methods work, let us first examine the two basic types of devices that can be attached to a local area network to gain an appreciation for the work the access method must accomplish.

**Listeners and Talkers**

We can categorize the operating mode of each device as being a 'listener' or a 'talker.' Some devices, like printers, only receive data and thus operate only as a listener. Other devices, such as personal computers, can either transmit or receive data and are capable of operating in both modes. In a baseband signaling environment where only one channel exists or on an individual channel on a broadband system, if several talkers wish to communicate at the same time a collision will occur unless a scheme is employed that defines when each device can talk and, in the event of a collision, what events must transpire to avoid its recurrence.

For data to correctly reach its destination, each listener must have a unique address and its network equipment must be designed to respond to a message on the net only when it recognizes its address, thus, the primary goals in the design of an access method are to minimize the potential for data collision and provide a mechanism for corrective action when data collides, as well as to ensure that an addressing scheme is employed to enable messages to reach their destination.

### Carrier-Sense Multiple Access with Collision Detection (CSMA/CD)

Carrier-Sense Multiple Access with Collision Detection can be categorized as a 'listen' then 'send' access method. CSMA/CD is one of the earliest-developed access techniques and is used in Ethernet, which is the local area network developed by the Xerox Corporation whose technology has been licensed to many companies, and was standardized by the Institute of Electrical and Electronic Engineers (IEEE) under its 802.3 standard.

Under the CSMA/CD concept, when a station has data to send it first listens to determine if any other station on the network is talking; the fact that the channel is idle is determined in one of two ways based upon whether the network is broadband or baseband.

In a broadband network, the fact that a channel is idle is determined by noting the absence of a carrier tone on the cable. Carrier-sensing thus provides the mechanism to determine whether or not the channel is busy.

Ethernet, like other baseband systems, uses one channel for data transmission and does not employ the use of a carrier. Instead, Ethernet encodes data using a Manchester code in which a timing transition always occurs in the middle of each bit as previously illustrated in Figure 1.7. Although Ethernet does not transmit data via the use of a carrier, the continuous transitions of the Manchester code can be considered as equivalent to a carrier signal. Carrier-sensing on a baseband network is thus performed by monitoring the line for activity.

In a CSMA/CD network, if the channel is busy, the station will wait until it becomes idle prior to transmitting data. Since it is possible for two stations to listen at the same time and discover an idle channel, it is also possible that the two stations could then transmit at the same time. When this situation arises, a collision will occur. Upon sensing that a collision has occurred, a delay scheme will be employed to prevent a repetition of the collision. Typically, each station will use either a randomly generated or predefined time-out period prior to attempting to retransmit the message that previously collided. Since this access method requires hardware capable of detecting the occurrence of a collision, additional circuitry required to perform collision detection adds to the cost of such hardware.

Figure 1.9 illustrates a CSMA/CD bus-based local area network. Here each workstation is attached to the transmission medium, such as coaxial cable, by a device known as a bus interface unit (BIU). To illustrate the operation of a CSMA/CD network assume station A is currently using the channel and stations C and D wish to transmit. The BIUs connecting stations C and D to the network would listen to the channel and note it was busy. Once station A completes its transmission, stations C and D would attempt to gain access to the channel. Since station A's signal takes longer than C's to propagate down the cable to station D, then C's BIU notices that the channel is free slightly before station D's BIU. However, as station C gets ready to transmit, station D now assumes the channel is free. Within an infinitesimal period of time C starts transmission followed by D, resulting in a collision. Here the collision is a function of the propagation delay of the signal and the distance between two competing stations. Due to this CSMA/CD networks work better as the main cable length decreases.

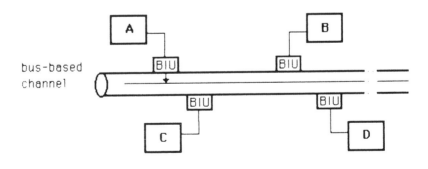

BIU = bus interface unit

**Figure 1.9** CSMA/CD network operation. In a CSMA/CD network, as the distance between workstations increases the resulting increase in propagation delay time increases the probability of the occurrence of collisions.

Although there are several versions of CSMA/CD marketed, by far the most common version is based upon licensed technology from Xerox Corporation, with over 50 other vendors developing products based upon Xerox's Ethernet specifications.

When the IEEE developed its 802.3 standard for CSMA/CD systems it did not precisely follow Xerox's original Ethernet specifications, although there is an extremely high degree of similarity between the two. Unfortunately, most 802.3-compatible hardware is not compatible with older Ethernet equipment, although many manufacturers now support both.

The CSMA/CD access technique is best suited for networks with intermittent transmission, since an increase in traffic volume causes a corresponding increase in the probability of the cable being occupied when a station wishes to talk. In addition, as traffic volume builds under CSMA/CD, throughput may decline, since there will be longer waits to gain access to the network as well as additional time-outs required to resolve collisions that occur.

### Carrier-Sense Multiple Access with Collision Avoidance (CSMA/CA)

Carrier-Sense Multiple Access with Collision Avoidance represents a modified version of the CSMA/CD access technique. Under the CSMA/CA access technique, each of the hardware devices attached to the talkers on the network estimates when a collision is likely to occur and avoids transmission during those times. Since this technique eliminates the requirement for collision-detection hardware, the cost of hardware to implement this access technique is usually less than for CSMA/CD hardware.

### Token Passing

In a token-passing access method, each time the network is turned on a token is generated. Consisting of a unique bit pattern, the token travels the length of the network, either around a ring or along the length of a bus. When a station on the network has data to transmit it must first seize a free token. On a Token-Ring network, the token is then transformed to indicate it is in use and information is added to produce a frame which represents data being transmitted from one station to another. On an FDDI network, the token is removed from the network by the station that will transmit data—a process known as absorption. Then, the FDDI station can transmit one or more frames based upon several factors described later in this and other chapters prior to placing the token back onto the network. During the time the token is in use or absorbed the other stations on the network remain idle, eliminating the possibility of collisions occurring. Once the transmission is completed the token is either converted back into its original form by the station that transmitted the frame on the Token-Ring network or placed back onto an FDDI network and becomes available for use by the next station on the network.

Figure 1.10 illustrates the general operation of a token-passing Token-Ring network using a ring topology. Since a station on the network can only transmit when it has a free token, token passing eliminates the requirement for collision detection hardware. Due to the dependence of the network upon the token, the loss of a station can bring the entire network down. To avoid this, the design characteristics of Token-Ring networks include circuitry that automatically removes a failed or failing station from the network as well as other 'self-healing' features.

Due to the variety of transmission media, network structures and access methods, there is no one best network for all users. Table 1.2 should be used by the reader to obtain a generalized comparison of the advantages and disadvantages of the technical characteristics of local area networks, using the transmission medium as a frame of reference.

## Advantages of token passing

When comparing CSMA/CD to token passing there are several advantages to the latter type of LAN that makes it an attractive choice in comparison to Ethernet-type local area networks. One of the key advantages of token passing is its deterministic access method. Unlike Ethernet in which access is non-predictable, Token-Ring network stations gain access to a network by acquiring a free token whose rotation around the ring is predictable. This means performance will not significantly degrade as traffic increases. In comparison, as traffic increases on a CSMA/CD network, the probability of collisions increases, decreasing throughput.

Currently, Ethernet adapter cards are half the cost of Token-Ring cards. Although this cost difference makes

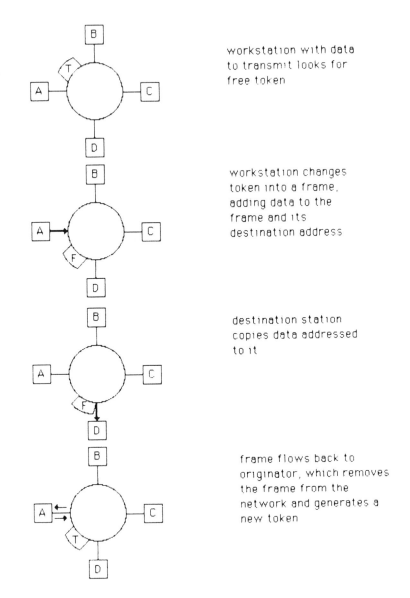

workstation with data
to transmit looks for
free token

workstation changes
token into a frame,
adding data to the
frame and its
destination address

destination station
copies data addressed
to it

frame flows back to
originator, which removes
the frame from the
network and generates a
new token

**Figure 1.10**   Token-Ring operation.

CSMA/CD networks more popular than Token-Ring networks, the predictability and consistency of Token-Ring networks makes them the preferred LAN for organizations with high utilization or a potential requirement for adding applications that can increase network utilization. In addition, the operating rate of some Token-Ring networks provides a data transfer

**Table 1.2**  Technical characteristics of LANs having different transmission media.

| Characteristic | Twisted-pair wire | Baseband coaxial cable | Broadband coaxial cable | Fiber optic cable |
|---|---|---|---|---|
| Topology | Bus, star or ring | Bus or ring | Bus or ring star | Bus, ring or |
| Channels | Single channel | Single channel | Multichannel | Single, multichannel |
| Data rate | Normally 2 to 4 Mbps, up to 16 Mbps obtainable | Normally 2 to 10 Mbps, up to 100 Mbps obtainable | Up to 400 Mbps | Up to Gbps |
| Maximum nodes on net | Usually <255 | Usually <1024 | Several thousand | Several thousand |
| Geographical coverage | In thousands of feet | In miles | In tens of miles | In tens of miles |
| Major advantages | Low cost, may be able to use existing wiring | Low cost, simple to install | Supports voice, data, video applications simultaneously | Supports voice, data, video applications simultaneously |
| Major advantages | Limited bandwidth, requires conduits, low immunity to noise | Low immunity to noise | High cost, difficult to install, requires RF modems and headend | Cable cost, difficult to splice |

capability considerably beyond that obtainable from the use of different types of Ethernet local area networks. For example, Token-Ring and FDDI networks can operate at 16 Mbps and 100 Mbps. In comparison, the maximum Ethernet operating rate is currently limited to 10 Mbps.

## 1.3 TOKEN-RING NETWORKS

Since this book is about Token-Ring networks, we would be remiss if we did not conclude this chapter with an overview of the different types of these networks. In doing so we will discuss the manner in which we will focus our attention on different types of Token-Ring networks.

## Types of networks

We can categorize Token-Ring networks based upon the media used as well as their network topology and data rate. Although the first two network features, as we will soon note, do not provide a clear distinction between networks, the data rate of the network currently provides a mechanism for differentiating major types of Token-Ring networks. Thus, we will discuss Token-Ring networks in terms of their operating rate.

There are three distinct data rates at which Token-Ring networks operate: 4, 16, and 100 million bits per second (Mbps). Token-Ring networks that operate at 4 Mbps are standardized under the IEEE 802.4 and 802.5 standards for operation on a bus and ring structure and use copper media as a data transport mechanism. However, both networks can be extended through the use of fiber optic repeaters in which electrical signals are converted to light pulses for transmission over fiber strung between repeaters. In addition, IBM's 16-Mbps Token-Ring network follows the IEEE 802.5 standard but incorporates several extensions, such as a 16-Mbps operating rate and a feature known as early token release that were being considered as extensions to the 802.5 standard at the time this book was written. Token-Ring networks that operate at 100 Mbps are referred to as Fiber Distributed Data Interface (FDDI) networks. Although FDDI is currently partially standardized as a token-passing network which uses fiber as the transmission media, at the time this book was written a developing standard known as CDDI for Copper Distributed Data Interface was under development to permit the transmission of data at 100 Mbps according to the FDDI standard via copper-based media.

In this book we will primarily focus our attention upon ring networks. In doing so we will refer to networks operating at 4 and 16 Mbps as Token-Ring networks, while networks operating at 100 Mbps will be referred to as FDDI or CDDI based upon the media used by each network.

## Bus operation

When used with a bus topology the token bus LAN provides access to the network as if it were a ring. Under the IEEE

802.4 specification for a token bus network a token circulates from end-to-end on the bus and provides a station with the ability to use the bus for a predefined period of time to send or receive data. Under this standard all stations on the network can receive all signals transmitted—a condition known as broadcasting. However, the token access method can be structured to form a logical ring which bypasses one or more stations as illustrated in Figure 1.11. In this illustration all stations can receive frames; however, stations C and G will not be able to initiate a transmission as they will never receive a token. Here a logical ring is formed consisting of workstations A, D, E, F and B. During normal operations a station which completes its use of a token passes it on to a designated station known as the successor. By passing the token from station to station the logical ring was formed as shown in Figure 1.11.

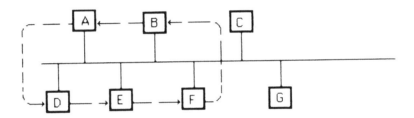

**Figure 1.11** Logical ring formation on a physical bus. Token passing on a physical bus enables a logical ring to be formed which may or may not include all stations on the bus.

The IEEE 802.4 standard for a physical bus employing token passing as the access method is quite similar to the manufacturing automation protocol (MAP) developed by General Motors. Although this standard has achieved a high degree of usage in industrial applications, its use is considerably overshadowed by the use of a physical ring for token passing and the higher level of requirements to interconnect that type of network. Due to this we will focus our attention upon Token-Ring structured networks in this book, including FDDI.

## Token-Ring vs. FDDI ring operations

There are a large number of similarities, as well as differences, between Token-Ring and FDDI networks. Both types of network are based upon the use of a ring topology and require the acquisition of a free token prior to a station on the network being able to transmit information. Differences between the two networks include the method of attachment of stations to each network and the type of transmission medium used, the number of rings and use of rings by each network, their frame format and frame transmission capability, and the operating rate of each network. Other differences between the two networks range in scope from the standard defining the operation of the ring network to the maximum number of stations supported by each network. Since an extensive comparison of Token-Ring and FDDI network features occurs at appropriate locations throughout this book, in this introductory chapter we will focus our attention upon obtaining a general level of knowledge concerning the operation of each network. Thus, we will defer detailed information about each network to later chapters in this book.

*Ring structure*

In a Token-Ring network, stations are first connected to a device known as a multistation access unit (MAU). When the number of stations required to be attached to the network exceeds the capacity of an MAU, an additional MAU is added to the network and MAUs are cabled together to form a ring. In an FDDI network, stations can be attached either directly to the ring or through the use of a concentrator—a device similar to a Token-Ring MAU.

Although both a Token-Ring and an FDDI ring contain two paths, the use of the secondary path differs between networks. In an FDDI network the secondary ring can be automatically used in the event of a primary ring failure—a process commonly referred to as self-healing. In comparison, the use of a Token-Ring backup ring path requires manual intervention.

*Media and operating rate*

Token-Ring networks are primarily constructed using copper wire, with optical fiber repeaters capable of being used to extend the transmission distance on the ring. In comparison, an FDDI network uses fiber optic media. Concerning operating rates, as previously mentioned, Token-Ring networks operate at 4 and 16 Mbps, while FDDI networks operate at 100 Mbps.

*Transmission*

Although both Token-Ring and FDDI networks require a station to acquire a free token prior to transmitting information, the manner in which information can be transmitted differs between networks. On a Token-Ring network the acquisition of a free token enables the acquiring station to transmit one frame. That frame as with all data movements occurs asynchronously. On an FDDI network a free token is removed by the transmitting station prior to the station transmitting a frame. The frame can be transmitted either synchronously or asynchronously, with the former used when a guaranteed bandwidth is required, while the latter can only occur when traffic on the ring drops below a predefined level. When the station transmits synchronously, it can transmit multiple frames until a predefined time allocation period expires. At that time the station releases the free token to enable another station to transmit data onto the network. Thus, an FDDI network has the capability to allocate network bandwidth.

*Token and frame use*

In a Token-Ring network a token is either free or unavailable and carried within a frame. Thus, it is always flowing around the ring. In comparison, an FDDI token is removed from the ring while a station transmits one or more frames.

Another difference between Token-Ring and FDDI networks concerns the maximum frame length. At 4 Mbps a Token-Ring frame can be up to 4500 bytes in length, while at 16 Mbps a Token-Ring frame can be up to 18 000 bytes in length. In comparison, the maximum FDDI frame is limited to 4500 bytes.

**Station support**

The maximum number of stations supported by a Token-Ring network is limited to 260. To support additional stations requires the use of bridges, routers, or other equipment to interconnect separate networks. In comparison, the maximum number of stations supported by an FDDI network is 500.

**Encoding method**

Token-Ring networks encode data using a technique known as Differential Manchester encoding. That coding technique would require 200 million signal changes per second to provide a 100-Mbps FDDI operating rate. Since this would drive up the cost of FDDI networks, a different coding technique known as 4B/5B is used on FDDI networks. This technique results in data being transmitted as a series of four-bit symbols, with each symbol encoded within a five-bit pattern. Under 4B/5B encoding a signaling rate of 125 million signal changes is required to produce an operating rate of 100 Mbps and provides an 80% efficiency. In comparison, Differential Manchester encoding is 50% efficient since two signal changes are required to represent one bit.

Although both Token-Ring and FDDI networks are token based, as indicated in our prior overview there are significant differences between the features of each network. Table 1.3 summarizes those differences and provides readers with a quick summary of the operational capability of each network with respect to their operating rates, token acquisition and release mechanism, frame size, and other parameters that are more fully covered in later chapters in this book.

**Table 1.3** Comparison of major Token-Ring and FDDI features.

| Feature | Token-Ring | FDDI |
| --- | --- | --- |
| Standard | IEEE 802.5 | ANSI X3T9.5 |
| Ring connection | Via a multistation access unit | directly or via a concentrator |
| Ring topology | Single ring with backup path | dual ring with self-healing capability |
| Ring operating rate | 4/16 Mbps | 100 Mbps |
| Media | Copper, optical fiber available for use by repeaters | Optical fiber |
| Token acquisition | After receive (4 Mbps) or transmit (16 Mbps) | After transmit |
| Maximum frame size | 4500 bytes (4 Mbps) 18 000 bytes (16 Mbps) | 4500 bytes |
| Maximum number of stations | 260 | 500 |
| Data encoding | Differential Manchester 50% efficient | 4B/5B 80% efficient |

# 2

---

# NETWORK STANDARDS

---

Standards can be viewed as the 'glue' which binds hardware and software from different vendors so they can interoperate. The importance of standards and the work of standards organizations have proved essential for the growth of both local and worldwide communications. In the United States and many other countries, national standards organizations have defined physical and operational characteristics that enable vendors to manufacture equipment compatible with line facilities provided by communications carriers as well as equipment produced by other vendors and which may be connected to a local or wide area network. At the international level, standards organizations have promulgated several series of communications–related recommendations. These recommendations, while not mandatory for following, have become highly influential on a worldwide basis for the development of equipment and facilities and have been adopted by hundreds of public companies and communications carriers.

In addition to national and international standards, a series of *de facto* standards has evolved through the licensing of technology among companies. Such *de facto* standards, as an example, have facilitated the development of communications software for use on personal computers. Today, consumers can purchase communications software that can control modems manufactured by hundreds of vendors since most modems are now constructed to respond to a core set of uniform control codes.

## 2.1 STANDARDS ORGANIZATIONS

In this chapter we will first focus our attention upon two national and two international standards organizations. The national standards organizations we will briefly discuss in this section are the American National Standards Institute (ANSI) and the Institute of Electrical and Electronic Engineers (IEEE). The work of each organization has been a guiding force in the rapid expansion in the use of local area networks due to a series of standards developed by those organizations. In the international area, we will discuss the role of the Consultative Committee for International Telephone and Telegraph (CCITT) and the International Standards Organization (ISO), both of which have developed numerous standards which facilitate the operation of local and wide area networks.

Due to the importance of the ISO's Open Systems Interconnection (OSI) Reference Model and the IEEE's 802 Committee lower layer standards we will examine each as separate entities in this chapter. Since we must understand the OSI Reference Model prior to examining the effect of the efforts of the IEEE and ANSI upon the lower layers of that model, we will look at the OSI Reference Model prior to examining the Reference Model layer subdivisions performed by the IEEE and ANSI.

## National standards organizations

The two national standards organizations we will briefly discuss are the American National Standards Institute and the Institute of Electrical and Electronic Engineers. In the area of local area networking standards, both ANSI and the IEEE work in conjunction with the ISO to standardize LAN technology.

The ISO delegated the standardization of local area networking technology to ANSI. ANSI in turn delegated lower speed LAN standards, defined as operating rates at and below 50 Mbps, to the IEEE. This resulted in ANSI developing standards for the Fiber Distributed Data Interface (FDDI), while the IEEE developed standards for Ethernet, Token-Ring, and other local area networks.

Once the IEEE develops and approves a standard it is sent to ANSI for review. If ANSI approves the standard it is then sent to the ISO. Then, the ISO solicits comments from all member countries to ensure the standard will work at the international level, resulting in an IEEE- or ANSI-developed standard becoming an ISO standard.

*ANSI*

The principal standards-forming body in the United States is the American National Standards Institute (ANSI). Located in

New York City, this non-profit, non-governmental organization was founded in 1918 and functions as the representative of the United States to the ISO.

ANSI standards are developed through the work of its approximately 300 Standards Committees or from the efforts of associated groups, such as the Electronic Industry Association (EIA). Recognizing the importance of the computer industry, ANSI established its X3 Standards Committee in 1960. That committee consists of 25 Technical Committees, each assigned to develop standards for a specific technical area. One of those Technical Committees is the X3S3 committee, more formally known as the Data Communications Technical Committee, which was responsible for the ANSI X3T9.5 standard which governs FDDI operations and which is now recognized as the ISO 9314 standard.

*IEEE*

The Institute of Electrical and Electronic Engineers (IEEE) is a US-based engineering society that is very active in the development of data communications standards. In fact, the most prominent developer of local area networking standards is the IEEE, whose subcommittee 802 began its work in 1980 prior to the establishment of a viable market for the technology.

The IEEE Project 802 efforts are concentrated upon the physical interface of equipment and the procedures and functions required to establish, maintain, and release connections among network devices, including defining data formats, error control procedures, and other control activities governing the flow of information. This focus of the IEEE actually represents the lowest two layers of the ISO model, physical and link, which are discussed later in this chapter.

## International standards organizations

Two important international standards organizations are the Consultative Committee for International Telephone and Telegraph (CCITT) and the International Standards Organization (ISO). The CCITT can be considered as a governmental body as it functions under the auspices of an agency of the United Nations. Although the ISO is a non-governmental agency, its work in the field of data communications is well recognized.

*CCITT*

The Consultative Committee for International Telephone and Telegraph (CCITT) is a group within the International Telecommunications Union (ITU), the latter being a specialized agency of the United Nations headquartered in Geneva, Switzerland. The CCITT is tasked with direct responsibility for developing data communications standards and consists of 15 Study Groups, each tasked with a specific area of responsibility.

The work of the CCITT is performed on a four-year cycle which is known as a Study Period. At the conclusion of each Study Period, a Plenary Session occurs. During the Plenary Session, the work of the CCITT during the previous four years is reviewed, proposed recommendations are considered for adoption, and items to be investigated during the next four-year cycle are considered.

The CCITT's Ninth Plenary Session met in 1988 and its Tenth Session during 1992. Although approval of recommended standards is not intended to be mandatory, CCITT recommendations have the effect of law in some Western European countries and many of its recommendations have been adopted by both communications carriers and vendors in the United States.

*ISO*

The International Standards Organization (ISO) is a non-governmental entity that has consultative status within the UN Economic and Social Council. The goal of the ISO is to 'promote the development of standards in the world with a view to facilitating international exchange of goods and services.'

The membership of the ISO consists of the national standards organizations of most countries, with approximately 100 countries currently participating in its work.

Perhaps the most notable achievement of the ISO in the field of communications is its development of the seven-layer Open Systems Interconnection (OSI) Reference Model.

## 2.2 THE ISO REFERENCE MODEL

The International Standards Organization (ISO) established a framework for standardizing communications systems called the Open Systems Interconnection (OSI) Reference Model. The OSI architecture defines the communications process as a set of seven layers, with specific functions isolated and associated with each layer. Each layer, as illustrated in Figure 2.1, covers lower layer processes, effectively isolating them from higher-layer functions. In this way, each layer performs a set of functions necessary to provide a set of services to the layer above it.

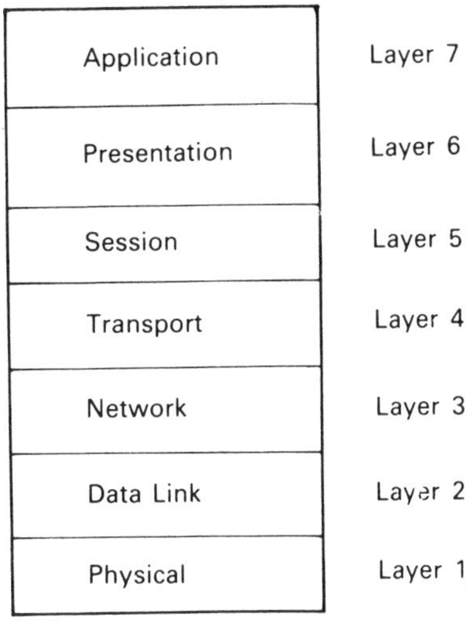

| | |
|---|---|
| Application | Layer 7 |
| Presentation | Layer 6 |
| Session | Layer 5 |
| Transport | Layer 4 |
| Network | Layer 3 |
| Data Link | Layer 2 |
| Physical | Layer 1 |

**Figure 2.1**  ISO reference model.

Layer isolation permits the characteristics of a given layer to change without impacting the remainder of the model, provided that the supporting services remain the same. One major advantage of this layered approach is that users can mix and match OSI conforming communications products to tailor their communications systems to satisfy a particular networking requirement.

The OSI Reference Model, while not completely viable with many current network architectures, offers the potential to directly interconnect networks based upon the use of different vendor equipment. This interconnectivity potential will be of substantial benefit to both users and vendors. For users, interconnectivity will remove the shackles that in many instances tie them to a particular vendor. For vendors, the ability to easily interconnect their products will provide them with access to a larger market. The importance of the OSI model is such that it has been adopted by the CCITT as Recommendation X.200.

## Layered architecture

As previously discussed, the OSI Reference Model is based upon the establishment of a layered, or partitioned, architecture. This partioning effort can be considered as being derived from the scientific process whereby complex problems are subdivided into functional tasks that are easier to implement on an aggregate individual basis than as a whole.

As a result of the application of a partitioning approach to communications network architecture, the communications process was subdivided into seven distinct partitions, called layers. Each layer consists of a set of functions designed to provide a defined series of services which relate to the mission of that layer. For example, the functions associated with the physical connection of equipment to a network are referred to as the physical layer.

With the exception of layers 1 and 7, each layer is bounded by the layers above and below it. Layer 1, the physical layer, can be considered to be bound below by the interconnecting medium over which transmission flows, while layer 7 is the upper layer and has no upper boundary. Within each layer is a group of functions which can be viewed as providing a set of defined services to the layer which bounds it from above, resulting in layer $n$ using the services of layer $n - 1$. Thus, the design of a layered architecture enables the characteristics of a particular layer to change without affecting the rest of the system, assuming the services provided by the layer do not change.

## OSI layers

An understanding of the OSI layers is best obtained by first examining a possible network structure that illustrates the components of a typical wide area network. Figure 2.2 illustrates a network structure which is only typical in the sense that it will be used for a discussion of the components upon which networks are constructed.

The circles in Figure 2.2 represent nodes which are points where data enters or exits a network or is switched between two

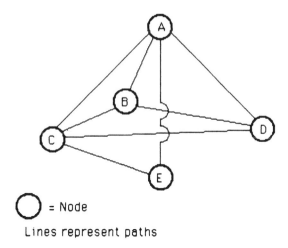

Figure 2.2   Network components.

networks connected by one or more paths. Nodes are connected to other nodes via communications cables or circuits and can be established on any type of communications media, such as cable, microwave, or radio.

From a physical perspective, a node can be based upon the use of one of several types of computers, including a personal computer, minicomputer, mainframe computer, or specialized computer, such as a front-end processor. Connections to network nodes into a wide area network can occur via the use of terminals directly connected to computers, terminals connected to a node via the use of one or more intermediate communications devices or via paths linking one network to another network. In fact, a workstation on a Token-Ring network that provides access into a wide area network can be considered a network node. In this situation the workstation can be a bridge, router, or gateway and provides a connectivity mechanism between other stations on the Token-Ring network and the wide area network.

The routes between two nodes, such as C–E–A, C–D–A, C–A, and C–B–A, which could be used to route data between nodes A and C, are information paths. Due to the variability in the flow of information through a wide area network, the shortest path between nodes may not be available for use or may represent a non-efficient path with respect to other paths constructed through intermediate nodes between a source and destination node. A temporary connection established to link two nodes whose route is based upon such parameters as current network activity is known as a logical connection. This logical connection represents the use of physical facilities, including paths and node switching capability on a temporary basis.

The major functions of each of the seven OSI layers are described in the following seven paragraphs.

### Layer 1—the physical layer

At the lowest or most basic level, the physical layer (level 1) is a set of rules that specifies the electrical and physical connection between devices. This level specifies the cable connections and the electrical rules necessary to transfer data between devices. Typically, the physical link corresponds to previously established interface standards, such as the RS–232/V.24 interface which governs the attachment of data terminal equipment, such as the serial port of personal computers, to data communications equipment, such as modems, at data rates below 19.2 kbps.

### Layer 2—the data link layer

The next layer, which is known as the data link layer (level 2), denotes how a device gains access to the medium specified in the physical layer; it also defines data formats, including the framing of data within transmitted messages, error control procedures, and other link control activities. From defining data formats, including procedures to correct transmission errors, this layer becomes responsible for the reliable delivery of information. Two examples of data link control protocols that can reside in this layer include IBM's Binary Synchronous Communications (BSC) and the CCITT's High-level Data Link Control (HDLC).

Since the development of OSI layers was originally targeted towards wide area networking, its applicability to local area networks required a degree of modification. Under the IEEE 802 standards, the data link layer was divided into two sublayers— logical link control (LLC) and media access control (MAC). Under the ANSI FDDI standard this subdivision was retained while the physical layer was also subdivided into two sublayers to better reflect the use of optical fiber. The LLC layer is responsible for generating and interpreting commands which control the flow of data and perform recovery operations in the event of errors. In comparison, the MAC layer is responsible for providing access to the local area network, which enables a station on the network to transmit information. In Sections 2.3 and 2.4 we will examine the IEEE 802 and ANSI standards, including the functions and operation of the LLC and MAC layers as well as the subdivision of the physical layer under the FDDI standard.

### Layer 3—the network layer

The network layer (level 3) is responsible for arranging a logical connection between a source and destination on the network, including the selection and management of a route for the flow of information between source and destination based upon the available data paths in the network. Services provided by this layer are associated with the movement of data packets through a network, including addressing, routing, switching, sequencing, and flow control procedures. In a complex network, the source and destination may not be directly connected by a single path, but instead require a path to be established that consists of many subpaths. Thus, routing data through the network onto the correct paths is an important feature of this layer.

Several protocols have been defined for layer 3, including the CCITT X.25 packet switching protocol and the CCITT X.75 gateway protocol. X.25 governs the flow of information through a packet network, while X.75 governs the flow of information between packet networks.

### Layer 4—the transport layer

The transport layer (level 4) is responsible for guaranteeing that the transfer of information occurs correctly after a route has been established through the network by the network level protocol. Thus, the primary function of this layer is to control the communications session between network nodes once a path has been established by the network control layer. Error control, sequence checking, and other end-to-end data reliability factors are the primary concern of this layer which enables the transport layer to provide a reliable end-to-end data transfer capability.

*Layer 5—the session layer*

> The session layer (level 5) provides a set of rules for establishing and terminating data streams between nodes in a network. The services that this session layer can provide include establishing and terminating node connections, message flow control, dialogue control, and end-to-end data control.

*Layer 6—the presentation layer*

> The presentation layer (level 6) services are concerned with data transformation, formatting, and syntax. One of the primary functions performed by the presentation layer is the conversion of transmitted data into a display format appropriate for a receiving device. This can include any necessary conversion between ASCII and EBCDIC codes. Data encryption/decryption and data compression and decompression are additional examples of the data transformation that could be handled by this layer.

*Layer 7—the application layer*

> Finally, the application layer (level 7) acts as a window through which the application gains access to all of the services provided by the model. Examples of functions performed at this level include file transfers, resource sharing, and database access. While the first four layers are fairly well defined, the top three layers may vary considerably, depending upon the network used. Figure 2.3 illustrates the OSI model in schematic format, showing the various levels of the model with respect to a terminal accessing an application on a host computer system.

## Data flow

> As data flows within an ISO network each layer appends appropriate heading information to frames of information flowing within the network while removing the heading infor.nation added by a lower layer. In this manner, layer $n$ interacts with layer $n-1$ as data flows through an ISO network.
>
> Figure 2.4 illustrates the appending and removal of frame header information as data flows through a network constructed

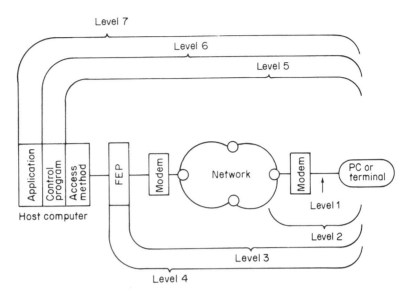

**Figure 2.3** OSI model schematic.

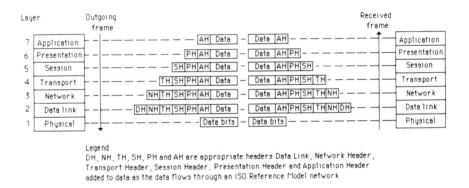

**Figure 2.4** Data flow within an OSI Reference Model network.

according to the ISO Reference Model. Since each higher level removes the header appended by a lower level, the frame traversing the network arrives in its original form at its destination.

As the reader will surmise from the previous illustrations, the ISO Reference Model is designed to simplify the construction of data networks. This simplification is due to the eventual standardization of methods and procedures to append appropriate heading information to frames flowing through a network, permitting data to be routed to its appropriate destination following a uniform procedure.

## 2.3 IEEE 802 STANDARDS

The IEEE Committee 802 was formed at the beginning of the 1980's to develop standards for emerging technologies. By doing so the IEEE fostered the development of local area networking equipment from different vendors that can work together. In addition, IEEE LAN standards provided a common design goal for vendors to access a relatively larger market than if proprietary equipment was developed. This in turn enabled economies of scale to reduce the cost of products developed for larger markets.

### 802 committees

Table 2.1 lists the organization of IEEE 802 committees involved in local area networks. In examining the lists of committees listed in Table 2.1 it is apparent that the IEEE early on noted that a number of different systems would be required to satisfy the requirements of a diverse end-user population. Accordingly, the IEEE adopted the CSMA/CD, Token Bus and Token Ring as Standards 802.3, 802.4 and 802.5, respectively.

**Table 2.1**  IEEE Series 802 committees.

| | |
|---|---|
| 802.1 | High Level Interface |
| 802.2 | Logical Link Control |
| 802.3 | CSMA/CD |
| 802.4 | Token-Passing Bus |
| 802.5 | Token-Passing Ring |
| 802.6 | Metropolitan Area Networks |
| 802.7 | Broadband Technical Advisory Group |
| 802.8 | Fiber Optic Technical Advisory Group |
| 802.9 | Integrated Voice and Data Networks |
| 802.10 | Network Security |
| 802.11 | Wireless LANs |

The IEEE Committee 802 published draft standards for CSMA/CD and Token Bus local area networks in 1982. Standard 802.3, which describes a baseband CSMA/CD network similar to Ethernet, was published in 1983. Since then, several addenda to the 802.3 standard were adopted which govern the operation of CSMA/CD on different types of media. Those addenda include 10BASE-2 which defines a 10 Mbps baseband network operating on thin coaxial cable, 1BASE-5 which defines a 1 Mbps baseband network operating on twisted-pair and 10BROAD-36, a broadband 10 Mbps network that operates on thick coaxial cable.

The next standard published by the IEEE was 802.4, which describes a token-passing bus-oriented network for both baseband and broadband transmission. This standard is similar to the Manufacturing Automation Protocol (MAP) standard developed by General Motors.

The third LAN standard published by the IEEE was based upon IBM's specifications for its Token-Ring network. Known as the 802.5 standard, it defines the operation of token-ring networks on shielded twisted-pair cable at data rates of 1 and 4 Mbps. That standard will more than likely be modified by the time you read this book to acknowledge three IBM enhancements to Token-Ring network operations. Those enhancements include the 16-Mbps operating rate, the ability to release a token early on a 16-Mbps network, and a bridge-routing protocol known as source routing.

## Data link subdivision

One of the more interesting facets of IEEE 802 standards is the subdivision of the ISO Open System Interconnection Model's data link layer into two sublayers—logical link control and medium access control. Figure 2.5 illustrates the relationship between IEEE 802 local area network standards and the first three layers of the OSI Reference Model.

The separation of the data link layer into two entities provides a mechanism for regulating access to the medium independent of the method for establishing, maintaining and terminating the logical link between workstations. Here the method of regulating access to the medium is defined by the medium access control portion of each local area network standard. This enables the logical link control standard to be applicable to each type of network.

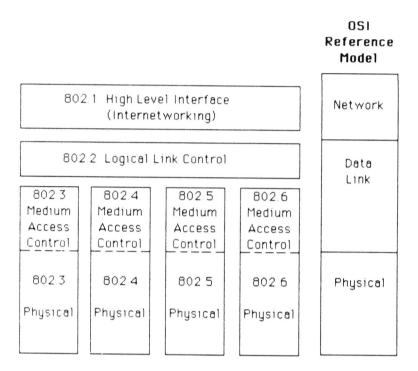

**Figure 2.5**   Relationship between IEEE standards and the OSI Reference Model.

*Medium access control*

The medium access control sublayer is responsible for controlling access to the network. To accomplish this it must ensure that a situation in which two or more stations attempt to simultaneously transmit data onto the network cannot occur. For Token-Ring networks this is accomplished by permitting only one token to flow on the LAN and by restricting the ability of stations on the network to transmit except when they are able to acquire a free token.

In addition to network access control, the MAC sublayer is responsible for the orderly movement of data onto and off the network. To accomplish this the MAC sublayer is responsible for MAC addressing, frame type recognition, frame control, frame copying, token priority, and network management.

The MAC address represents the physical address of each station connected to the network. That address can belong to a single station, represent a predefined group of stations (group address), all stations on the network (broadcast address), or a null address for frames which should be ignored by all stations on the network. Here a null address is normally used for ring testing. Through MAC addresses the physical source and destination of frames are identified.

Frame type recognition enables the type and format of a frame to be recognized. To ensure frames can be accurately processed, frame control prefixes each frame with a starting delimiter and terminates each frame with an ending delimiter. In addition, a frame check sequence (FCS) is computed based upon applying an algorithm to the contents of the frame, with the results of the operation placed into the frame. This enables a receiving station to perform a similar operation. If the locally computed FCS matches the FCS carried in the frame, then the frame is considered to have arrived without error.

Once a frame arrives at a station that has the same address as the destination address in the frame, the station must copy the frame. The copying operation moves the contents of the frame into a buffer area in a Token-Ring adapter card. The adapter card removes certain fields from the frame, such as the starting and ending delimiters, and passes the information field into a predefined memory area in the station into which the adapter card is inserted. To ensure that extended communications, such as a large file transfer, do not adversely affect other communications, such as a short electronic mail message routed between network stations, requires a priority mechanism. This priority mechanism is provided by the inclusion of a priority field within a token, with priority management at the MAC sublayer being responsible for permitting preferential access while maintaining fairness with respect to the ability of all network stations to gain access to the network.

A LAN is similar to any network in that error conditions can be expected to occur. To support the ability of Token-Ring networks to handle error conditions at the access control level, a number of network management features are included in Token-Ring networks. Those management features include MAC frames used to perform different tests, adapter card self-testing functions, signal loss and ring error detection and reporting capabilities, and the automatic appointment of a station to serve as an active monitor. The latter monitors token and frame transmissions, detects lost tokens and frames, and has the ability to purge circulating tokens and frames from the ring. Readers are referred to Chapter 4 for detailed

information concerning Token-Ring frame formats and the role
and operation of the active monitor.

*Logical link control*

Logical link control frames are used to provide a link between
network layer protocols and media access control. This linkage
is accomplished through the use of Service Access Points (SAPs)
which can be considered as operating similar to a mailbox. That
is, both network layer protocols and logical link control have
access to SAPs and can leave messages for each other in them.

Similar to mailboxes in a post office, each SAP has a distinct
address. For the logical link control a SAP represents the
location of a network layer process, such as the location of an
application within a workstation as viewed from the network.
From the network layer perspective, a SAP represents the place
to leave messages concerning the network services requested by
an application.

LLC frames contain two special address fields known as
the Destination Services Access Point and the Source Services
Access Point. The Destination Services Access Point (DSAP) is
one byte in length and specifies the receiving network layer
process. The Source Service Access Point (SSAP) is also one
byte in length. The SSAP specifies the sending network layer
process. Both DSAP and SSAP addresses are assigned by the
IEEE. Readers are referred to chapter 4 for detailed information
concerning LLC frame formats and data flow.

## 2.4 ANSI/ISO FDDI STANDARDS

The efforts of ANSI in developing FDDI have been internationally
recognized by the publication of ISO 9314. This standard is
divided into six parts; however, at the time this book was written
certain parts within ISO 9314 were still at a draft stage and had
not been accepted as an international standard.

Table 2.2 lists the ISO FDDI standards and pending
standards. Note that although Station Management was a
draft ANSI standard, that standard was solid enough for many
vendors to offer FDDI products in early 1993. Also note that
FDDI II represents a hybrid type of network that subdivides a
frame into slots that may be more suitable for carrying voice
and video than the original FDDI standard.

**Table 2.2**  FDDI standards status.

| Standard | ISO Number | Status |
|---|---|---|
| The physical layer | 9314-1 | International standard |
| MAC layer | 9314-2 | Draft |
| Physical medium dependent layer | 9314-3 | International standard |
| Use of FDDI on single-mode fiber | 9314-4 | Draft |
| FDDI II | 9314-5 | draft |
| Station management | n/a | Draft ANSI standard |

In examining the standards listed in Table 2.2, note the absence of a logical link control. In actuality it is there, since LLC is defined by the IEEE 802.2 standard.

The FDDI architecture is similar to Token-Ring in its relation to the lower layers of the OSI Reference Model. That is, FDDI has sublayers similar to the manner in which Token-Ring has sublayers. However, under FDDI, the two lowest OSI layers 1 and 2 are subdivided into four layers. Figure 2.6 illustrates the relationship between the two lower layers of the OSI Reference Model and FDDI.

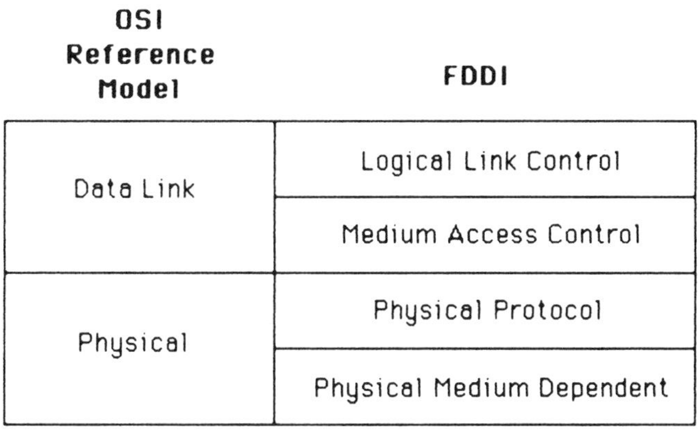

| OSI Reference Model | FDDI |
|---|---|
| Data Link | Logical Link Control |
| | Medium Access Control |
| Physical | Physical Protocol |
| | Physical Medium Dependent |

**Figure 2.6**  Comparing FDDI to the lower layer of the OSI Reference Model.

## Physical medium dependent layer

The Physical medium dependent layer specifies the type and size of optical fiber used by FDDI, the connectors, and the wavelength of the light used to transmit information.

## Physical layer

The physical layer defines the signaling rate, method of data encoding, and clocking on the network. The FDDI data rate is 100 Mbps, representing an increase by a factor of 25 over the 4-Mbps Token-Ring network. Unlike Differential Manchester encoding which is used on Token-Ring networks, FDDI uses a technique in which data is transmitted as a series of four-bit symbols encoded within a five-bit pattern—a method known as 4B/5B encoding. Readers are referred to Chapters 3 and 4 for specific information concerning the encoding of data on Token-Ring and FDDI networks.

## Medium access control

The FDDI MAC layer is very similar to the Token-Ring MAC layer with respect to its functionality. The major differences between the two concern the token-access process, frame size, frame structure, and priority mechanism employed with FDDI. Readers are referred to Chapters 4 and 5 for specific information concerning Token-Ring and FDDI frame formats and ring operations.

# 3

# TOKEN-RING CONCEPTS

One of the key factors associated with the successful setup of a Token-Ring network is a firm understanding of Token-Ring concepts. In this chapter we will focus our attention upon a broad range of Token-Ring concepts, examining the physical wiring and topology associated with this network and its hardware and software components. In addition, we will examine the use of a core set of internetworking devices whose utilization permits Token-Ring networks to be connected to other networks. Using that information as a base will enable us to design several rings as well as illustrate how such rings can be expanded.

## 3.1 TYPES OF TOKEN-RINGS

There are currently three major types of Token-Rings, with a fourth under development at the time this book was written. The first two types of Token-Ring networks are the focus of this chapter—4- and 16-Mbps Token-Ring networks that operate according to the IEEE 802.5 standard. Two additional Token-Ring networks are the Fiber Distributed Data Interface (FDDI) that operates at 100 Mbps and FDDI transmission over copper wiring—an evolving standard commonly referred to as Copper Distributed Data Interface (CDDI). Detailed information concerning FDDI and CDDI networks are presented in Chapter 4 as a separate entity.

## 3.2 NETWORK TOPOLOGY AND PHYSICAL WIRING

Two primary constraints associated with the design of Token-Ring networks are its topology and the wiring used in the network. A third major constraint is the operating rate of the network—4 or 16 Mbps. In examining the topology, wiring, and operating rate of Token-Ring networks we will soon note that each of these characteristics are related to one another. That is, the wiring used to cable devices on a Token-Ring network governs the maximum cabling distance between devices. The number of wiring concentrators, which are referred to as Multistation Access Units (MAUs), and their location govern the cable distance between MAUs and stations connected to MAUs. Finally, the operating rate of the network and the type of wiring used to cable devices together govern the distance between devices and the number of MAUs and stations permitted on the network.

## Topology considerations

Although the term 'Token-Ring' implies a ring structure, in actuality this type of LAN is either a star or star-ring structure, with the actual topology based upon the number of stations to be connected. The term 'star' is derived from the fact that a grouping of stations and other devices, including printers, plotters, repeaters, bridges, routers, and gateways, are connected in groups to a common device called a Multistation Access Unit (MAU).

Figure 3.1 illustrates a single ring formed through the use of one MAU in which up to eight devices are interconnected. Thus, for a very small Token-Ring LAN consisting of a mixture of eight or less devices the structure actually resembles a star.

When IBM introduced its 4-Mbps Token-Ring network its first MAU, known as the 8228, was a 10-port device, of which 2 ports were used for Ring-In (RI) and Ring-Out (RO) connectors which enable multiple MAUs to be connected to one another to expand the network. The remaining eight ports on the 8228 are designed for connecting devices to the ring. Since IBM's eight-port 8228 reached the market, other vendors have introduced similar products with different device support capacities. You can now commonly obtain MAUs that support 4, 8, and 16 devices.

In examining Figure 3.1, note that an eight-port MAU is illustrated, which enables up to eight devices to be interconnected to a Token-Ring LAN. The MAU can be considered the main ring path, as data will flow from one port to another via each device connected to the port. If you have more than eight devices, you

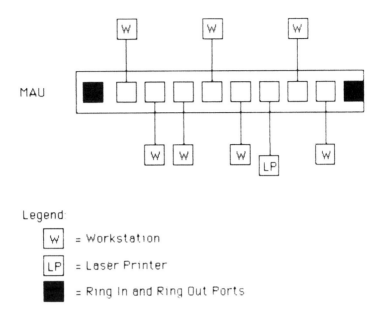

**Figure 3.1** Single-ring LAN. A single-ring LAN can support up to eight devices through their attachment to a common MAU.

can add additional MAUs, interconnecting the MAUs via the Ring-In and Ring-Out ports located at each side of each MAU. When this interconnection occurs by linking two or more MAUs together you form a star-ring topology as illustrated in Figure 3.2. In this illustration the stations and other devices form a star structure, while the interconnection of MAUs forms the ring; hence you obtain a star-ring topology.

## Redundant vs. non-redundant main ring paths

When two or more MAUs are interconnected, the serial path formed by those interconnections is known as the main ring path. Connections between MAUs can be accomplished through the use of one or two pairs of wiring. One pair will be used as the primary data path, while the other pair functions as a backup data path.

The top of Figure 3.3 illustrates the formation of a ring consisting of two MAUs in which both primary and backup paths are established to provide a redundant main ring path. If one of the cables linking the MAUs becomes disconnected,

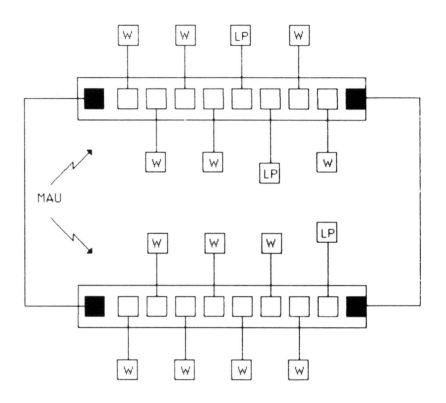

Legend

W = Workstation

LP = Laser Printer

■ = Ring In and Ring Out Ports

**Figure 3.2**  Developing the star-ring.

cut, or crimped, the network can continue to operate since the remaining wiring pair provides a non-redundant main ring path capability as shown in the lower portion of Figure 3.3.

The backup capability provided by redundant main ring paths is established through the use of loopback plugs or a built-in MAU self-shorting feature, both of which are discussed in additional detail later in this chapter. Since it is both difficult and tedious to draw wire pairs, in the remainder of this chapter we will use a single line to indicate wiring pairs between MAUs and MAUs and stations connected to MAUs.

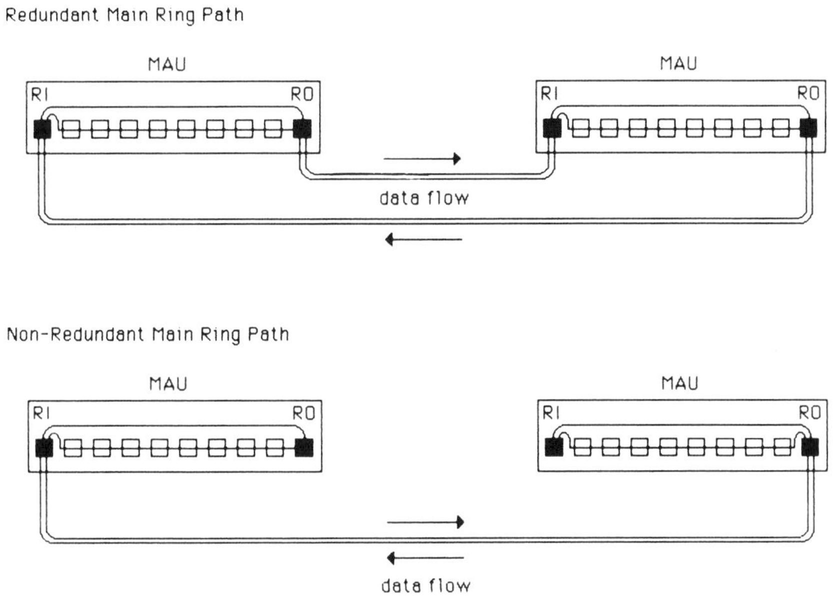

Redundant Main Ring Path

Non-Redundant Main Ring Path

**Figure 3.3**   Redundant and non-redundant main-ring paths.

Regardless of whether you use one, two, or a large number of MAUs, there are certain physical cabling restrictions you must consider in laying out the structure of your network. In addition, you must also consider the number of MAUs in your network and their placement in wiring closets as well as your projected communications requirements to determine if you will require bridges, routers, or gateways or if multiple rings will be interconnected via one or more of the previously mentioned devices. First let us examine some of the cabling and device restrictions associated with the use of Token-Ring networks. Then let us consider how we can apply our knowledge of cabling and device restrictions to satisfy representative communications requirements of an organization to develop a Token-Ring structure.

## Cabling and device restrictions

The type of cable or wiring used to connect devices to MAUs and interconnect MAUs is a major constraint that governs the size of a Token-Ring network. Since the IBM cabling system provides a large number of common types of wiring, let us first examine the type of cable defined by that cabling system.

## IBM cabling system

The IBM cabling system was introduced in 1984 as a mechanism to support the networking requirements of office environments. By defining standards for cables, connectors, faceplates, distribution panels, and other facilities IBM's cabling system is designed to support the interconnection of personal computers, conventional terminals, mainframe computers, and office systems. In addition, this system permits devices to be moved from one location to another or added to a network through a simple connection to the cabling system's wall plates or surface mounts.

### Cable Types

The IBM cabling system specifies seven different cabling categories. Depending upon the type of cable selected you can install the selected wiring indoors, outdoors, under a carpet, or in ducts and other air spaces.

The IBM cabling system uses wire which conforms to the American wire gauge or AWG. AWG is a unit of measurement with respect to the wire diameter. As the wire diameter gets larger the AWG number decreases, in effect resulting in an inverse relationship between wire diameter and AWG. The IBM cabling system uses wire between 22 AWG (0.644 mm) and 26 AWG (0.405 mm). Since a larger diameter wire has less resistance to current flow than a smaller wire diameter, a smaller AWG permits cabling distances to be extended in comparison to a higher AWG cable.

### Type 1

The IBM cabling system Type 1 cable contains two twisted pairs of 22 AWG conductors. Each pair is shielded with a foil wrapping and both pairs are surrounded by an outer braided shield or with a corrugated metallic shield. One pair of wires uses shield colors of red and green, while the second pair of wires uses shield colors of orange and black. The braided shield is used for indoor wiring, while the corrugated metallic shield is used for outdoor wiring. Type 1 cable is available in two different designs—plenum and non-plenum. Plenum cable can be installed without the use of a conduit while non-plenum cable requires a conduit. Type 1 cable is typically used to connect a distribution panel or multistation access unit and the faceplate or surface mount at a workstation.

### Type 2

Type 2 cable is actually a Type 1 indoor cable with the addition of four pairs of 22 AWG conductors for telephone usage. Due to this, Type 1 cable is also referred to as data-grade twisted-pair cable, while Type 2 cable is known as two data-grade and four-grade twisted pair. Due to its voice capability, Type 2 cable can support PBX interconnections. Like Type 1 cable, Type 2 cable supports plenum and non-plenum designs. Type 2 cable is not available in an outdoor version.

### Type 3

Type 3 cable is conventional twisted pair, telephone wire, with a minimum of two twists per foot. Both 22 AWG and 24 AWG conductors are supported by this cable type. One common use of Type 3 cable is to connect PCs to MAUs in a Token-Ring network.

### Type 5

Type 5 cable is fiber optic cable. Two $100/140$ $\mu$m optical fibers are contained in a Type 5 cable. This cable is suitable for indoor, non-plenum installation or outdoor aerial installation. Due to the extended transmission distance obtainable with fiber optic cable, Type 5 cable is used in conjunction with the IBM 8219 Token-Ring Network Optical Fiber Repeater to interconnect two MAUs up to 6600 feet (2 km) from one another.

### Type 6

Type 6 cable contains two twisted pairs of 26 AWG conductors for data communications. It is available for non-plenum applications only and its smaller diameter than Type 1 cable makes it slightly more flexible. The primary use of Type 6 cable is for short runs as a flexible path cord. This type of cable is often used to connect an adapter card in a personal computer to a faceplate which, in turn, is connected to a Type 1 or Type 2 cable which forms the backbone of a network.

## Type 8

Type 8 cable is designed for installation under a carpet. This cable contains two individually shielded, parallel pairs of 26 AWG conductors with a plastic ramp designed to make undercarpet installation as unobtrusive as possible. Although Type 8 cable can be used in a manner similar to Type 1, it only provides half of the maximum transmission distance obtainable through the use of Type 1 cable.

## Type 9

Type 9 cable is essentially a low-cost version of Type 1 cable. Like Type 1, Type 9 cable consists of two twisted pairs of data cable; however, 26 AWG conductors are used in place of the 22 AWG wire used in Type 1 cable. As a result of the use of a smaller diameter cable, transmission distances on Type 9 cable are approximately two-thirds that obtainable through the use of Type 1 cable. The color coding on the shield of Type 9 cable is the same as that used for Type 1 cable.

All seven types of cables defined by the IBM cabling system can be used to construct Token-Ring networks. However, the use of each type of cable has a different effect upon the ability to connect devices to the network, the number of devices that can be connected to a common network, the number of wiring closets in which MAUs can be installed to form a ring, and the ability of the cable to carry separate voice conversations. The latter capability enables a common cable to be routed to a user's desk where a portion of the cable is connected to their telephone while another portion of the cable is connected to their computer's Token-Ring adapter card.

Table 3.1 summarizes the performance characteristics of the cables defined by the IBM cabling system. The drive distance entry indicates the relative relationship between different types of cables with respect to the maximum cabling distance between a workstation and an MAU as well as between MAUs. Type 1 cable provides a maximum drive distance of 100 m between a workstation and an MAU and 300 m between MAUs for a network operating at 4 Mbps. Other drive distance entries in Table 3.1 are relative to the drive distance obtainable when Type 1 cable is used.

**Table 3.1** IBM cable system cable performance characteristics.

| Performance characteristics | Cable type | | | | | | |
|---|---|---|---|---|---|---|---|
| | 1 | 2 | 3 | 5 | 6 | 8 | 9 |
| Drive distance (relative to type 1) | 1.0 | 1.0 | 0.45 | 3.0 | 0.75 | 0.5 | 0.66 |
| Data rate (Mbps) | 16 | 16 | 4* | 250 | 16 | 16 | 16 |
| Maximum devices per ring | 260 | 260 | 72 | 260 | 96 | 260 | 260 |
| Maximum closets per ring | 12 | 12 | 2 | 12 | 12 | 12 | 12 |
| Voice support | no | yes | yes | no | no | no | no |

*Note: Although 16-Mbps operations are not directly supported by Type 3 cable, its use is quite common when drive distances are very short.

**Connectors**

The IBM cabling system includes connectors for terminating both data and voice conductors. The data connector has a unique design based upon the development of a latching mechanism which permits it to mate with another, identical connector.

Figure 3.4 illustrates the IBM cabling system data connector. Its design makes it self-shorting when disconnected from another connector. This provides a Token-Ring network with electrical continuity when a station is disconnected. Unfortunately, the data connector is very expensive in comparison to RS-232 and RJ telephone connectors with the typical retail price of the data connector between $8 and $10, whereas RS-232 connectors cost approximately $3 and an RJ telephone connector can be purchased for a dime or so.

Due to the high cost of data connectors and cable the acceptance of the IBM cabling system by end-users has been slow to materialize. Since it provides a standard system of office interconnectivity its usage may significantly increase if it becomes more economical in comparison to the cost of conventional connectors and cable.

Now that we have reviewed the types of cabling specifed by the IBM cabling system, let us focus our attention upon cabling and device restrictions you must consider in designing

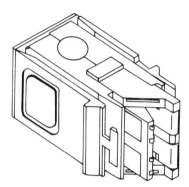

**Figure 3.4**   Cabling system data connector.

an appropriate Token-Ring network to ensure the network will
work correctly. First, you must consider the maximum cabling
distance between each device and an MAU that will service the
device. The cable between the MAU and the device is referred
to as a lobe, with the maximum lobe distance being 100 m
or 330 feet at both 4 and 16 Mbps. This means that you
must consider the lobe distance in conjunction with the cabling
distance restrictions between MAUs if you have more than eight
devices to be connected to a Token-Ring LAN. In addition, for
larger networks, you must also consider restrictions on the
number of MAUs in the network and their placement in wiring
closets as well as a parameter known as the adjusted ring length
since they collectively govern the maximum number of devices
that can be supported.

*Intra-MAU cabling distances*

Table 3.2 lists the maximum intra-MAU cabling distances
permitted on a Token-Ring network for the two most commonly
used types of IBM cables. Those distances can be extended
through the use of repeaters, however, their use adds both to
the complexity and cost of the network. In addition, by adding
more devices in a serial structure, you add to the probability
that one device will fail, which can bring down your network.

   As indicated in Table 3.2, the cabling distance between MAUs
depends upon both the operating rate of the LAN—4 Mbps or 16
Mbps—and the type of cable used. Type 1 is a double-shielded
pair cable, while Type 3 is non-shielded twisted-pair telephone
wire.

**Table 3.2**  Intra-MAU cabling distance (feet).

| | Type of cable | |
| Operating Rate | Type 1 | Type 3 |
| --- | --- | --- |
| 4 Mbps | 330 | 1000 |
| 16 Mbps | 330 | 250 |

In examining the entries in Table 3.2, it may appear odd that the maximum intra-MAU cable distance is the same for both 4- and 16-Mbps networks when Type 1 cable is used. This situation occurred because, at the time IBM set a 100-m recommended limit for a 4-Mbps network, the company took into consideration the need to reuse the same cabling when customers upgraded to a 16-Mbps operating rate. When using Type 3 cable, distances are shorter since signal line noise increases in proportion to the square root of frequency. Thus, upgrading the operating rate from 4 to 16 Mbps with Type 3 cable decreases the maximum permissible distance.

As you plan to extend your network to interconnect additional devices, you must also consider the maximum number of MAUs and devices supported by a Token-Ring network. If you use Type 1 cable, you are limited to a maximum of 33 MAUs and 260 devices. If you use Type 3 cable, you are limited to a maximum of 9 MAUs and 72 devices. These limitations are applicable to both 4- and 16-Mbps networks; however, they represent a maximum number of MAUs and devices and do not indicate reality in which a lesser number of MAUs may be required due to the use of multiple wiring closets or a long adjusted ring length. Due to the role played by the adjusted ring length in governing the number of MAUs, let us examine what an adjusted ring length is and how it functions as a constraint.

*Adjusted ring length*

To fully understand the reason why we must consider the adjusted ring length (ARL) of a Token-Ring network requires a discussion on the network's ability to operate with a faulty cabling section. To illustrate this capability, consider the three-MAU network illustrated in Figure 3.5a. Under normal network operation, data is transmitted from RO to RI between MAUs and over the main ring path which connects the last MAU's RO port to the first MAU's RI port.

If an attached device or a lobe cable fails, the lack of voltage on the MAU's port causes the port to be bypassed, permitting information from other stations to flow on the main ring path. If an MAU or a cable interconnecting two MAUs fails, the previously described built-in backup capability of MAUs permits the network to continue operating. This backup capability permits the Token-Ring to be reestablished in one of two ways dependent upon the capability of the MAUs used in the network. Some MAUs have a 'self-shorting' capability, which means that RI and RO connectors are joined together without requiring the use of a cable or plug to complete a ring. Other MAUs require the use of a cable or plug between the RI and RO connectors. By using the 'self-shorting' capability, or using a cable or plug in the input and output connectors of the MAUs located at both ends of a failed cable, the ring can be reconfigured for operation. Figure 3.5b illustrates the reconfigured ring. Note that the total cable length of the main ring path and available cable segments represents the adjusted ring length.

In actuality, the adjusted ring length is the total ring length (main ring path plus all cable segments) less the shortest cable segment between MAUs. The reason we subtract the shortest cable segment is that doing so provides the longest total cable distance for a reconfigured ring. It is that distance that a signal must be capable of flowing around a ring without excessive distortion adversely affecting the signal. For example, suppose the main ring path is 300 feet and cable segments A and B are 200 and 150 feet, respectively. Then, the total drive distance is 300+200+150, or 650 feet, and the adjusted ring length is 650–150, or 500 feet.

*Other ring size considerations*

The adjusted ring length as well as the length of the main ring path are two constraints that govern the size of a Token-Ring network. Other constraints include the operating rate of the ring, the length of the longest lobe, the type and number of MAUs in the network, and the number of distinct locations where the MAUs are installed—the latter referred to by IBM as wiring closets. The type of MAU is equivalent to the type of cabling used. A Type 1 MAU is cabled using Type 1

### a. Normal network operation

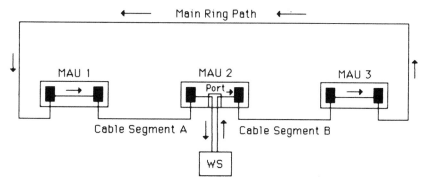

Total cable length = Main ring path + Cable segment A + Cable segment B

### b. Reconfigured ring due to faulty cable segment

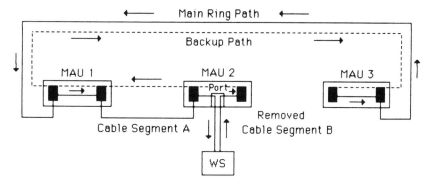

Adjusted ring length = Main ring path + Cable segment A

**Figure 3.5**  Computing the adjusted ring length.

(double-shielded pair cable), while a Type 3 MAU uses Type 3 (non-shielded twisted-pair telephone wire) cable.

When Type 1 MAUs are used for 4- or 16-Mbps operation and all lobe cables terminate in a single wiring closet, you can interconnect up to 33 IBM 8228 MAUs, which can serve 260 devices, with each device cabled using up to a 100-m lobe cable. Here, the number of 8228s is:

$$8228s = \text{Int}\frac{(\text{device} + 0.5)}{8} \leq 33.$$

For 2 to 12 wiring closets, IBM provides a series of charts in the firm's *Token-Ring Network, Introduction and Planning Guide*, which supplies details about the relationship between the lobe length, adjusted ring length, number of MAUs, and wiring closets when Type 1 cable is used. Those charts are two-dimensional arrays with the number of wiring closets listed across the horizontal heading and number of MAUs listed down the vertical heading. Each entry in the array provides in feet the sum of the longest lobe cable and adjusted ring length permitted. For example, a two-wiring-closet network with two MAUs can have a total of 1192 feet of cable made up of the sum of the longest lobe and the adjusted ring length. For a network with two wiring closets and three MAUs, the maximum cable distance decreases to 1163 feet, while a three-wiring-closet three-MAU network has a maximum cable distance of 1148 feet.

Although IBM does not supply formulas, they can be derived through linear regression. The top of Table 3.3 provides the formulas for 4- and 16-Mbps Token-Ring networks that indicate the relationship between the adjusted ring length, longest lobe, number of wiring closets, and number of MAUs. Those formulas can be rearranged as indicated in the lower portion of Table 3.3 to determine if your network is within the cable distance specification. As long as the cabling distance represents a positive surplus, your network is within IBM guidelines.

**Table 3.3**  Token-Ring network type 1 cable constraints. (All numeric values in feet.)

---

*Parameter constraints*
4 Mbps: ARL + LLobe $\leq$ 1278.5 $-$ (15.1 $\times$ WC + 28.5 $\times$ MAUs)
16 Mbps: ARL + LLobe $\leq$ 607.5 $-$ (16.42 $\times$ WC + 21.85 $\times$ MAUs)

*Cable surplus*
4 Mbps: 1278.5 $-$ (ARL + LLobe + 15.1 $\times$ WC + 28.5 $\times$ MAUs)
16 Mbps: 607.5 $-$ (ARL + LLobe + 16.42 $\times$ WC + 21.85 $\times$ MAUs)

---

ARL = adjusted ring length        WC = number of wiring closets
LLobe = longest lobe distance      MAUs = number of MAUs

*Networks based on other cable types*

Two other common types of cable used to construct Token-Ring networks are Type 3 cable and patch cables connected to an adapter cable consisting of 8 feet of Type 6 cable. Using

Type 3 cable, a Token-Ring network can consist of up to 72 devices using up to nine MAUs at both 4 and 16 Mbps. MAU cabling distances can be up to 1000 feet at 4 Mbps and 250 feet at 16 Mbps. When patch cables connected to adapter cables using Type 6 cable are used, the maximum number of stations is limited to 96, while the maximum number of 8228 MAUs is limited to 12. The maximum patch cable lobe distance is 150 feet, while the maximum patch cable distance between two MAUs is also limited to 150 feet. Although up to 12 MAUs can be used in this type of network, the maximum patch cable distance permitted for connecting all MAUs is limited to 400 feet. This type of cable-based network provides users with a small movable cabling system and operates at both 4 and 16 Mbps. Table 3.4 summarizes the maximum number of devices and MAUs based upon different types of cable.

**Table 3.4**   Device and MAU limits versus cable type.

|        | Maximum devices | Maximum number of MAUs |
|--------|-----------------|------------------------|
| Type 1 | 260             | 33                     |
| Type 3 | 72              | 9                      |
| Type 6 | 96              | 12                     |

*Cable considerations*

Most organizations constructing Token-Ring networks are usually faced with considering two key cable-related areas. First, a decision concerning the use of Type 1 versus Type 3 cable must be made. Secondly, a decision concerning the use of the IBM cabling system connector versus the common telephone system RJ connector must be made.

Until recently, the selection of Type 1 versus Type 3 cable was governed by the operating rate of the network. That is, Type 3 cable was originally limited by IBM for 4 Mbps operations. Thus, users of the IBM cabling system were forced to use Type 1 shielded cable for constructing 16-Mbps networks. Unfortunately, shielded twisted-pair (STP) is heavier and costlier than unshielded twisted-pair (UTP) cable. Thus, UTP has become the preferred choice for constructing 4-Mbps networks and is commonly used in constructing 16-Mbps networks that have relatively short lobe and intra-MAU cabling distances. In fact, at the time this book was written IBM was said to be considering introducing a new 16-Mbps adapter card which would support the use of UTP cable for large networks.

A second issue facing many organizations is the type of cable connector to use. Due to the relatively high cost of the IBM cabling system connector, the use of RJ connectors is now commonly used to connect cable to MAUs. In fact, many vendors that manufacture MAUs now build-in RJ connector sockets as well as IBM cabling connector sockets, providing users with the ability to choose either type of connector for terminating their cables.

## 3.3 TOKEN-RING NETWORK HARDWARE

In discussing some basic Token-Ring concepts, we previously examined a few of the hardware components used in a Token-Ring network, such as different types of cable and the role and use of MAUs. While cable and MAUs provide the foundation for constructing Token-Ring networks, they only represent two of many hardware components used to construct such networks. Thus, in this section we will examine the operation and utilization of additional hardware components as well as review some previously discussed products.

### Adapter cards

A Token-Ring adapter card, referred to by many vendors as a network interface card (NIC), is a printed circuit board which is installed in the expansion slot of a computer.

The first adapter card marketed by IBM for connecting personal computers to a Token-Ring network was limited to supporting a 4-Mbps network operating rate. When IBM announced its 16-Mbps Token-Ring network, the company introduced its 16/4 Adapter which can transmit data over Token-Ring networks at either 4 or 16 Mbps to match the data rate of the network it is cabled to. The 16/4 Adapter contains a total of 64 kbytes of RAM, of which 63.5 kbytes are available to the user's computer by addressing the high memory area between 640 kbytes and 1 Mbytes. Although the 16/4 Adapter is similar to many other vendor products in that all 64 kbytes of its RAM reside in the address space of the computer it is inserted into, this adapter also supports RAM paging. This feature organizes the adapter's RAM into four 16-kbyte pages that are presented to a network application program one page at a time, which makes available 48 kbytes of RAM to other programs.

When using DOS and switching between programs, the additional memory obtained by RAM paging can make the difference between being able to switch between a LAN program and a large database or word processing program. Since the use of the adapter's full 64-kbyte block of RAM is slightly more efficient than mapping data transfers through 16-kbyte pages, the decision to use RAM paging involves balancing performance against memory availability. You can avoid making this decision by using an adapter card that has a bus mastering capability. With this capability, data can be transferred directly between the network and the computer's memory without requiring the computer's microprocessor to be involved. Thus, bus mastering eliminates the necessity to have additional memory on an adapter card; however, it requires the use of standard memory which can be at a premium on some DOS machines. According to industry data, bus mastering adapter cards will provide a level of data transfer around 200 kbps when using a DOS COPY statement to transfer a file. An adapter card using a full 64 kbytes of shared RAM will provide a data transfer between 175 and 200 kbps depending upon vendor, while the use of paged RAM will reduce performance to approximately 165 kbps.

All Token-Ring adapter cards contain several specially designed chip sets used to transmit and receive data to and from the network, perform self-checking operations, and generate different error messages when certain error conditions are observed.

The adapter card is cabled to a port on an MAU, enabling the computer in which it is installed to transmit and receive information to and from the network. Currently, over 50 companies manufacture Token-Ring adapter cards for use in a large variety of computers, including workstations, personal computers, minicomputers, and mainframe computers. Figure 3.6 illustrates three Token-Ring adapter cards manufactured by Intel Corporation for Industry Standard Architecture (ISA), Micro Channel Architecture (MCA), and Extended Industry Standard Architecture (EISA) expansion slots. Other common Token-Ring adapter cards are manufactured for use in different Apple Macintosh computers and Sun Microsystems workstations.

**Figure 3.6** Three Intel Token-Ring adapter cards. Clockwise from upper right are Industry Standard Architecture (ISA), Extended Industry Standard Architecture (EISA), and Microchannel Architecture (MCA) adapter cards. (Photograph courtesy of Intel Corporation.)

*Self-contained adapters*

Until 1991, network users wishing to share a printer on a Token-Ring network were required to connect the printer to a computer which in turn was connected to the network. In late 1991, Intel introduced a self-contained adapter card that can be directly connected to a printer. Known as NetPort and illustrated in Figure 3.7, this device permits up to two printers or plotters to be connected to a network without requiring the use of a computer. Through the use of NetPort or similar products manufactured by other vendors you can locate printers and plotters in areas accessible to many persons without requiring the placement of a computer in a common area.

*Wireless adapters*

Recognizing that at times the routing of a cable may be difficult or impossible, several vendors have developed wireless adapter cards. Some vendor products include an antenna connected to

**Figure 3.7** Intel NetPort printer server. The Intel NetPort contains a Token-Ring adapter card and other hardware components which enables two plotters or printers to be connected to a network without requiring the use of a computer. (Photograph courtesy of Intel Corporation.)

a special Token-Ring adapter card in which a chipset was added to perform spread spectrum transmission. Placing a similar adapter card and antenna into a server permits the support of a workstation at a distance of up to 800 feet in all directions from the server. Here the actual transmission distance will depend upon the number of walls through which the signal must pass and the composition of the walls.

A second type of wireless adapter card obtains its transmission capability through a connection to an infrared transmitter/receiver. Although this method of transmission is limited to a line-of-sight operation, it provides a mechanism to link stations onto a network from areas where it may be difficult or impractical to install cable, such as a computer located on a receptionist's desk in the atrium of a hotel lobby.

*Adapter operation*

When a computer containing a Token-Ring adapter is powered-on, the adapter performs a self-check operation. If it passes its self-check, it generates a +5 V signal onto the cable connecting the card to a port on the MAU. This voltage causes a relay on the MAU port to open, which switches the port from its bypass mode to its ring access mode of operation. Thus, the computer containing the adapter then becomes connected to the Token-Ring network. Conversely, if the adapter fails its self-check it will not transmit a +5 V signal and will not be connected to the network.

Once connected to the network, the adapter will look for a free token when it has data to transmit and converts that data into a frame which will contain information in a predefined format. Readers are referred to Chapter 4 for specific information on the flow of data within a Token-Ring network.

Although many vendors would like customers to believe that the performance of all Token-Ring adapter cards is equal such that price should be a key selection factor, this is not always true. While most adapter cards are manufactured using common chip sets produced by a few semiconductor vendors, differences in software drivers and hardware adapter board design can result in significant differences between the performance capability of different adapter cards. For example, by improving software drivers, the transfer of information between the adapter and the computer can be enhanced. In fact, in 1992 IBM announced that a new driver increased the efficiency of its Token-Ring adapter by 80%. This increase in performance was accomplished by using the driver to reduce the number of adapter interrupts on the computer's bus from four to two for each frame transmitted into the computer's memory. Concerning hardware design, several vendors manufacture adapters that support a bus mastering direct memory access (DMA) capability. As previously noted in this chapter, through the use of a bus mastering DMA capability data can be transferred directly into the computer's memory without requiring the intervention of the computer's processor. This technique is more efficient than the use of shared memory and programmed I/O, since those techniques require the computer's processor to be interrupted to effect a data transfer operation.

## Multistation access unit

Figure 3.8 illustrates a 10-port MAU referred to as a Madge Networks Ring Hub by this vendor. This device contains eight network ports, one RI port, and one RO port. In examining the ports on this MAU, readers will note they are designed to receive an IBM cable system connector.

**Figure 3.8** Madge Networks Ring Hub. The 10-port Madge Networks Ring Hub supports eight Token-Ring network device connections through the insertion of cables terminated with an IBM cable system connector. (Photograph courtesy of Madge Networks.)

The MAU can be considered to function as a wiring concentrator which serves as the building block for constructing Token-Ring networks. Each MAU contains both a main ring path and a backup path for transmitting signals over the ring. Although the MAU illustrated in Figure 3.8 was limited to using IBM cabling system connectors, other vendors provide media connections for unshielded twisted-pair cable using RJ11 and RJ45 jacks.

In addition to cable connector support, MAUs also differ concerning the presence or absence of AC power. Passive MAUs are unpowered and obtain power from the adapter cards connected to the network. Active MAUs contain an AC adapter and receive power from a standard electrical outlet. Signal jitter—a form of distortion in which bits are displaced from the position where they are expected to be located—may be more pronounced when using passive MAUs, and some vendors specify longer permissible cable distances when their active MAUs are used. Other differences between MAUs concerns the number of network ports supported and the physical placement of RI and RO ports. As previously mentioned in this chapter, commonly marketed MAUs support 4, 8, and 16 Token-Ring device connections. Concerning the physical placement of RI and RO ports, some vendors place those ports at opposite ends of the MAU. Other vendors place the RI and RO ports next to one another at one end of the MAU. The latter placement makes it easier to interconnect MAUs when several are mounted in a common rack.

## Controlled access unit

The controlled access unit is a term used by IBM to represent a wiring concentrator that can be used in place of a group of MAUs to support a large number of Token-Ring cable connections. The IBM model 8230 is that vendor's nomenclature for its controlled access unit. The 8230 is a rack-mountable device which consists of a base unit and up to four lobe attachment modules (LAMs). Each LAM supports the connection of up to 20 devices to the ring, permitting one 8230 to attach up to 80 workstations to a Token-Ring network.

Similar to the IBM 8228, the 8230 contains one RI and one RO port. Those ports enable the 8230 to be connected to conventional eight-port MAUs—the latter being used to satisfy the connectivity requirements of groups of users located in small clusters. In addition to providing the support formerly required through the use of up to ten 8228s, the 8230 works with IBM's LAN Network Manager program. That program enables an operator to list the adapter addresses connected to each 8230 in a network, set 8230 parameters, control access to the network through the 8230, and perform other functions.

The 8230 supports both 4- and 16-Mbps networks and can function as a repeater in both directions. This device is similar to the 8228 in that it can work with both copper and optical fiber cables in the IBM cabling system. In addition, 8230 lobe attachment modules are available with IBM cabling system connectors as well as RJ45 connectors—the latter supporting twisted-wire lobe connections.

Figure 3.9 illustrates the use of the IBM 8230 in conjunction with a 8228 to construct a Token-Ring network. In this example, it was assumed that up to 20 network users were located in a relatively small clustered area in a corner of a floor and would be cabled to a one-LAM 8230. At the opposite end of the floor, a small group of eight or less users is located. Here you could use a single 8228 to service those users. By using the 8228 at the second location instead of expanding the 8230, you would minimize lobe runs and could both significantly reduce the cost of cabling devices to the network as well as ensure you do not violate network cabling constraints.

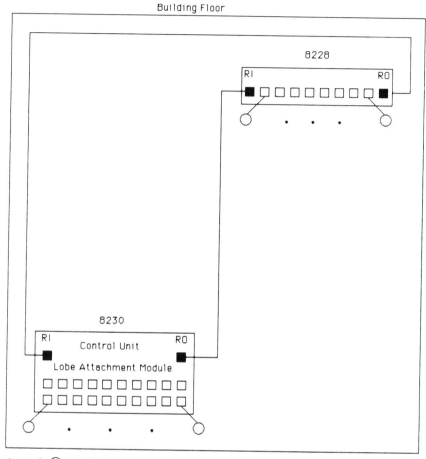

**Figure 3.9** Using IBM 8228 and 8230 devices to build a ring. The IBM 8230 Controlled Access Unit can be expanded to support the connection of up to 80 devices into a Token-Ring network, while the 8228 MAU supports up to 8 devices.

## Repeaters

A repeater represents the simplest type of hardware component in terms of design, operation, and functionality. This device operates at the physical layer of the ISO Open Systems Interconnection Reference Model, regenerating a signal received on one cable segment and then retransmitting the signal onto another cable segment. Figure 3.10a illustrates the operation of a repeater with respect to the ISO OSI Reference Model.

**a. At OSI level**

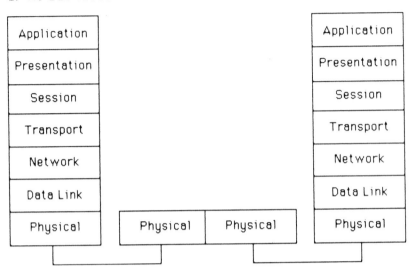

**b. Copper repeater signal regeneration process**

**Figure 3.10**  Repeater operation.

Repeaters are used to increase the geographical distance a Token-Ring network can cover. They can be used on both 4- and 16-Mbps networks to extend the lobe length between an MAU and a workstation, the distance between MAUs, or the distance between an MAU and a CAU.

*Types*

There are two basic types of repeaters. An electrical or copper repeater—the latter being a term used to denote the media it supports—simply receives an electrical signal and then regenerates the signal. During the signal regeneration process a new signal is formed which matches the original characteristics of the received signal. This process is illustrated in Figure 3.10b. By transmitting a new signal, the repeater removes any previous distortion and attenuation, enabling an extension in the permissible transmission distance.

The second type of repeater commonly used is an electrical–optical device commonly referred to as a fiber optic repeater due to its support of fiber media. This type of repeater converts an electrical signal into an optical signal for transmission and performs a reverse function when receiving a light signal. Similar to an electrical repeater, the electrical–optical repeater extends the distance that a signal can be carried on a local area network. Fiber optic repeaters are restricted to use on the main ring path of Token-Ring networks and must be used in pairs. Copper repeaters must also be used in pairs to extend the main ring path; however, they can be used on an individual basis to extend the permissible lobe distance.

Since a repeater is restricted to operating at the OSI physical layer, it is transparent to data flow. This restricts the use of a repeater to linking identical networks or network segments. For example, you could use repeaters to connect two Ethernet or two Token-Ring networks but not to connect an Ethernet network to a Token-Ring network.

*Distance extension*

The cabling distance obtained from the use of a copper repeater to extend lobe and main ring path distances depends upon the operating rate of the network and the type of wiring used as well as the particular vendor product selected. For example, Table 3.5 lists the maximum repeater transmission distances obtainable on a lobe and on the main ring path through the use of certain Andrew Corporation repeater products. Although the distances listed in Table 3.5 are representative of several vendor products, readers should check vendor specifications prior to using copper repeaters. In fact, some vendors manufacturing copper repeaters permit their daisy-chaining, in which the distance between MAUs may be extended up to 5000 feet.

To obtain extended main ring path distances you can consider the use of fiber optic repeaters. The IBM 8219 Token-Ring optical fiber repeater permits MAUs to be located up to 6600 feet from one another when the network operates at 16 Mbps and 10 000 feet when the network operates at 4 Mbps. Since fiber

**Table 3.5** Andrew Corporation maximum repeater transmission distances in feet.

| | Operating rate | |
| --- | --- | --- |
| Wiring | 4 Mbps | 16 Mbps |
| When used on lobes: | | |
| Type 1 | 2400 | 900 |
| Type 3 | | |
| 19 AWG | 1100 | 450 |
| 22 AWG | 1000 | 420 |
| 24 AWG | 900 | 390 |
| 26 AWG | 800 | 360 |
| When used on main ring path: | | |
| Type 1 | 2400 | 1000 |
| Type 3 | | |
| 19 AWG | 1275 | 480 |
| 22 AWG | 1200 | 450 |
| 24 AWG | 1100 | 420 |
| 26 AWG | 975 | 390 |

optic cable transports signals in the form of light energy, such signals are immune to electrical interference. Thus, the routing of fiber optic cable can include its placement near machinery and other types of electromagnetic energy generators that may cause havoc to signals transported on copper cable.

*Topology considerations*

When using repeaters between MAUs, you can consider two topologies—using either a pair of repeaters in a wiring closet or a single repeater in a wiring closet. The top of Figure 3.11 illustrates the use of a pair of repeaters, while the lower portion illustrates the use of single repeaters. For simplicity of illustration, workstations attached to MAUs are not shown in Figure 3.11.

When a pair of repeaters is used to interconnect wiring closets, the ring is completed by cabling the repeaters to form a circular ring. When only one pair of repeaters is used, the repeaters are cabled together and the ring is completed using either the self-shorting feature of some MAUs or the use of loopback plugs on the last MAU in each wiring closet. Doing so results in the ring operating on the built-in backup path; however, while this saves

## Using repeater pairs

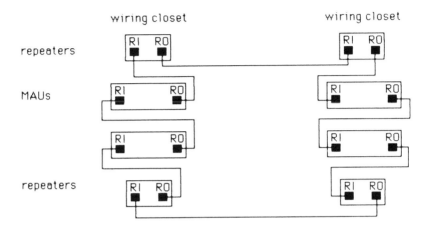

## Using a single pair of repeaters

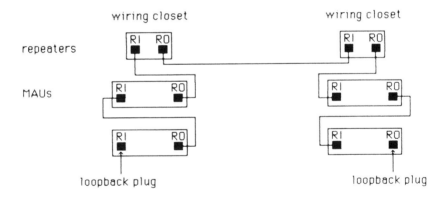

**Figure 3.11**   Extending wiring closet distances.

a pair of repeaters it also eliminates the use of the backup path if a cable failure occurs.

## Bridges

In comparison to a repeater which lacks intelligence and is restricted to linking similar local area networks, bridges are intelligent devices that can connect similar and dissimilar local area networks. To obtain an appreciation for the functions performed by bridges, let us examine the use of this type of networking product.

*Operation*

Figure 3.12 illustrates the operation of a bridge with respect to the OSI Reference Model as well as its use to connect two separate Token-Ring networks. The use of a bridge to connect two Token-Ring networks is shown as a logical connection. From a physical perspective the bridge contains two Token-Ring adapter cards, with each card cabled to a port on an MAU or CAU connected to different rings.

When a bridge begins to operate, it examines each frame transmitted on connected local area networks at the data link layer—a process beyond the capability of a repeater which operates transparent to data. By reading the source address included in each frame, the bridge assembles a table of local addresses for each network. In addition to reading each source address, the bridge also reads the destination address contained in the frame. If the destination address is not contained in the local address table that the bridge constructs, this fact indicates that the frame's destination is not on the current network. In this situation, the bridge transmits the frame onto the other network it is attached to. If the destination address is contained in the local address table, this indicates that the frame should remain on the local network. In this situation the bridge simply repeats the frame without altering its routing.

The previously described method of bridging operation is referred to as transparent bridging. Readers are referred to Chapter 6 for detailed information concerning different methods of bridge operations.

We can summarize the operation of the bridge illustrated in the lower portion of Figure 3.12 as follows:

- Bridge reads all frames transmitted on network A.
- Frames with destination address on network A are repeated back onto that network.
- Frames with destination address on network B are removed from network A and retransmitted onto network B.
- The above process is reversed for traffic on network B.

**Filtering and Forwarding**

The process of examining each frame is known as filtering. The filtering rate of a bridge is directly related to its level of performance. That is, the higher the filtering rate of a bridge

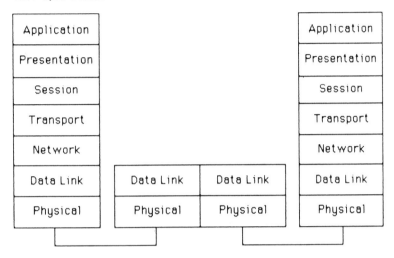

**a.   OSI operation**

**b.   Application Example**

**Figure 3.12**   Bridge operation. A bridge connects two local area networks or network segments at the data link layer.

the lower the probability it will become a bottleneck to network performance. A second performance measurement associated with bridges is their forwarding rate. The forwarding rate is expressed in frames per second and denotes the maximum capability of a bridge to transmit traffic from one network to another.

*Types*

There are two general types of bridges—transparent and translating. Each type of bridge can be obtained as a local or remote device, with a remote device including a wide area network (WAN) interface as well as the ability to convert frames into a WAN transmission protocol.

**Transparent Bridge**

A transparent bridge provides a connection between two local area networks that employ the same data link protocol. Thus, the bridge shown in the lower portion of Figure 3.12 can be considered to be a transparent bridge. This type of bridge is used to connect two or more local area networks that employ identical protocols at the data link layer. At the physical layer, some transparent bridges have multiple ports that support different media. Thus, a transparent bridge does not have to be transparent at the physical level although the majority of such bridges are.

Although a transparent bridge provides a high level of performance for a small number of network interconnections, its level of performance decreases as the number of interconnected networks increases. The rationale for this loss in performance is based upon the method used by transparent bridges to develop a route between LANs. Readers are referred to Chapter 6 for specific information concerning bridge routing and performance issues.

**Translating Bridge**

A translating bridge provides a connection capability between two local area networks that employ different protocols at the data link layer. Since networks using different data link layer protocols normally use different media, a translating bridge will also provide support for different physical layer connections.

Figure 3.13 illustrates the use of a translating bridge to interconnect a Token-Ring network to an Ethernet local area network. In this example, the bridge functions as an Ethernet node on the Ethernet network and as a Token-Ring node on the Token-Ring network. When a frame from one network has a destination on the other network, the bridge will perform a series of operations, including frame and transmission rate conversion. For example, consider an Ethernet frame destined to the Token-Ring network. The bridge will strip fields not applicable to Token-Ring operations, such as the frame's preamble and Frame Check Sequence (FCS). Then it will convert the remainder of the frame into a Token-Ring frame format. Once the bridge receives a free token the new frame will be transmitted onto the Token-Ring network; however, the transmission rate will be at the Token-Ring network rate and not at the Ethernet rate. For frames going from the Token-Ring to the Ethernet the process would be reversed.

One of the problems associated with the use of a translating bridge is the conversion of frames from their format on one network to the format required for use on another network. For example, the information field of an Ethernet frame can vary from 64 to 1500 bytes, while a Token-Ring can have a maximum information field size of 4500 bytes when the ring operates at 4 Mbps and 18 000 bytes when the ring operates at 16 Mbps. If a station on a Token-Ring network has a frame whose information field exceeds 1500 bytes in length, the bridging of that frame onto an Ethernet network cannot occur. This is because there is no provision within either protocol to inform a station that a frame flowing from one network to another was fragmented and requires reassembly. To effectively use a bridge in this situation requires software on each station on each network to be configured to use the smallest maximum frame size of any network to be connected together. In this example, Token-Ring workstations would not be allowed to transmit information fields greater than 1500 bytes.

*Features*

The functionality of a bridge is based upon the features incorporated into this device. Table 3.6 lists 11 major bridge features which define both the functionality and performance level of a bridge.

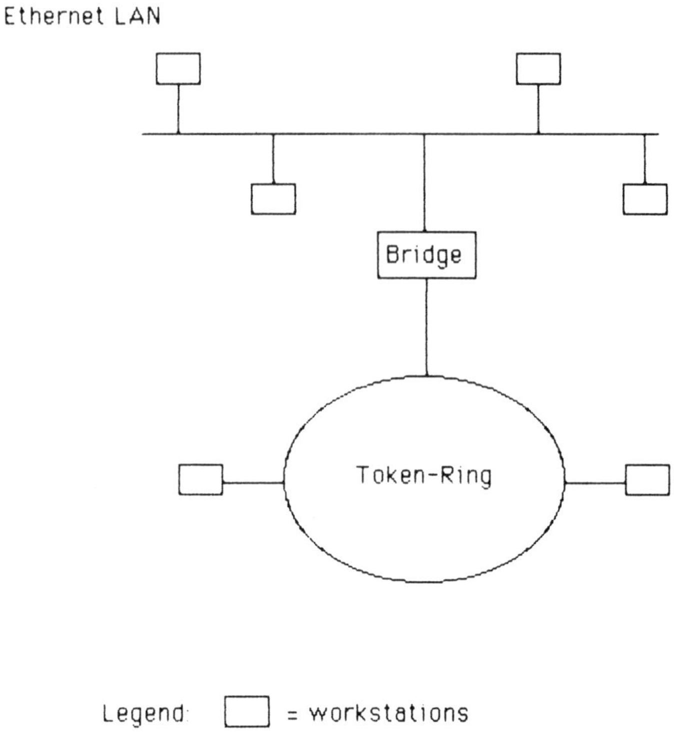

Ethernet LAN

Legend:  [ ] = workstations

**Figure 3.13** Translating bridge operation. A translating bridge connects local area networks that employ different protocols at the data link layer. In this example the translating bridge is used to connect an Ethernet local area network to a Token-Ring network.

**Table 3.6**  Bridge features.

Filtering and forwarding rate
Selective forwarding capability
Multiple port support
Wide area network interface support
Local area network media interface support
Transparent operation at the data link layer
Translating operation to link dissimilar networks
Encapsulation operation to support wide area network usage
Standalone and adapter based fabrication
Self-learning (transparent) routing
Source routing

### Filtering and Forwarding

The filtering and forwarding rate indicates the ability of the bridge to accept, examine, and regenerate frames on the same network (filtering) and transfer frames onto a different network (forwarding). A higher filtering and forwarding rate indicates a higher-performing bridge.

### Selective Forwarding

Some bridges have a selective forwarding capability. Bridges with this feature can be configured to selectively forward frames based upon predefined source and destination addresses. Through the use of a selective forwarding capability you can develop predefined routes for frames to take when flowing between networks as well as enable or inhibit the transfer of information between predefined workstations.

Figure 3.14 illustrates the use of the selective forwarding capability of two bridges to provide two independent routes for data transfer between an Ethernet and a Token-Ring network. In this example, you might enable all workstations with source address 1 and 2 connected to the Ethernet network to have data destined to the Token-Ring flow over bridge 1, while workstations with a source address of 3 and 4 that are transmitting data to the Token-Ring are configured to use bridge 2.

### Multiple Port Support

The multiple port support capability of a bridge is related to its local and wide area network media interface support. Some bridges support additional ports beyond the two that make up a basic bridge. Doing so enables a bridge to provide connectivity between three or more local area networks.

Figure 3.15 illustrates one potential use of a multiple port bridge to link an Ethernet network to two Token-Ring networks.

### Local and Wide Area Interface Support

Local area media interfaces supported by bridges can include thin and thick Ethernet coaxial cable, IEEE 10BASE-T,

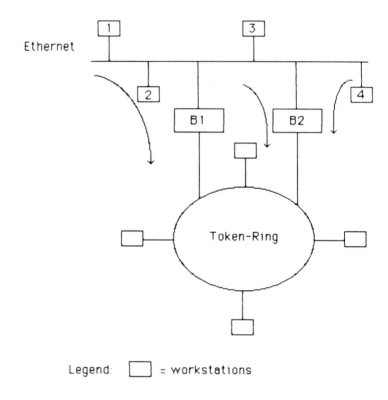

**Figure 3.14**  Using bridge selective forwarding capability. Using the selective forwarding capability of bridges enables the data flow between networks to be distributed based upon source or destination addresses.

and shielded and unshielded twisted-pair cable. Wide area network interfaces are incorporated into remote bridges that are designed to provide an internetworking capability between two or more geographically dispersed LANs linked by a WAN. Common WAN media interfaces can include RS-232 for data rates at or below 19.2 kbps, CCITT X.21 for packet network access at data rates up to 128 kbps, CCITT V.35 for data rates between 48 kbps and 128 kbps, and a T1/E1 interface for operations at 1.544 Mbps and 2.048 Mbps, respectively.

**Transparent Operation**

Although bridges are thought of as transparent to data, this is not always true. For interconnecting different networks located in the same geographical area bridges are normally transparent

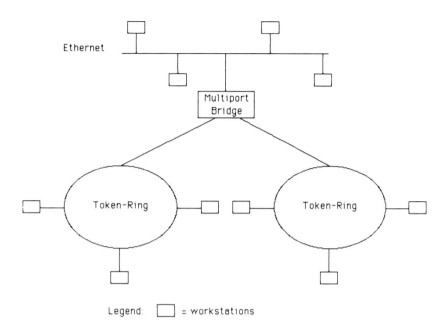

**Figure 3.15** Using a multiport bridge. Through the use of a multiport bridge you can interconnect three or more local area networks.

to data. However, some remote bridges use data compression algorithms to reduce the quantity of data transmitted between bridges connected via a wide area network. Such compression-performing bridges are not transparent to data, although they restore data to its original form.

**Frame Translation**

For interconnecting different types of local area networks, bridges must perform a translation of frames. For example, an Ethernet frame must be changed into a Token-Ring frame when the frame is routed from an Ethernet to a Token-Ring network. As previously mentioned, since frames cannot be fragmented at the data link layer you must set the workstations on the Token-Ring network to the smallest maximum frame size of the Ethernet, or 1500 bytes.

When data is transferred between colocated local area networks the frame format on one network is suitable for transfer onto the other network or modified for transfer when the media access control layers differ. When a bridge is used to connect two local area networks via a wide area network facility a WAN protocol is employed to control data transfer. The wide area network protocol is better suited for transmission over the WAN as it will normally incorporate error detection and correction, enable a large number of unacknowledged 'WAN' frames to exist to speed information transfer, support full-duplex data transfers, and is standardized. Examples of such wide area network protocols include IBM's SDLC, Digital Equipment Corporation's DDCMP, and the CCITT's HDLC and X.25.

### Frame Encapsulation

Figure 3.16 illustrates the operation of a pair of remote bridges connecting two local area networks via a wide area network. For transmission from network A to network B user data from a network A station is first converted into logical link control and media access control frames. The bridge then encapsulates one or more LAN frames into the bridging protocol frame used for communications over the wide area network. Since the local area network frame is wrapped in another protocol, we say the LAN frame is tunneled within the WAN protocol. At the opposite end of the wide area network the distant remote bridge performs a reverse operation, removing the WAN protocol header and trailer from each frame.

### Fabrication

Some bridges are manufactured as standalone products. Such devices can be considered as 'plug and play,' as you simply connect the bridge to the media and power it on. Other bridges are manufactured as adapter cards for insertion into the system unit of a personal computer, workstation, or reduced instruction set computer (RISC). Through the use of software developed in conjunction with hardware you may obtain more flexibility in the use of this type of bridge than a standalone device whose software is fixed in ROM.

### Routing Method

The routing capability of a bridge governs its capability to interconnect local area networks as well as its level of

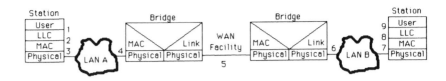

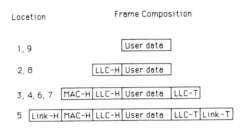

Legend:
LLC = logical link control
MAC = media access control
H = header
T = trailer

**Figure 3.16** Remote bridge operation. A remote bridge wraps the logical link control (LLC) and media access control (MAC) frames in another protocol for transmission over a wide area network.

performance. A transparent bridge automatically develops routing tables. Thus, this device is known as a self-learning bridge and represents the most elementary type of bridge routing. In the IBM Token-Ring frame (see Chapter 5) there is an optional routing field that can be used to develop routing information for frames routed through a series of bridges. Readers are referred to Chapter 6 for an in-depth discussion of bridge routing methods.

## Routers

A router is a device that operates at the network layer of the ISO OSI Reference Model as illustrated in Figure 3.17. Although this level of operation may appear to be insignificant in comparison to a bridge which operates at the data link layer, in actuality, there is a considerable difference in the routing capability of bridges and routers.

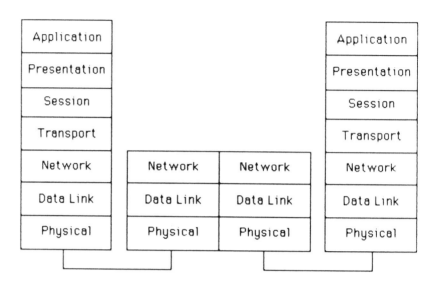

**Figure 3.17** Router operation. A router operates at the network layer of the ISO OSI Reference Model. This enables a router to provide network layer services, such as flow control and frame fragmentation.

The ability to operate at the network layer enables a router to extend internetworking across multiple data links in an orderly and predefined manner. This means that a router can determine the best path through a series of data links from a source network to a destination network. To accomplish this the router operates using a network protocol, such as the Internet Protocol (IP), Digital Equipment Corporation's DECnet Phase V, and Novell's IPX. This networking protocol must operate on both the source and destination network when protocol-dependent routers are used. If protocol-independent routers are used you can interconnect networks using different protocols. The protocol-independent router can be considered as a sophisticated transparent bridge. Its operation and utilization is described in detail in Chapter 7. In comparison, since a bridge operates at the data link layer, it can always be used to transfer information between networks operating different network protocols. This makes a bridge more efficient for linking networks that only have one or a few paths, while a router is more efficient for interconnecting multiple network links via multiple paths.

*Network address utilization*

Unlike a bridge which must monitor all frames at the media access control layer, a router is specifically addressed at the network layer. This means that a router only has to examine frames explicitly addressed to that device. In communications terminology, the monitoring of all frames is referred to as a promiscuous mode of operation, while the selective examination of frames is referred to as a non-promiscuous mode of operation.

Another difference between the operation of bridges and routers is the structure of the addresses they operate upon. Bridges operate at the data link layer, which means that they typically examine physical addresses that are contained in read-only memory on adapter cards and used in the generation of frames. In comparison, routers operate at the network layer where addresses are normally assigned by a network administrator to a group of stations having a common characteristic, such as being connected on an Ethernet in one area of a building and a Token-Ring network in another area in a building. This type of address is known as a logical address and can be assigned and modified by the network administrator.

*Table operation*

Similar to bridges, routers make forwarding decisions using tables. Unlike a bridge that may employ a simple table look-up procedure to determine if a destination address is on a particular network, a router may employ a much more sophisticated forwarding decision criteria. For example, a router may be configured to analyze several paths based upon an algorithm and dynamically select a path based upon the results of the algorithm. Routing algorithms and protocols are discussed in Chapter 7.

*Advantages of use*

The use of routers provides a number of significant advantages in comparison to the use of bridges. To illustrate those advantages we will examine the use of routers shown in Figure 3.18 in which four corporate offices containing seven local area networks are interconnected through the use of four routers. In this example networks A and B are located in a building in Los Angeles, networks C and D are located in New York, network E

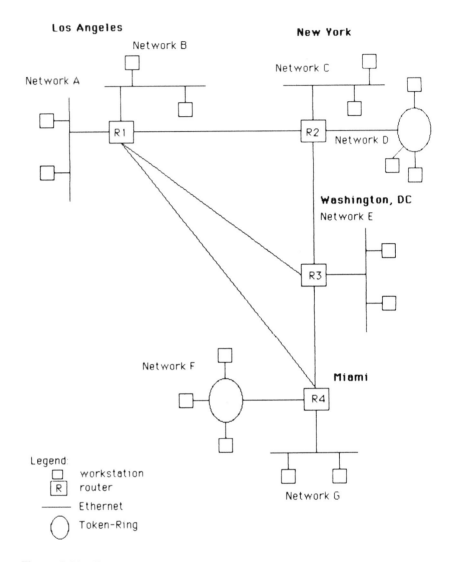

**Figure 3.18** Building an internet using routes. Routers can be used to establish complex networks in which traffic is varied over network facilities based upon the operational status and utilization of different network paths.

is located in Washington, DC, and networks F and G are located in Miami.

### Multiple Path Transmission and Routing Control

Suppose a station on network A in Los Angeles requires transmission to a station on network G in Miami. Initially, router R1 might use the path R1–R4 to transmit data between networks. If the path should fail or if an excessive amount of traffic flows between Los Angeles and Miami using that path, router R1 can seek to establish other paths, such as R1–R3–R4 or even R1–R2–R3–R4. In fact, many routers will consider each packet as a separate entity, routing the packet to its destination over the best available path at the time of transmission. Although this could conceivably result in packets arriving at R4 out of sequence, routers have the capability to resequence packets into their original order prior to passing data onto the destination network.

### Flow Control

As data flows through multiple paths towards its destination it becomes possible for a link to become congested. For example, data from a station on network C and network E routed to network G might build up to the point where the path R3–R4 becomes congested. To eliminate the possibility of packet loss, routers will use flow control. That is, they will inhibit transmission onto a link as well as notify other routers to inhibit data flow until there is an available level of bandwidth for traffic.

### Frame Fragmentation

As previously mentioned, bridges cannot break a frame into a series of frames when transmission occurs between networks with different frame sizes. This situation requires workstations to be configured to use the smallest maximum frame size of any network to be connected together. In comparison, most network protocols supported by routers include a provision for fragmentation of packets and their reassembly.

The higher level of functionality of routers over bridges is not without a price. That price is in terms of packet processing, software complexity, and cost. Since routers provide a more complex series of functions than bridges their ability to process packets is typically one-half to two-thirds of the processing capability of bridges. In addition, the development time required to program a more complex series of functions adds to the cost of routers. Thus, routers are generally more expensive than bridges. Table 3.7 summarizes the major differences between bridges and routers in terms of their operation, functionality, complexity, and cost.

**Table 3.7**  Bridge/router comparison

| Characteristic | Bridge | Router |
|---|---|---|
| Routing based upon an algorithm or protocol | Normally no | Yes |
| Protocol transparency | Yes | Only protocol-independent router |
| Uses network addresses | No | Yes |
| Promiscuous mode of operation | Yes | No |
| Forwarding decision | elementary | Can be complex |
| Multiple path transmission | Limited | High |
| Routing control | Limited | High |
| Flow control | No | Yes |
| Frame fragmentation | No | Yes |
| Packet processing rate | High | Moderate |
| Cost | Less expensive | More expensive |

## Brouters

A brouter can be considered a hybrid device, representing a combination of bridging and routing capabilities.

*Operation*

When a brouter receives a frame it examines it to determine if it is destined for another local area network. If so, it then checks the protocol of the frame to determine if it is supported at the network layer supported by the router function. If supported, the brouter will route the frame similar to the manner in which a router operates. However, if the brouter does not support the protocol it will bridge the frame using layer 2 information.

In comparison to routers, brouters provide an additional level of connectivity between networks, although that connectivity takes place at a lower level in the OSI Reference Model hierarchy. This is because a router would simply ignore a frame for which it does not support the network protocol, while a brouter would bridge the frame.

*Utilization*

The key advantage from the use of brouters is obtained from the ability of this device to both bridge and route data. Its ability to perform this dual function enables a brouter to replace the use of separate bridges and routers in some networking applications. For example, consider the use of a separate bridge and router in the top portion of Figure 3.19. In this example the bridge provides an interconnection capability between two relatively colocated networks, while the router provides an interconnection capability to distant networks. By replacing the separate bridge and router with a brouter the same level of functionality is obtained as illustrated in the lower portion of Figure 3.19. Of course, you want to ensure that the filtering and forwarding rate of the brouter is sufficient to be used in the manner illustrated. Otherwise, the replacement of separate bridges and routers by brouters may introduce delays that affect network performance. Readers are referred to Chapters 6 and 7 for information concerning the processing requirements of bridges and routers.

**Gateway**

The well known phrase 'one person's passion is another's poison' can in many ways apply to gateways. The term 'gateway' was originally coined to reference a device which provides a communications path between two local area networks or a LAN and a mainframe computer from the physical through the application layer. Figure 3.20 illustrates the operation of a gateway with respect to the ISO OSI Reference Model. Since its original operational description, the term 'gateway' has been used more loosely to describe a range of products ranging from bridges that simply interconnect two local area networks to protocol converters that provide asynchronous dial-up access into an IBM SNA network.

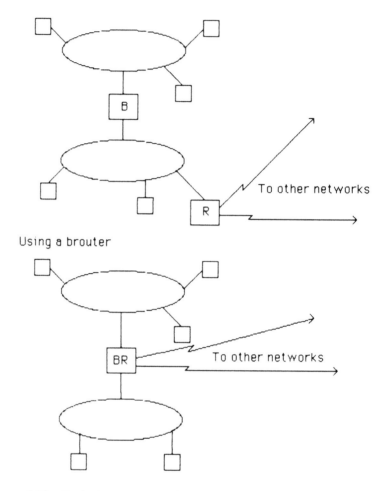

**Figure 3.19**   Replacing a separate bridge and router with a brouter.

*Definition*

In this book we will use the term 'gateway' as it was originally intended, to describe a product that performs protocol conversion through all seven layers of the ISO OSI Reference Model. As such, a gateway performs all of the functions of a router as well as protocol conversion.

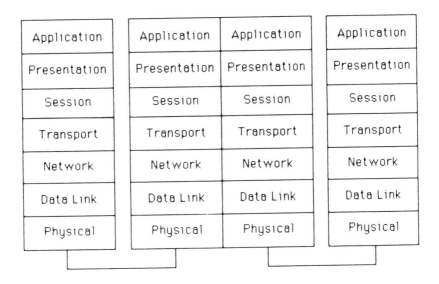

**Figure 3.20**  Gateway operation. A gateway operates at all seven layers of the ISO OSI Reference Model.

*Operation*

Gateways are protocol specific in function, typically used to provide access to a mainframe computer. Some vendors manufacture multi-protocol gateways. Such products are normally manufactured as adapter cards containing separate processors that are installed in the system unit of a personal computer or a specially designed vendor hardware platform. When used in conjunction with appropriate vendor software, this type of gateway is actually an $N$-in-1 gateway, where $N$ references the number of protocol conversions and separate connections the gateway can perform.

Figure 3.21 illustrates the use of a multi-protocol gateway to link stations on a Token-Ring network to an IBM mainframe via an SDLC link and via an X.25 connection to a packet switching network. Once connected to the packet switching network, LAN traffic may be further converted by gateway facilities built into that network or traffic may be routed to a packet network node and transmitted from that node to its final destination in its X.25 packet format.

Gateways are primarily designed and used for LAN–WAN connections and not for inter-LAN communications. Due to the more sophisticated functions performed by gateways, they

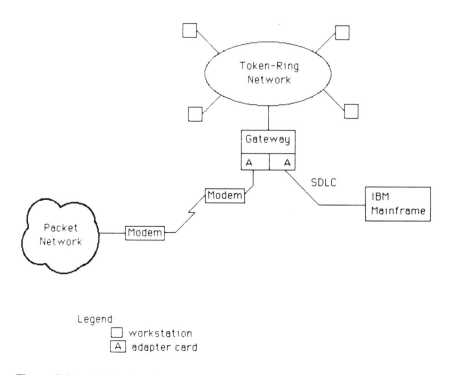

**Figure 3.21** Multi-protocol gateway operation. A multi-protocol gateway can be used to provide local area network stations access to different computational facilities, either directly or through the use of a packet network.

are slower than routers in providing network throughput. In addition, due to the large number of protocol options that may require consideration when configuring a gateway, its installation is considerably more difficult than the setup of a router. Readers are referred to Chapter 8 for specific information concerning the operation and utilization of gateways.

## File server

The file server can be considered as the central repository of information upon which a local area network is normally constructed. The file server is normally a personal computer or minicomputer that has a very powerful microprocessor, such as an Intel 486 or a RISC chip, as well as a large amount of fast-access on-line storage. The on-line storage is used to hold the local area network operating system and application programs that other stations on the network may use. In doing so several software vendors have split application programs, enabling portions of a program to be run on a network station, while other portions, such as the updating of a database, occur on the server. This technique is known as client–server processing.

*Connectivity functions*

As the heart of a local area network, the server supports every network application. Thus, it is in an ideal position to perform connectivity functions. Some servers are designed to function as an asynchronous gateway, providing access to one or a group of modems that individual network stations can access for communications via the switched telephone network. Here, software on the server considers the group of modems as a pool for access purposes. Hence, the term 'modem pooling' is used to refer to a server used to provide this functionality. Other servers contain software and hardware to provide access to mainframe computers via a specific protocol, such as SDLC, X.25, or TCP/IP.

## 3.4 SOFTWARE COMPONENTS

The installation of a local area network requires a variety of hardware and software products. As a minimum, each station on the network requires the installation of a network interface or adapter card into its system unit. This interface card contains a number of ROM modules and specialized circuitry as well as a microprocessor that implements the access method used to communicate on the common cable.

In some local area networks, one personal computer must be reserved to process the network commands and functions. Since it services these commands and functions, it is normally called the network server. A combination of specialized software, that overlays the operating system on each workstation connected to the network as well as software placed upon the server, governs the operation of the network. To understand the role of the network server and the functions of LAN software, let us first review how a personal computer operates under a conventional version of the disk operating system (DOS) used in the IBM PC and compatible personal computer environment.

DOS is a single-user operating system that is designed to provide access to peripherals attached to the system as well as control of those peripherals, the interpretation of commands to perform various functions on the system, and management of disk storage and memory. Under DOS, your keyboard is the standard input device and your display is the standard output device, with the control of the personal computer limited to one user.

As soon as a networked personal computer is initialized, its network software routines are added to DOS, permitting the computer to interact with the rest of the network. Prior to the introduction of DOS version 3.1, this software was normally an overlay to DOS that served to filter commands. Thus, when a command was issued to perform a function on the PC the software overlay permitted the command to pass directly to DOS for execution. If a command is issued that references the network, the software overlay intercepts or filters the command from reaching DOS and in conjunction with the adapter board transmits the command onto the network. If the network is server based, the non-local commands must be sent to a server for additional processing. The left-hand portion of Figure 3.22 illustrates the hardware and software components required when LAN software is designed as an overlay to DOS.

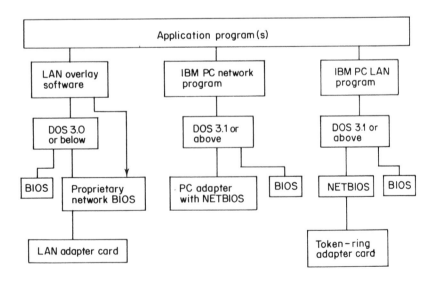

**Figure 3.22** Potential PC LAN hardware and software relationships in an IBM PC environment.

Prior to the introduction of DOS 3.1, most LAN vendors either developed proprietary methods to lock files and records or ignored incorporating such features, in effect limiting their networks to simple file-swapping and printer-sharing applications. Since there was no Network Basic Input/Output System (NETBIOS), a proprietary network BIOS was developed and accessed via the vendor's LAN overlay software to send and receive data from the LAN adapter card. Here NETBIOS is the lowest level of software on a local area network, translating commands to send and receive data via the adapter card into the instructions that actually perform the requested functions.

With the introduction of IBM's first local area network referred to as the PC Network in August 1984, IBM released all three components required to implement an IBM local area network using IBM equipment—the IBM PC Network Program, PC DOS 3.1, and the IBM PC Network Adapter. The IBM PC Network Program was actually a tailored version of Microsoft Corporation's Microsoft Networks (MS-NET) software which is essentially a program that overlays DOS and permits workstations on a network to share their disks and peripheral devices. DOS 3.1, also developed by Microsoft, added file- and record-locking capabilities to DOS, permitting multiple users to access and modify data. Without file- and record-locking capability in DOS, custom software was required to obtain these functions, since their absence would result in the last person saving data onto a file overwriting changes made by other persons to the file. Thus, DOS 3.1 provided networking and application programmers with a set of standards they could use in developing network software.

Included on the IBM PC Network Adapter card in ROM is an extensive amount of programming instructions known as NETBIOS. The middle portion of Figure 3.22 illustrates the hardware and software components of an IBM PC LAN network.

When the IBM Token-Ring Network was introduced, NETBIOS was removed from the adapter card and incorporated as a separate software program which was activated from DOS. The right-hand column of Figure 3.22 illustrates the hardware and software relationship for the IBM Token-Ring local area network. Here, the network operating system for the Token-Ring was renamed as the IBM PC LAN Program from its former name of the IBM PC Network Program.

Due to the standardization of file and record locking under DOS 3.1, any multi-user software program written for DOS 3.1 or later versions of that operating system will execute on any LAN that supports this version of DOS. Although DOS 3.1 supports many networking functions, it is not a networking operating system. In fact, a variety of networking operating systems support DOS 3.1 and later versions of DOS, including MS-NET, IBM's PC Network Program, IBM's Token-Ring Program, and Novell's NetWare. This permits the user to select a third-party network operating system to use with IBM network hardware or the user can consider obtaining both third-party hardware and software to construct his or her local area network.

## Network operating system

A modern network operating system operates as an overlay to the personal computer's operating system, providing the connectivity which enables personal computers to communicate with one another and to share such network resources as hard disks, CD-ROM drives and printers, and can even obtain access to mainframes and minicomputers. Two of the more popular LAN operating systems are Microsoft Corporation's LAN Manager (a later version of that vendor's MS-NET) and Novell Corporation's NetWare.

Both LAN Manager and NetWare are file server-based network operating systems. This means that most network modules reside on the file server. A shell program is loaded into each workstation and works in conjunction with the server modules. The shell program workstation filters commands, directing user-entered commands to DOS or to the network modules residing on the server. Communications between the shell and the server modules can be considered as occurring at the OSI Reference Model's network layer. Microsoft's LAN Manager uses the IP protocol, while Novell's NetWare uses its Internetwork Packet Exchange (IPX) protocol as the language with which the workstation communicates with the file server. In fact, both IP and IPX are sophisticated network protocols which enable multiple servers to be located on a network and route information to their appropriate destination on a network or between networks.

*Services*

The process by which the shell enables a workstation to communicate with a set of services residing on a server is known as a client–server relationship. Services provided by network modules on the server can range in scope from file access and transfer, shared printer utilization, and printer queuing to electronic mail. Other features available in most network operating systems include the ability to partition disk storage and allocate such storage to different network users, the assignment of various types of security levels for individual network users and groups of users as well as on directories, files, and printers. Some network operating systems include a disk mirroring feature as well as a remote console dial-in capability.

Since file information in the form of updated accounting, payroll, and engineering data can be critical to the health of a company, it is often very important to have duplicate copies of information in the event a hard disk should fail. Disk mirroring is a feature which duplicates network information on two or more disks simultaneously. Thus, if one disk should fail network operations can continue.

A remote console dial-in capability enables a network user to gain access to the network from a remote location. This feature can be particularly advantageous for persons who travel and wish to transmit and receive messages with persons back at the office or obtain access to information residing on the network. Since the administration of a network can be a complex process, a remote dial-in feature may also make life less taxing for a network administrator. Working at home or at another location, the administrator can reassign privileges and perform other network functions that may not be possible in an eight-hour day.

## Looking at NetWare

Since the best way to obtain information concerning the relationship of a network operating system to network hardware is by examining the software, we will do so. In doing so we will discuss Novell Corporation's NetWare, as that network operating system (NOS) is by far the most popular of all NOSs used.

### Architecture

The architecture or structure of NetWare can be mapped to the OSI Reference Model and provides an indication of the method

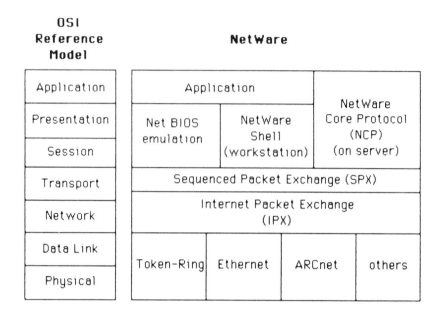

**Figure 3.23** NetWare and the OSI Reference Model.

by which this network operating system provides support for different types of hardware and includes the capability for the routing of packets between networks. Figure 3.23 illustrates the general relationship between NetWare and the OSI Reference Model.

In examining Figure 3.23, note that NetWare supports numerous types of local area networks. This means that you can use NetWare as the network operating system on Token-Ring, Ethernet, ARCnet, and other types of networks. In fact, NetWare also supports different types of operating systems, such as DOS, OS/2, UNIX, and Macintosh's Finder. This means that NetWare is capable of supporting different types of local area networks as well as workstations that use different operating systems.

At the network layer, Novell's IPX protocol performs addressing and internet routing functions. To accomplish this, an IPX packet contains both the source and destination network addresses. Those addresses are assigned by a network administrator and provide the mechanism for the routing of data between networks by routers which examine the network layer.

IPX is a connectionless network layer protocol that does not guarantee the delivery of data. To provide a reliable delivery mechanism, Novell developed its Sequenced Packet eXchange

(SPX)—a transport level interface which provides a connection-oriented packet delivery service.

At the session and presentation layers, NetWare uses a NETBIOS emulator which provides an interface between application programs written in compliance with NETBIOS and NetWare. As previously mentioned, the NetWare shell operates on each workstation and communicates with a core set of modules that reside on servers. That core set of modules is known as the NetWare Core Protocol (NCP). NCP provides such functions as workstation and network naming management, file partitioning, access and locking capability, accounting, and security.

**Versions**

Several versions of NetWare have been marketed during the past few years. NetWare 286, which was renamed NetWare 2.2, is designed to operate on Intel 286-based servers. This operating system supports up to 100 users. A more modern version of NetWare, NetWare 386, which was renamed NetWare 3.1, operates on Intel 386-based servers. This network operating system supports up to 250 users.

**Application Software**

The third major component of software required for productive work to occur on a local area network is application software. In the form of programs that support electronic mail, multiple access to database records, or the use of spreadsheet programs, application programs operate at the top layer of the OSI Reference Model.

Until the mid-1980s, most application programs used on LANs were not tailored to operate correctly in a multi-user environment. A large part of their inability to work correctly was due to the absence of file- and record-locking capability of PC operating systems—a situation that was corrected with the introduction of DOS 3.1. A second problem associated with application programs occurs when the program was written to bypass the personal computer's BIOS. Although this action in many instances would speed up screen displays, disk access, and other operations, it resulted in non-standardized program actions. This made it difficult, if not impossible, for some network operating systems to support ill-defined programs as an interrupt clash could bring the entire network to a rapid halt. Today, most application programs use BIOS calls and can be considered well defined. Such programs are easily supported by network operating systems. A few programs that bypass BIOS may also be supported due to the popularity of the application program which resulted in operating system vendors tailoring their software to support those applications.

## 3.5 DESIGNING TOKEN-RING NETWORKS

As previously discussed in this chapter, there are a number of constraints that must be considered in designing Token-Ring networks. Although those constraints are most important, equally important is the planning process required to establish a network. This is because the planning process provides the information required to design the network consistent with the constraints imposed by the wiring, MAU placement, network operating rate, and lobe distances.

### Locating users and equipment

One of the first, if not the first, steps you should take in designing a Token-Ring network is to locate your network users and the equipment that will be connected to the network. The location of users actually refers to user stations that will be cabled to the network, while we use the term 'equipment' to collectively refer to devices such as network servers, optical disks, laser printers, plotters, and other peripheral devices that may be shared by many users.

In locating users and equipment, it is important to either draw or obtain a schematic diagram of the floor plan of the building where different networks or network segments will reside. If no schematic is available, you should take care to inspect walls and ceilings to observe the possibility or impossibility of routing cable to user stations and common equipment. Even when a floor plan schematic is available, you should carefully review the work areas, focusing on walls and ceilings as many schematics do not illustrate load-bearing walls that cannot have cable routed through the wall nor electrical power conduits in ceilings which data cable routings should avoid.

## Data flow survey

Once you locate user stations and common equipment that will be connected to a network, you should conduct a survey of proposed network users. This survey should examine the connectivity requirements of users to other users, gateways to mainframes, and access to common equipment. Although each organization will have unique requirements, we can illustrate how you can easily express connectivity requirements in terms of one or more simple matrixes. For example, assume you have located users and equipment on two floors in a building that will be connected to a common network, while your organization has a mainframe computer in a distant city. Using a matrix similar to that illustrated in Figure 3.24, you can note the communications requirements for each user on one floor with respect to other users and equipment on that floor, the gateway to the mainframe, and to users and equipment on the second floor.

| Floor 1 | User 1 | User 2 | • • • | User N | Server A | Gateway | Floor 2 |
|---------|--------|--------|-------|--------|----------|---------|---------|
| User 1 | N/A | | • | | | | |
| User 2 | | N/A | • | | | | |
| : | | | N/A | | | | |
| User N | | | : | N/A | | | |
| Server A | | | | | N/A | | |

Figure 3.24  Communications requirements matrix. Through the use of one or more communications requirements matrixes you can denote the volume of traffic flow on the network. This will enable you to plan your network to avoid potential communications bottlenecks.

In completing the matrix illustrated in Figure 3.24 you can estimate the flow of data between users and network equipment or you can use H, M, and L to indicate predefined high, medium, and low traffic requirements, while N/A would indicate communications between two entries is not applicable nor required. Since communications between the same entities would not occur, N/A was entered for common vertical and horizontal entries for users on Floor 1. Readers are referred to Chapter 10 for information concerning techniques that can be used to estimate the data flow on Token-Ring networks.

Upon completion of the communications requirements matrix for each floor you will obtain a valuable indication of the data flow requirements for the network you wish to establish. You can now use this information in conjunction with your previously developed location schematic to design your network topology, including the placement of any required bridges, routers, and gateways as well as determining cable runs and the locations to install MAUs.

## Locating MAUs

Once you have identified the location of your stations and other devices to be networked, obtained a general idea of their communications requirements, and are familiar with your network cabling restrictions, you are ready to begin your network design. During this process your primary area of concern is to locate the MAUs that will form the backbone of your network. In doing so you should consider two methods of MAU installation: centralized and decentralized.

A centralized location for MAUs usually results in the use of one or a few 'wire closets' for their location. This provides a high degree of physical security as well as minimizing the potential for violating intra-MAU cabling restrictions. When one wiring closet is used, this method of installation also ensures you will not require repeaters to interconnect MAUs. However, this approach also requires some lobe runs that may exceed the maximum lobe distance. Thus, you may require repeaters on some of your lobe runs. In addition, since all devices have to be cabled to a central wire closet you may require a considerable amount of cable. For example, eight devices in one corner of a floor may require eight separate cables, each up to several hundred feet in length, to interconnect to a MAU located in a wire closet on the other side of the floor.

A second MAU location method you may wish to consider is the decentralized MAU installation approach. Under the decentralized MAU approach you would attempt to locate each MAU at an optimum distance near a cluster of devices that require a connection to the network. For example, if your organization has eight devices 300 feet from a wire closet, you could locate a MAU in close proximity to those eight devices.

This would reduce the requirement to install eight lengthy cables to only two—one for Ring-In and one for Ring-Out—which would connect that MAU to another MAU. In addition to saving cabling cost, the use of a decentralized MAU installation process may be practiced when your existing wiring closet runs out of space. Some disadvantages associated with decentralized MAUs include the need to go to each location when problems occur, and you are attempting to locate a faulty device, as well as potential physical security problems.

## Subdividing the network

When utilization or equipment constraints preclude one network from satisfying your connectivity requirements, you should consider subdividing the network into two or more rings. In addition to removing cabling and device restrictions, network subdivision is a practical technique to consider when the volume of communications may cause poor performance on a single network. To illustrate this let us return to our two-floor organization example. Let us assume that based upon an analysis of projected communications, intra-floor communications is expected to be very high. Thus, although we might be able to interconnect all devices on both floors to one network, we might want to establish independent networks on each floor and interconnect the networks through the use of a pair of bridges.

Assume that one floor has 48 devices to be attached to a network and the second floor has 60 devices to be attached to a network, resulting in a total of 108 devices. If the network is being established using Type 3 cable you can only have up to 72 devices and 9 MAUs. Thus, to overcome those constraints you must subdivide the network into two. Figure 3.25 illustrates from a physical perspective how you might establish two networks and interconnect those networks through the use of two bridges. Figure 3.26 illustrates from a logical perspective the interconnection of the two separate networks. Although you could use one bridge to interconnect the two networks, we purposely illustrated the use of two bridges as many organizations prefer to have a backup route for internetwork connectivity in the event one bridge should fail. Readers are again referred to Chapter 7 for detailed information concerning the operation and utilization of bridges.

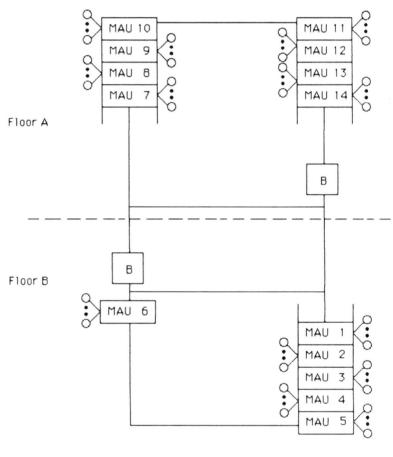

Floor A

Floor B

Legend:
    ○ = network devices
    B = bridge

**Figure 3.25**   Using bridges to interconnect separate networks.

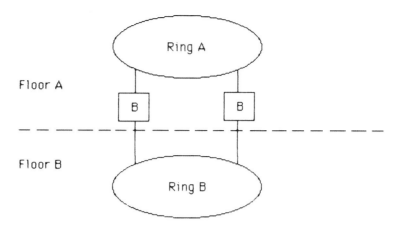

**Figure 3.26** Logical network view. This is the logical view of the physical components of the two interconnected Token-Ring networks illustrated in Figure 3.25.

# TOKEN-RING FRAME
# OPERATIONS

Until now we have primarily limited our discussion concerning the Token-Ring frame to a level of detail necessary to illustrate general concepts. In this chapter we will examine frame operations on a much more detailed basis, enabling us to understand the manner in which different frame fields are used for such functions as access control, error checking, routing of data between interconnected networks, and other Token-Ring network functions. In addition, by obtaining an understanding of the composition of Token-Ring frames, we will obtain the ability to recognize the cause of different types of problems, their potential effect upon a network, and actions we can consider to correct such problems.

## 4.1 TRANSMISSION FORMATS

Three types of transmission formats are supported on a Token-Ring network—token, abort, and frame. The token format as illustrated in the top of Figure 4.1 is the mechanism by which access to the ring is passed from one computer attached to the network to another device connected to the network. Here the token format consists of three bytes, of which the starting and ending delimiters are used to indicate the beginning and end of a token frame. The middle byte of a token frame is an access control byte. Three bits are used as a priority indicator, three bits are used as a reservation indicator, while one bit is used for the token bit, and another bit position functions as the monitor bit.

**a. Token format**

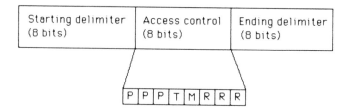

**b. Abort token format**

| Starting delimiter | Ending delimiter |
|---|---|

**c. Frame format**

| Starting delimiter (8 bits) | Access control (8 bits) | Frame control (8 bits) | Destination address (48 bits) | Source address (48 bits) | Routing information (optional) |
|---|---|---|---|---|---|

| Information variable | Frame check sequence (32 bits) | Ending delimiter (8 bits) | Frame status (8 bits) |
|---|---|---|---|

**Figure 4.1** Token, abort, and frame formats (P: priority bits, T: token bit, M: monitor bit, R: reservation bits).

When the token bit is set to a binary 0 it indicates that the transmission is a token. When it is set to a binary 1 it indicates that data in the form of a frame is being transmitted.

The second Token-Ring frame format signifies an abort token. In actuality there is no token, since this format is indicated by a starting delimiter followed by an ending delimiter. The transmission of an abort token is used to abort a previous transmission. The format of an abort token is illustrated in Figure 4.1b.

The third type of Token-Ring frame format occurs when a station seizes a free token. At that time the token format is converted into a frame which includes the addition of frame control, addressing data, an error detection field and a frame status field. The format of a Token-Ring frame is illustrated in Figure 4.1c. By examining each of the fields in the frame we will also examine the token and token abort frames due to the commonality of fields between each frame.

## Starting/ending delimiters

The starting and ending delimiters mark the beginning and ending of a token or frame. Each delimiter consists of a unique code pattern which identifies it to the network. To understand the composition of the starting and ending delimiter fields requires us to review the method by which data is represented on a Token-Ring network using Differential Manchester encoding.

### Differential Manchester encoding

Figure 4.2 illustrates the use of Differential Manchester encoding, comparing its operation to non-return to zero (NRZ) and conventional Manchester encoding.

At the top of Figure 4.2, NRZ coding illustrates the representation of data by holding a voltage low (–V) to represent a binary 0 and high (+V) to represent a binary 1. This method of signaling is called non-return to zero since there is no return to a 0 V position after each data bit is coded.

One problem associated with NRZ encoding is the fact that a long string of 0 or 1 bits does not result in a voltage change. Thus, to determine that bit $m$ in a string of $n$ bits of 0's or 1's is set to a 0 or 1 requires sampling at predefined bit times. This in turn requires each device on a network using NRZ encoding to have its own clocking circuitry.

To avoid the necessity of building clocking circuitry into devices, a mechanism is required for encoded data to carry clocking information. One method by which encoded data carries clocking information is obtained from the use of Manchester encoding which is illustrated in Figure 4.2b. In Manchester encoding, each data bit consists of a half-bit time signal at a low voltage (–V) and another half-bit time signal at the opposite positive voltage (+V). Every binary 0 is represented by a half-bit time at a low voltage and the remaining bit time at a high voltage. Every binary 1 is represented by a half-bit time at a high voltage followed by a half bit time at a low voltage. By

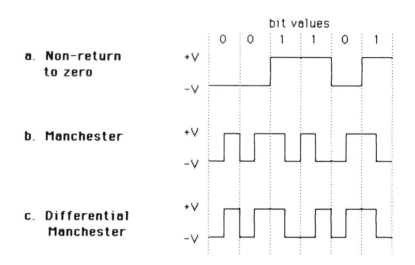

**Figure 4.2** Differential Manchester encoding. In differential Manchester encoding, the direction of the signal's voltage transition changes whenever a binary 1 is transmitted but remains the same for a binary 0.

changing the voltage for every binary digit, Manchester encoding ensures that the signal carries self-clocking information.

In Figure 4.2c, Differential Manchester encoding is illustrated. The difference between Manchester encoding and Differential Manchester encoding occurs in the method by which binary 1's are encoded. In Differential Manchester encoding, the direction of the signal's voltage transition changes whenever a binary 1 is transmitted, but remains the same for a binary 0. The IEEE 802.5 standard specifies the use of Differential Manchester encoding and this encoding technique is used on Token-Ring networks at the physical layer to transmit and detect four distinct symbols—a binary 0, a binary 1, and two non-data symbols.

*Non-data symbols*

Under Manchester and Differential Manchester encoding there are two possible code violations that can occur. Each code violation produces what is known as a non-data symbol and is used in the Token-Ring frame to denote starting and ending delimiters similar to the use of the flag in an HDLC frame. However, unlike the flag whose bit composition 01111110 is uniquely maintained by inserting a 0 bit after every sequence of five set bits and removing a 0 following every sequence of five set bits, Differential Manchester encoding maintains the uniqueness of frames by the use of non-data J and non-data K symbols. This eliminates the bit stuffing operations required by HDLC.

The two non-data symbols each consist of two half-bit times without a voltage change. The J symbol occurs when the voltage is the same as that of the last signal, while the K symbol occurs when the voltage becomes opposite of that of the last signal. Figure 4.3 illustrates the occurrence of the J and K non-data symbols based upon different last bit voltages. Readers will note in comparing Figure 4.3 to Figure 4.2c that the J and K non-data symbols are distinct code violations that cannot be mistaken for either a binary 0 or a binary 1.

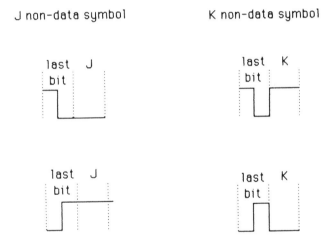

**Figure 4.3** J and K non-data symbol composition. J and K non-data symbols are distinct code violations that cannot be mistaken for data.

Now that we have an understanding of the operation of Differential Manchester encoding and the composition of the J and K non-data symbols, we can focus our attention upon the actual format of each frame delimiter.

The start delimiter field marks the beginning of a frame. The composition of this field is the bits and non-data symbols JK0JK000. The end delimiter field marks the end of a frame as well as denoting whether or not the frame is the last frame of a multiple frame sequence using a single token or if there are additional frames following this frame. The format of the end delimiter field is JK1JK1IE, where I is the intermediate frame bit. If I is set to 0, this indicates it is the last frame transmitted by a station. If I is set to 1, this indicates that additional frames follow this frame. E is an Error-Detected bit. The E bit is initially set to 0 by the station transmitting a frame, token, or abort sequence. As the frame circulates the ring, each station checks the transmission for errors. Upon detection of a Frame Check Sequence (FCS) error, inappropriate non-data symbol, illegal framing, or another type of error, the first station detecting the error will set the E bit to a value of 1. Since stations keep track of the number of times they set the E bit to a value of 1, it becomes possible to use this information as a guide to locating possible cable errors. For example, if one workstation accounted for a very large percentage of E bit settings in a 72-station network, there is a high degree of probability that there is a problem with the lobe cable to that workstation. The problem could be a crimped cable or a loose connector and represents a logical place to commence an investigation in an attempt to reduce E bit errors.

## Access control

The second field in both token and frame formats is the access control byte. As illustrated at the top of Figure 4.1, this byte consists of four subfields and serves as the controlling mechanism for gaining access to the network. When a free token circulates the network the access control field represents one-third of the length of the frame since it is prefixed by the start delimiter and suffixed by the end delimiter.

The lowest priority that can be specified by the priority bits in the access control byte is 0 (000), while the highest is seven (111), providing eight levels of priority. Table 4.1 lists the normal use of the priority bits in the access control field. Workstations have a default priority of three, while bridges have a default priority of four.

To reserve a token, a workstation inserts its priority level in the priority reservation subfield. Unless another station with a higher priority bumps the requesting station, the reservation will be honored and the requesting station will obtain the token. If the token bit is set to 1, this serves as an indication that a frame follows instead of the ending delimiter.

**Table 4.1** Priority bit settings.

| Priority bits | Priority |
| --- | --- |
| 000 | Normal user priority, MAC frames that do not require a token and response type MAC frames |
| 001 | Normal user priority |
| 010 | Normal user priority |
| 011 | Normal user priority and MAC frames that require tokens |
| 100 | Bridge |
| 101 | Reserved |
| 110 | Reserved |
| 111 | Specialized station management |

A station that needs to transmit a frame at a given priority can use any available token that has a priority level equal to or less than the priority level of the frame to be transmitted. When a token of equal or lower priority is not available, the ring station can reserve a token of the required priority through the use of the reservation bits. In doing so the station must follow two rules. First, if a passing token has a higher priority reservation than the reservation level desired by the workstation, the station will not alter the reservation field contents. Secondly, if the reservation bits have not been set or indicate a lower priority than that desired by the station, the station can now set the reservation bits to the required priority level.

Once a frame is removed by its originating station, the reservation bits in the header will be checked. If those bits have a non-zero value, the station must release a non-zero priority token, with the actual priority assigned based upon the priority used by the station for the recently transmitted frame, the reservation bit settings received upon the return of the frame, and any stored priority.

On occasion, the Token-Ring protocol will result in the transmission of a new token by a station prior to that station having the ability to verify the settings of the access control field in a returned frame. When this situation arises, the token will be issued according to the priority and reservation bit settings in the access control field of the transmitted frame.

Figure 4.4 illustrates the operation of the priority (P) and reservation (R) bit fields in the access control field. In

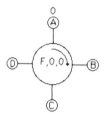

a. Station A generates a frame
using a non-priority token  P,R=0,0.

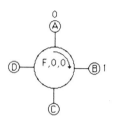

b. Station B reserves a priority
1 in the reservation bits in
the frame  P,R=0,1, Station A
enters a priority-hold state.

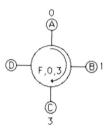

c. Station C reserves a priority of 3,
overriding B's reservation of  1; P,R=0,3.

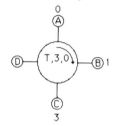

d. Station A removes its frame and
generates a token at reserved
priority level 3;  P,R=3,0.

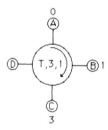

e. Station B repeats priority token and
makes a new reservation of priority
level 1;  P,R=3,1.

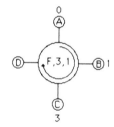

f. Station C grabs token and
transmits a frame with a priority
of 3,  P,R=3,1.

**Figure 4.4**   Priority and reservation field utilization.

this example, the prevention of a high-priority station from monopolizing the network is illustrated by station A entering a Priority–Hold state. This occurs when a station originates a token at a higher priority than the last token it generated. Once in a Priority–Hold state, the station will issue tokens that will bring the priority level eventually down to zero as a mechanism to prevent a high-priority station from monopolizing the network.

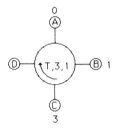

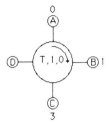

g. Upon return of frame to Station C it is removed. Station C generates a token at the priority just used; P,R=3,1.

h. Station A in a priority-hold state grabs token and changes its priority to 1; P,R=1,0. Station A stays in priority-hold state until priority reduced to 0

Legend:

Ⓐ, Ⓑ, Ⓒ, Ⓓ = stations

Numeric outside station identifier indicates priority level.

**Figure 4.4** *continued*

*The monitor bit*

The monitor bit is used to prevent a token with a priority exceeding zero or a frame from continuously circulating on the Token-Ring. This bit is transmitted as a 0 in all tokens and frames, except for a device on the network which functions as an active monitor and thus obtains the capability to inspect and modify that bit. When a token or frame is examined by the active monitor it will set the monitor bit to a 1 if it was previously found to be set to 0. If a token or frame is found to have the monitor bit already set to 1 this indicates that the token or frame has already made at least one revolution around the ring and an error condition has occurred, usually caused by the failure of a station to remove its transmission from the ring or the failure of a high-priority station to seize a token. When the active monitor finds a monitor bit set to 1 it assumes an error condition has occurred. The active monitor then purges the token or frame and releases a new token onto the ring. Now that we have an understanding of the role of the monitor bit in the access control field and the operation of the active monitor on that bit, let's focus our attention upon the active monitor.

*Active monitor*

The active monitor is the device that has the highest address on the network. All other stations on the network are considered as standby monitors and watch the active monitor.

As previously explained, the function of the active monitor is to determine if a token or frame is continuously circulating the ring in error. To accomplish this the active monitor sets the monitor count bit as a token or frame goes by. If a destination workstation fails or has its power turned off the frame will circulate back to the active monitor, where it is then removed from the network. In the event the active monitor should fail or be turned off, the standby monitors watch the active monitor by looking for an active monitor frame. If one does not appear within seven seconds, the standby monitor that has the highest network address then takes over as the active monitor.

## Frame control

The frame control field informs a receiving device on the network of the type of frame that was transmitted and how it should be interpreted. Frames can be either logical link control (LLC) or reference physical link functions according to the IEEE 802.5 media access control (MAC) standard. A media access control frame carries network control information and responses, while a logical link control frame carries data. Under IEEE 802 standards the data link layer of the OSI Open System Reference Model described in Chapter 1 was subdivided into LLC and MAC layers. The rationale for this split and additional information concerning the LLC and MAC layers are included in Sections 4.2 and 4.3.

The eight-bit frame control field has the format FFZZZZZZ, where FF are frame definition bits. The top of Table 4.2 indicates the possible settings of the frame bits and the assignment of those settings. The ZZZZZZ bits convey media access control (MAC) buffering information when the FF bits are set to 00. When the FF bits are set to 01 to indicate an LLC frame, the ZZZZZZ bits are split into two fields, designated rrrYYY. Currently, the rrr bits are reserved for future use and are set to 000. The YYY bits indicate the priority of the logical link control (LLC) data. The lower portion of Table 4.2 indicates the value of the Z bits when used in MAC frames to notify a Token-Ring adapter that the frame is to be expressed buffered.

**Table 4.2** Frame control field subfields.

| F bit settings | Assignment |
|---|---|
| 00 | MAC frame |
| 01 | LLC frame |
| 10 | Undefined (reserved for future use) |
| 11 | Undefined (reserved for future use) |

| Z bit settings | Assignment[*] |
|---|---|
| 000 | Normal buffering |
| 001 | Remove ring station |
| 010 | Beacon |
| 011 | Claim token |
| 100 | Ring purge |
| 101 | Active monitor present |
| 110 | Standby monitor present |

[*] When F bits set to 00, Z bits are used to notify an adapter that the frame is to be expressed buffered.

## Destination address

Although the IEEE 802.5 standard supports both 16-bit and 48-bit address fields, IBM's implementation requires the use of 48-bit address fields. IBM's destination address field is made up of five subfields as illustrated in Figure 4.5. The first bit in the destination address identifies the destination as an individual station (bit set to 0) or as a group (bit set to 1) of one or more stations. The latter provides the capability for a message to be broadcast to a group of stations.

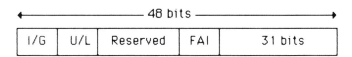

**Figure 4.5** Destination address subfields (I/G: individual or group bit address identifier, U/L: universally or locally administered bit identifier, FAI: functional address indicator). The reserved field contains the manufacturer's identification in 22 bits represented by 6 hex digits.

*Universally administered address*

The universally administered address is a unique address permanently encoded into an adapter's ROM. Because it is placed into ROM, it is also known as a burned-in address. The IEEE assigns blocks of addresses to each vendor manufacturing Token-Ring equipment, which ensures that Token-Ring adapter cards manufactured by different vendors are uniquely defined. Some Token-Ring adapter manufacturers are assigned universal addresses that contain an organizationally unique identifier. This identifier consists of the first six hex digits of the adapter card address and is also referred to as the manufacturer identification. For example, cards manufactured by IBM will begin with the address X08005A or X10005A, whereas adapter cards manufactured by Texas Instruments will begin with the address X400014. Table 4.3 lists vendor universal address prefixes assigned by the IEEE.

*Locally administered address*

A key problem with the use of universally administered addresses is the requirement to change software coding in a mainframe computer whenever a workstation connected to the mainframe via a gateway is added or removed from the network. To avoid constant software changes, locally administrated addressing can be used. This type of addressing temporarily overrides universally administrated addressing; however, the user is now responsible for ensuring the uniqueness of each address.

*Functional address indicator*

The functional address indicator subfield in the destination address identifies the function associated with the destination address, such as a bridge, active monitor or configuration report server.

The functional address indicator indicates a functional address when set to 0 and the I/G bit position is set to a 1—the latter indicating a group address. This condition can only occur when the U/L bit position is also set to a 1 and results in the ability to generate locally administered group addresses that are called functional addresses. Table 4.4 lists the functional addresses defined by the IEEE. Currently, 14

**Table 4.3**  Vendor universal address prefixes.

| 6-digit Address Prefix | Vendor | 6-digit Address Prefix | Vendor |
|---|---|---|---|
| 00000D | RND | 480009 | HP |
| 0000A6 | NwkGnl | 48000A | Nestar |
| 0000C9 | Prteon | 480010 | AT&T |
| 00013A | Agilis | 480014 | Exceln |
| 0001C8 | TmsCrd | 480017 | NSC |
| 00DD00 | UB | 48001E | Apollo |
| 00DD01 | UB | 480020 | Sun |
| 08005A | IBM | 480025 | CDC |
| 100058 | DG | 480028 | TI |
| 10005A | IBM | 48002B | DEC |
| 1000D8 | DG | 480036 | Intrgr |
| 48000C | Cisco | 480039 | Spider |
| 400014 | TI | 480045 | Xylogx |
| 400022 | VisTec | 480047 | Sequnt |
| 40002A | TRW | 480049 | Univtn |
| 400065 | NwkGnl | 48004C | Encore |
| 40009F | Amrstr | 48004E | BICC |
| 4000A9 | NSC | 480067 | ComDes |
| 4000AA | Xerox | 480068 | Ridge |
| 4000B3 | Cimlin | 480069 | SilGrf |
| 4000C0 | WstDig | 48006A | AT&T |
| 4000C9 | Prteon | 48006E | Exceln |
| 4000DD | Gould | 48007C | Vtalnk |
| 420701 | Intrln | 480089 | Kinetx |
| 42608C | 3Com | 48008B | Pyramd |
| 42CF1F | CMC | 48008D | Xyvisn |
| 480002 | Bridge | 480090 | Retix |
| 480003 | ACC | 500014 | TI |
| 480005 | Symblx | EA0003 | DEC |
| 480008 | BBN | EA0004 | DECnet |

functional addresses have been defined out of a total of 31 that are available for use, with the remaining addresses available for user definitions or reserved for future use.

*Address values*

The range of addresses that can be used on a Token-Ring primarily depends upon the settings of the I/G, U/L, and FAI

**Table 4.4**  IEEE functional addresses.

| | |
|---|---|
| Active monitor | XC000 0000 0001 |
| Ring parameter server | XC000 0000 0002 |
| Network server heartbeat | XC000 0000 0004 |
| Ring error monitor | XC000 0000 0008 |
| Configuration report server | XC000 0000 0010 |
| Synchronous bandwidth manager | XC000 0000 0020 |
| Locate - directory server | XC000 0000 0040 |
| NETBIOS | XC000 0000 0080 |
| Bridge | XC000 0000 0100 |
| IMPL server | XC000 0000 0200 |
| Ring authorization server | XC000 0000 0400 |
| LAN gateway | XC000 0000 0800 |
| Ring wiring concentrator | XC000 0000 1000 |
| LAN manager | XC000 0000 2000 |
| User-defined | XC000 0000 8000 |
| | through |
| | XC000 4000 0000 |

bit positions. When the I/G and U/L bit positions are set to 00 the manufacturer's universal address is used. When the I/G and U/L bits are set to 01, individual locally administered addresses are used in the defined range listed in Table 4.4. When all three bit positions are set, this situation indicates a group address within the range contained in Table 4.5. If the I/G and U/L bits are set to 11 but the FAI bit is set to 0, this indicates that the address is a functional address. In this situation the range of addresses is bit-sensitive, permitting only those functional addresses previously listed in Table 4.4.

In addition to the previously mentioned addresses, there are two special destination address values that are defined. An address of all 1's (FFFFFFFFFFFF) identifies all stations as destination stations. If a null address is used in which all bits are set to 0 (X000000000000), the frame is not addressed to any workstation. In this situation it can only be transmitted but not received, enabling you to test the ability of the active monitor to purge this type of frame from the network.

## Source address

The source address field always represents an individual address which specifies the adapter card responsible for the

**Table 4.5**  Token-Ring addresses.

| | Bit settings | | | |
|---|---|---|---|---|
| | I/G | U/L | FAI | Address/address range |
| Individual, universal administered | 0 | 0 | 0/1 | Manufacturer's serial no. |
| Individual, locally administered | 0 | 1 | 0 | X4000 0000 0000 to X4000 7FFF FFFF |
| Group address | 1 | 1 | 1 | XC000 8000 0000 to XC000 FFFF FFFF |
| Functional address | 1 | 1 | 0 | XC000 0000 0001 to XC000 0000 2000 (bit-sensitive) |
| All-stations broadcast | 1 | 1 | 1 | XFFFF FFFF FFFF |
| Null address | 0 | 0 | 0 | X0000 0000 0000 |

transmission. The source address field consists of three major subfields as illustrated in Figure 4.6. When locally administered addressing occurs, only 24 bits in the address field are used since the 22 manufacturer identification bit positions are not used.

**Figure 4.6**  Source address field (RI: routing information bit identifier, U/L: universally or locally administered bit identifier). The 46 address bits consist of 22 manufacturer identification bits and 24 universally administered bits when the U/L bit is set to 0. If set to 1, a 31-bit locally administered address is used with the manufacturer's identification bits set to 0.

The routing information bit identifier identifies the fact that routing information is contained in an optional routing information field. This bit is set when a frame is routed across a bridge using IBM's source routing technique.

## Routing information

The routing information field is optional and is included in a frame when the RI bit of the source address field is set. Figure 4.7 illustrates the format of the optional routing information field. If this field is omitted, the frame cannot leave the ring it was originated on under IBM's source routing bridging method. Under transparent bridging, the frame can be transmitted onto another ring. Both source routing bridging and transparent bridging are covered in detail in Chapter 6. The routing information field is of variable length and contains a control subfield and one or more two-byte route designator fields when included in a frame as the latter are required to control the flow of frames across one or more bridges.

The maximum length of the routing information field (RIF) supported by IBM is 18 bytes. Since each RIF field must contain a two-byte routing control field, this leaves a maximum of 16 bytes available for use by up to eight route designators. As illustrated in Figure 4.7, each two-byte route designator consists of a 12-bit ring number and a four-bit bridge number. Thus, a maximum total of 16 bridges can be used to join any two rings in an Enterprise Token-Ring network.

## Information field

The information field is used to contain Token-Ring commands and responses as well as carry user data. The type of data carried by the information field depends upon the F bit settings in the frame type field. If the F bits are set to 00 the information field carries media access control (MAC) commands and responses that are used for network management operations. If the F bits are set to 01 the information field carries logical link control (LLC) or user data. Such data can be in the form of portions of a file being transferred on the network or an electronic mail message being routed to another workstation on the network. The information field is of variable length and can be considered to represent the higher level protocol enveloped in a Token-Ring frame.

In the IBM implementation of the IEEE 802.5 Token-Ring standard the maximum length of the information field depends upon the Token-Ring adapter used and the operating rate of the network. Token-Ring adapters with 64 kbytes of memory can handle up to 4.5 kbytes on a 4 Mbps network and up to 18 kbytes on a 16 Mbps network.

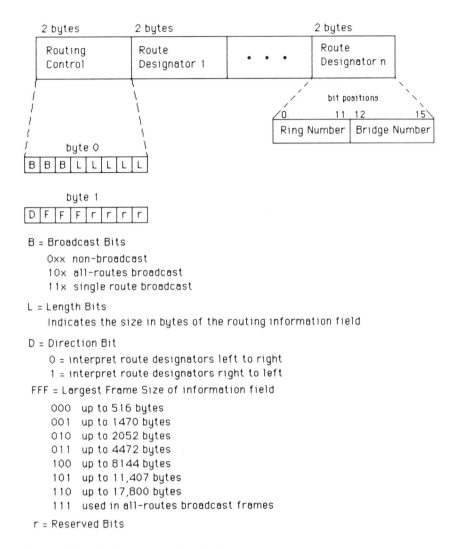

**Figure 4.7** Routing information field.

## Frame check sequence

The frame check sequence field contains four bytes which provide the mechanism for checking the accuracy of frames flowing on the network. The cyclic redundancy check data included in the frame check sequence field covers the frame control, destination address, source address, routing information and information fields. If an adapter computes a cyclic redundancy check that does not match the data contained in the frame check sequence field of a frame, the destination adapter discards the frame information and sets an error bit (E bit) indicator. This error bit indicator, as previously discussed, actually represents a ninth bit position of the ending delimiter and serves to inform the transmitting station that the data was received in error.

## Frame status

The frame status field serves as a mechanism to indicate the results of a frame's circulation around a ring to the station that initiated the frame. Figure 4.8 indicates the format of the frame status field. The frame status field contains three subfields that are duplicated for accuracy purposes since they reside outside of CRC checking. One field (A) is used to denote whether an address was recognized, while a second field (C) indicates whether the frame was copied at its destination. Each of these fields is one bit in length. The third field, which is two bit positions in length (rr), is currently reserved for future use.

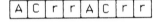

A = Address-Recognized Bits
B = Frame-Copied Bits
r = Reserved Bits

**Figure 4.8** Frame status field. The frame status field denotes whether the destination address was recognized and whether the frame was copied. Since this field is outside of CRC checking its subfields are duplicated for accuracy.

## 4.2 MEDIUM ACCESS CONTROL

As previously discussed, a MAC frame is used to transport network commands and responses. As such, the MAC layer controls the routing of information between the LLC and the physical network. Examples of MAC protocol functions include the recognition of adapter addresses, physical medium access management, and message verification and status generation. A MAC frame is indicated by the setting of the first two bits in the frame control field to 00. When this situation occurs, the contents of the information field which carries MAC data is known as a vector.

## Vectors and subvectors

Only one vector is permitted per MAC frame. That vector consists of a major vector length (VL), a major vector identifier (VI), and zero or more subvectors.

As indicated in Figure 4.9, there can be multiple subvectors within a vector. The vector length (VL) is a 16-bit number that gives the length of the vector, including the VL subfield in bytes. VL can vary between decimal 4 and 65 535 in value. The minimum value that can be assigned to VL results from the fact that the smallest information field must contain both VL and VI subfields. Since each subfield is two bytes in length, the minimum value of VL is 4.

When one or more subvectors is contained in a MAC information field, each subvector contains three fields. The subvector length (SVL) is an eight-bit number which indicates the length of the subvector. Since an eight-bit number has a maximum value of 255 and cannot indicate a length exceeding 256 bytes (0–255), a method was required to accommodate subvector values (SVV) longer than 254 bytes. The method used is the placement of XFF in the SVL field to indicate that SVV exceeds 254 bytes. Then, the actual length is placed in the first two bytes following SVL. Finally, each SVV contains the data to be transmitted. The command field within the major vector identifier contains bit values referred to as code points which uniquely identify the type of MAC frame. Figure 4.9 illustrates the format of the MAC frame information field, while Table 4.6 lists currently defined vector identifier codes for six MAC control frames defined under the IEEE 802.5 standard.

## MAC control

As discussed earlier in this chapter, each ring has a station known as the active monitor which is responsible for monitoring tokens and taking action to prevent the endless circulation of a token on a ring. Other stations function as standby monitors and one such station will assume the functions of the active monitor if that device should fail or be removed from

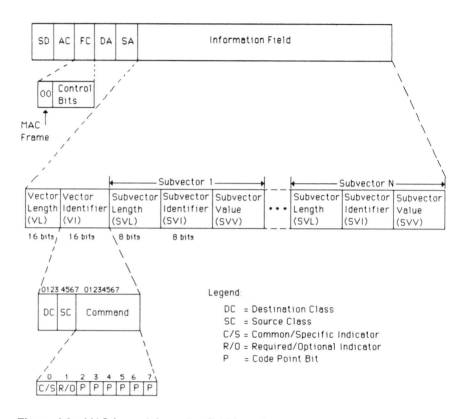

**Figure 4.9** MAC frame information field format.

**Table 4.6** Vector Identifier Codes.

| Code value | MAC frame meaning |
|---|---|
| 010 | Beacon (BCN) |
| 011 | Claim token (CL_TK) |
| 100 | Purge MAC frame (PRG) |
| 101 | Active monitor present (AMP) |
| 110 | Standby monitor present (SMP) |
| 111 | Duplicate address test (DAT) |

the ring. For the standby monitor with the highest network address to take over the functions of the active monitor, the standby monitor needs to know there is a problem with the active monitor. If no frames are circulating on the ring but the active monitor is operating, the standby monitor might falsely presume the active monitor has failed. Thus, the active monitor will periodically issue an active monitor present (AMP) MAC frame. This frame must be issued every seven seconds to inform the standby monitors that the active monitor is operational. Similarly, standby monitors periodically issue a standby monitor present (SMP) MAC frame to denote they are operational.

If an active monitor fails to send an AMP frame within the required time interval, the standby monitor with the highest network address will continuously transmit claim token (CL_TK) MAC frames in an attempt to become the active monitor. The standby monitor will continue to transmit CL_TK MAC frames until one of three conditions occurs:

- A MAC CL_TK frame is received and the sender's address exceeds the standby monitor's station address.
- A MAC beacon (BCN) frame is received.
- A MAC purge (PRG) frame is received.

If one of the preceding conditions occurs, the standby monitor will cease its transmission of CL_TK frames and resume its standby function.

*Purge frame*

If a CL_TK frame issued by a standby monitor is received back without modification and neither a beacon nor purge frame is received in response to the CL_TK frame, the standby monitor becomes the active monitor and transmits a purge MAC frame. The purge frame is also transmitted by the active monitor each time a ring is initialized or if a token is lost. Once a purge frame is transmitted, the transmitting device will place a token back on the ring.

*Beacon frame*

In the event of a major ring failure, such as a cable break or the continuous transmission by one station (known as jabbering), a beacon frame will be transmitted. The transmission of BCN frames can be used to isolate ring faults. For an example of the use of a beacon frame, consider Figure 4.10 in which a cable fault results in a ring break. When a station detects a serious problem with the ring, such as the failure to receive a frame or

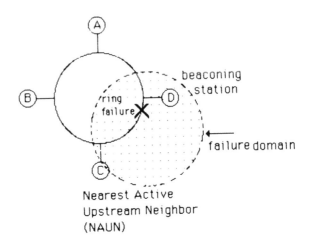

**Figure 4.10**  Beaconing. A beaconing frame indicates a failure occurring between the beaconing station and its nearest active upstream neighbor—an area referred to as a failure domain.

token, it transmits a beacon frame. That frame defines a failure domain which consists of the station reporting the failure via the transmission of a beacon and its nearest active upstream neighbor (NAUN), as well as everything between the two.

If a beacon frame makes its way back to the issuing station, that station will remove itself from the ring and perform a series of diagnostic tests to determine if it should attempt to reinsert itself into the ring. This procedure ensures that a ring error caused by a beaconing station can be compensated for by having that station remove itself from the ring. Since beacon frames indicate a general area where a failure occurred, they also initiate a process known as auto-reconfiguration. The first step in the auto-reconfiguration process is the diagnostic testing of the beaconing station's adapter. Other steps in the auto-reconfiguration process include diagnostic tests performed by other nodes located in the failure domain in an attempt to reconfigure a ring around a failed area.

*Duplicate address test frame*

The last type of MAC command frame is the duplicate address test (DAT) frame. This frame is transmitted during a station initialization process when a station joins a ring. The station joining the ring transmits a MAC DAT frame with its own address in the frame's destination address field. If the frame returns to the originating station with its address-recognized (A) bit in the frame control field set to 1, this means that another station on the ring is assigned that address. The station attempting to join the ring will send a message to the ring network manager concerning this situation and will not join the network.

## 4.3 LOGICAL LINK CONTROL

In concluding this chapter, we will examine the flow of information within a Token-Ring network at the logical link control (LLC) sublayer. The LLC sublayer is responsible for performing routing, error control, and flow control. In addition, this sublayer is responsible for providing a consistent view of a LAN to upper OSI layers, regardless of the type of media and protocols used on the network.

Figure 4.11 illustrates the format of an LLC frame which is carried within the information field of the Token-Ring frame. As previously discussed in this chapter, the setting of the first two bits in the frame control field of a Token-Ring frame to 01 indicates that the information field should be interpreted as an LLC frame. The portion of the Token-Ring frame which carries LLC information is known as a protocol data unit and consists of either three or four fields, depending upon the inclusion or omission of an optional information field. The control field is similar to the control field used in the HDLC protocol and defines three types of frames—information (I-frames) are used for sequenced messages, supervisory (S-frames) are used for status and flow control, while unnumbered (U-frames) are used for unsequenced, unacknowledged messages.

### Service access points

Service access points (SAPs) can be considered interfaces to the upper layers of the OSI Reference Model, such as the network layer protocols. A station can have one or more SAPs associated with it for a specific layer and can have one or more active sessions initiated through a single SAP. Thus, we can consider an SAP to function similar in scope to a mailbox, containing

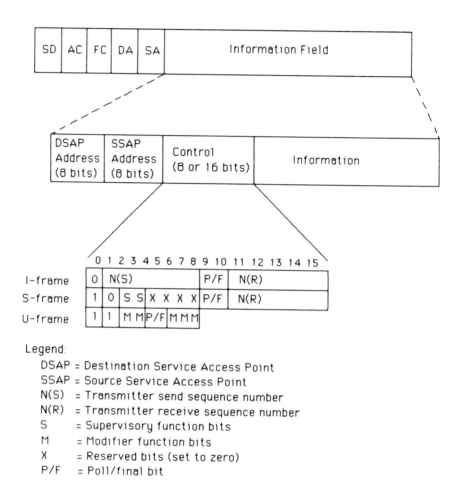

**Figure 4.11**  Logical link control frame format.

an address which enables many types of mailings to reach the box. However, instead of mail, SAP addresses identify different network layer processes and function as locations where messages can be left concerning desired network services.

*DSAP*

The first field in the LLC protocol data unit is the destination services access point (DSAP). The DSAP address field identifies one or more service access points for which information is to be delivered.

*SSAP*

The second field in the LLC protocol data unit is the source services access point (SSAP). The SSAP address field identifies the service access point which transmitted the frame. Both DSAP and SSAP addresses are assigned to vendors by the IEEE to ensure that each is unique.

Both DSAPs and SSAPs are eight-bit fields; however, only seven bits are used for addressing, which results in a maximum of 128 distinct addresses available for each service access point. The eighth DSAP bit indicates whether the destination is an individual or a group address, while the eighth SSAP bit indicates whether the PDU contains a request or a response.

The control field contains information which defines how the LLC frame will be handled. U-frames are used for what is known as connectionless service in which frames are not acknowledged, while I-frames are used for connection-oriented services in which frames are acknowledged.

## Connectionless service

Unacknowledged connectionless service is also known as a Type 1 operation. In this mode of operation there is no data link connection establishment between SAPs of the end stations prior to the transmission of information. Thus, this service can provide rapid data transfer since there is no connection overhead. Since there is no provision for acknowledgement or confirmation of data transfers, Type 1 service is not reliable and higher layer services must be used to provide error recovery operations.

## Connection-oriented service

Connection-oriented or Type 2 service requires a logical link layer connection to be established between a transmitting and receiving station prior to the flow of information occurring. Once a connection is established, each frame is acknowledged. Thus, a connection-oriented service provides frame acknowledgement and does not require the use of higher layer services to provide for error recovery.

## Acknowledged connectionless service

Acknowledged connectionless service, known as Type 3 service, has been proposed as an enhancement to current standards. Under a Type 3 service there is no connection establishment prior to the occurrence of the exchange of data. However, during data transfer individual frames are acknowledged.

## Flow control

Two techniques are used at the link layer to control the flow of data in an orderly manner and prevent transmitting stations from overwhelming receivers with data. The first technique is known as a sliding window and is employed by Type 2 LLC operations. Under the sliding window flow control method, up to 127 frames may be outstanding prior to requiring an acknowledgement from a destination station. This method is full-duplex and permits data to be simultaneously transmitted in each direction.

A second flow control method known as stop-and-wait is used in Type 3 services. Under the stop-and-wait method of flow control, the originating station cannot send more data until the destination station returns a positive acknowledgement.

In comparison to the sliding window method the stop-and-wait method of flow control is inefficient. This is because a receiver can acknowledge multiple PDUs in a single acknowledgement when using a sliding window protocol as well as transmit up to 127 frames without requiring an acknowledgement.

# FDDI CONCEPTS

As previously noted in the last section of Chapter 1, there are a number of similarities and differences between Token-Ring and FDDI networks. In this chapter we will focus our attention upon FDDI network components used to construct this local area network, the use of the FDDI token and timers to allocate network bandwidth, and other concepts which will illustrate the operation and utilization of this network and its similarities and differences with respect to Token-Ring networks. Again, readers are reminded that in this book we reference 4- and 16-Mbps operating rings collectively as Token-Ring networks, while referring to a ring network that operates at 100 Mbps based upon transmission over fiber optic cable as FDDI.

Fiber Distributed Data Interface (FDDI) is a relatively recent and evolving local area networking standard which provides a 100-Mbps operating rate. In addition, due to the design of FDDI networks which incorporate counter-rotating rings, reliability is increased, since one ring functions as a backup to the other.

Work on FDDI dates to 1982, during which both vendors and standards bodies recognized the need for higher speed LAN products and standards to govern the operation of those products. The FDDI standard was developed by the American National Standards Institute (ANSI) X3T9.5 Task Group. In addition, this standard is also being incorporated by the ISO as part of its OSI protocol suite.

The original intention of FDDI standards organizations was for the development of specifications for fiber optic media, optical transmitters and receivers, frame formats, protocols, and media access. However, recent developments in the use of twisted-pair has expanded the operation of FDDI to operate over that transmission medium. Known as CDDI with the C referencing copper, this technique has generated a considerable amount of interest. By 1992, several vendors had introduced FDDI over twisted-pair products and standards bodies were developing specifications that are expected to result in a new standard that will define 100-Mbps operations on twisted-pair cable.

## 5.1 NETWORK ADVANTAGES

The major advantages of FDDI relates to its operating rate, reliability, and immunity to electromagnetic interference.

### Operating rate

FDDI provides an approximate five- to twenty-fold increase in operating rates over previously developed Token-Ring local area networks. This makes an FDDI network into an attractive mechanism to provide an interconnection capability to link lower-speed networks as well as to interconnect minicomputers and mainframes via an attachment to their high-speed channels. When functioning as a mechanism to interconnect lower-speed local area networks, an FDDI network serves as a backbone net. One example of its use would be the situation where each floor in a building has its own local area network. An FDDI network might then be routed vertically within the building, providing a high-speed link between individual networks on each floor.

### Reliability

As previously mentioned, the FDDI standard specified dual fiber-optic counter-rotating rings. The dual rings provide an architecture which permits redundancy which can negate the effect of a network failure. In fact, the FDDI standard defines a ring self-healing mechanism which enables stations to identify a failure and take corrective action. In doing so a station that identifies a cable fault would wrap an incoming signal on its healthy side onto an outgoing fiber. Its neighbor on the other side of the fault would also wrap away from the failure, resulting in a dual ring being converted into a single ring which maintains network connectivity. This mechanism will be illustrated later in this chapter once we review the basic components of an FDDI network.

## Use of optical media

Other advantages of FDDI primarily relate to its use of optical media. Those advantages include the ability to install optical cable without the use of a conduit, the extended transmission distance of an optical system, its immunity to electrical interference and a high degree of security since an optical cable is almost impossible to tap.

# 5.2 HARDWARE COMPONENTS, NETWORK TOPOLOGY AND ACCESS

There is a range of hardware components used to construct an FDDI network. Those components include optical transmitters and receivers, the optical fiber used to carry information, single- and dual-attachment stations, and a concentrator. Other devices that can be used to expand the capability and functionality of an FDDI network, as well as interconnect FDDI networks and FDDI networks to other types of networks, include bridges, routers, and gateways. Since we covered the general operation of bridges, routers, and gateways in Chapter 3 and will present detailed information on each device in future chapters devoted to each network component, we will minimize our discussion of those devices in this chapter.

## Optical transmitters, receivers and cable

The physical medium dependent (PMD) layer discussed in Chapter 1 defines the fiber type and size used in an FDDI network. In addition, this layer defines the connectors used on the fiber cable and the wavelength of the light beam transmitted. Thus, to comply with the PMD layer, optical transmitters and receivers must be compatible with the PMD layer's specifications.

### Optical transmitters

The function of the optical transmitter is to convert electrical signals into light signals that can be carried by the optical fiber used with FDDI networks. FDDI standards specify the use of a light-emitting diode (LED) in the optical transmitter which generates a light signal at a wavelength of 1300 nanometers (nm). This wavelength is shorter than the 1550 nm wavelength produced by lasers and permits less expensive LEDs to be used as the driving light source.

Currently, LEDs are used with multimode optical fiber cables. Although not standardized for use, laser diodes (LDs) are usually used as the optical transmitter when single-mode optical fiber cables are used in an FDDI network. Both single-mode and multimode optical fiber cables are described later in this chapter.

*Optical receiver*

An optical receiver recognizes an optical signal and converts that signal into an electrical signal. To accomplish this task, an optical receiver includes a photodetector which recognizes an optical signal as well as circuitry to generate an electrical signal.

*Fiber optic cable*

Under the PMD standard the type of cable, the wavelength of the optical signal, and the amount of power loss in the cable, which is known as signal attenuation, are specified.

**The Standard Fiber**

The standard fiber specified by FDDI is a multimode fiber of $62.5/125$ $\mu$m ($10^{-6}$ m). Multimode fiber references the fact that multiple modes or rays of light can flow over the fiber at the same time. The first number (62.5) references the core of the fiber, while the second number (125) references the fiber's cladding diameter. Figure 5.1 illustrates the components of a fiber optic cable and their relationship to one another.

**Alternative fiber**

Although the PMD standard specifies the use of multimode $62.5/125$ $\mu$m fiber, fiber sizes of $50/125$, $82.5/125$, and $100/40$ $\mu$m are listed as alternatives. Smaller diameters provide a higher bandwidth capability; however, they are more expensive

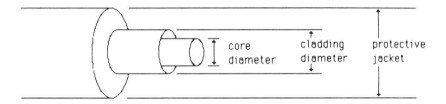

**Figure 5.1** Fiber optic cable. The FDDI Physical Medium Dependent (PMD) standard specifies the use of multimode 62.5 (core diameter)/125 (cladding diameter) $\mu$m cable.

to manufacture. Conversely, larger diameters provide a lower bandwidth capability and are less expensive to produce. At the time this book was written, the use of single-mode fiber was on the verge of approval as another PMD standard. Similarly, the use of copper or twisted wire was being developed as a 'CDDI' standard.

Single-mode fiber, known as monomode in Europe, permits only one ray to be transmitted and has a much smaller core than multimode fiber—typically between 8 and 10 $\mu$m. Such fibers are designed to operate at a wavelength of 1300 nm, similar to FDDI multimode fiber. Due to the small core size of single-mode fiber, its use requires an optical transmitter containing a laser which is capable of concentrating more power into a smaller area than obtainable through the use of an LED. The use of single-mode fiber and laser-based optical transmitters can significantly extend the transmission distance in comparison to the use of multimode fiber and LED-based optical transmitters.

**Power Loss**

In addition to specifying the type of cable and wavelength that flows on the cable, the PMD standard also specifies the permitted power loss of the cable. That loss, which is 1.5 dB per km at a wavelength of 1300 nm, results in a maximum fiber drive distance of 2 km between stations. Theoretically, this means that support of 500 stations representing the maximum number of stations on an FDDI network could result in a ring which extends over a 1000-km area. In reality, a total fiber length of 200 km is specified for FDDI networks, which means that many stations must be closer than 2 km from one another.

*Connectors*

A considerable amount of planning resulted in the specifications for connectors used for attaching physical stations to an FDDI ring. Physical connections between stations occur through the use of duplex connectors that are polarized to prevent transmitting and receiving fibers from being inadvertently interchanged. To both simplify cable assembly as well as prevent miswiring, cables are normally fabricated with different types of connectors. For example, the FDDI dual ring is implemented by a cable assembly which contains a type A connector on one end and a type B connector on the opposite end of the cable. Similarly, another type of cable assembly used to connect a single attached station to a concentrator has two different connectors. An M connector plugs into the M (master) port on a concentrator, while the S connector (slave) plugs into the S port on the single-attached station. Although the use of different connectors precludes miswiring, it should be noted that you can obtain a cable with S type connectors on each cable end. The S connector can be considered a universal FDDI connector and a cable with dual S connectors can be used to interconnect any two FDDI ports. However, this type of cable should be used with care since it does not provide the cabling protection afforded by the use of cables with different connectors on each end.

## Network topology

To obtain an appreciation of the use of different devices used to connect stations to an FDDI network requires a short discussion of the topology and flow of tokens on that network.

*Counter-rotating rings*

FDDI uses two rings which are formed in a ring–star topology. One ring is known as the primary, while the other ring is known as the secondary ring. The primary ring is similar to the main ring path in a Token-Ring network, while the secondary ring acts like the Token-Ring backup ring path. However, the FDDI backup ring unlike the Token-Ring backup path can automatically be placed into operation as a 'self-healing' mechanism. When this occurs, data flow is counter to the flow of data that occurred on the primary ring and results in many persons referring to FDDI as a counter-rotating ring topology.

_Token use_

Similar to the IEEE 802.5 token-ring standard, a rotating token is used to provide stations with permission to transmit data. When an FDDI station wants to transmit information it waits until it detects the token and captures or absorbs it. Once the station controls the token it can transmit information until it either has no more data to send or until a token holding timer expires. When either situation occurs, the station then releases the token onto the ring so it can be used by the next station that has data to transmit. This token-passing technique is more formally known as a timed-token passing technique and uses bandwidth more efficiently than the 802.5 token-passing method. This is because only one token and one frame can be present on a Token-Ring network. In comparison, although only one token is present on an FDDI network at any time, multiple frames from one or more stations can be traversing an FDDI network. Readers will find detailed information concerning the use of the token-holding timer and other timers used by FDDI stations to allocate bandwidth in Section 5.5.

_Network access_

Access to an FDDI network is accomplished through the use of three types of stations—a single attached station (SAS) and two types of dual-attached stations (DAS).

**Dual-attached Station**

A dual-attached station connects to both counter rotating rings used to form an FDDI ring. Each DAS contains two defined optical connection pairs. One pair, called the A interface or port, contains one primary ring input and the secondary ring output. The second pair, called the B interface or port, contains the primary ring output and the secondary ring input. Through the use of two optical transceivers each DAS can transmit and receive data on each ring.

A second type of DAS is known as a concentrator. In addition to the previously described A and B interfaces, a DAS concentrator contains a series of extra ports that are called M, or master ports. The M ports on a DAS concentrator provide connectivity to single attached stations (SASs), a DAS, or another concentrator. Thus, the concentrator provides additional ports which extends the ability to access the primary ring to other stations.

The connection between DAS nodes occurs through the use of two cable sheaths, each containing two fiber optic cables. One pair of cables functions as the primary ring, while the second pair of cables functions as a counter-rotating secondary ring used for backup operations. As previously noted, to ensure the correct cabling to form a dual ring, a main ring cable used to interconnect two dual-attached stations or a DAS to a concentrator contains a type A connector on one end and a type B connector on the other end of the cable.

### Single-attached Station

In comparison to dual attached stations that provide a connection to the dual FDDI rings, a single-attached station can only be connected to a single ring. The connection of single-attached stations to a DAS concentrator can resemble a star topology, even though the interconnection of DAS and DAS concentrators forms a ring. The connection between SAS nodes is accomplished through the use of a single cable sheath containing two fiber optic cables. Since a single-attached station only contains a single optical transceiver, its cost is less than a dual-attached station. However, its inability to connect to the dual ring lowers its reliability in comparison to the connection of workstations to an FDDI network through a dual-attached station.

One of the functions performed by the concentrator includes sensing when an attached SAS is not powered on. When this situation occurs, the concentrator electronically reroutes data to the next sequentially located station. This permits cable faults or a malfunctioning SAS to be electronically bypassed.

Figure 5.2 illustrates the major components of an FDDI network as well as how a ring can be reconfigured in the event of a cable fault or DAS failure. In this example, it was assumed that a cable fault occurred between the upper right and extreme right dual attached stations. Each of those stations has the

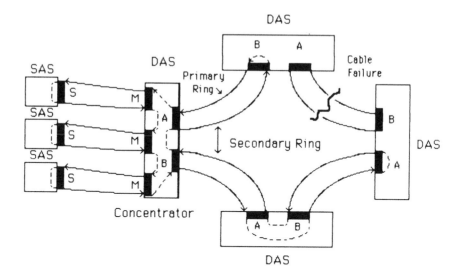

Legend:
A     – A interface contains primary ring input and secondary
        ring input
B     – B interface contains primary ring output and secondary
        ring input
M     – master port
S     – slave port
DAS – dual attached station
SAS – single attached station

**Figure 5.2** FDDI ring operation during cable fault failure. Two dual-attached stations can perform a wrap operation to convert a dual ring into a single ring which bypasses a cable or device failure.

capability to monitor light levels and recognize a cable failure. By two adjacent stations wrapping away from the failure, the dual ring becomes converted into a single ring and connectivity is restored. When the failure condition is corrected the restoral of an appropriate light level causes each DAS to remove the previously implemented wrap and restores the network to its dual ring operation.

## 5.3 DATA ENCODING

The transmission of data on fiber optic cable is accomplished through the use of intensity modulation. That is, a binary 1 is represented by a pulse of light, while a binary 0 is represented by the absence of an optical signal.

One of the key problems associated with any signaling technique that uses the presence or absence of voltage, current, or light to denote binary digits is the potential lack of synchronization from the coding method. Intensity modulation is no exception to this problem, since long strings of 1s or 0s produced by simply turning a light signal on and off will result in a situation where a receiver must either have clocking circuitry or it will lose synchronization with the transmitter. Since clocking circuitry can be costly, a more economical alternative to obtain synchronization between transmitters and receivers is to encode binary data in such a manner that it guarantees the presence of signal transitions even when there are few transitions in the data being transmitted.

As previously explained in Chapters 1 and 4, Token-Ring networks use Differential Manchester encoding to obtain signal transitions that enable clocking to be derived from an incoming data stream. Although intensity modulation could be performed to encode data according to Differential Manchester encoding, doing so would result in a baud rate of 200 M signals per second to obtain a 100-Mbps operating rate. This high signaling rate would be expensive to implement; designers therefore looked for another method to encode data and obtain the required level of signal transitions for receivers to derive clocking from a transmitted signal. That encoding and signaling method is first obtained by placing each group of four bits into a five-bit code (4B/5B encoding). Then, the five-bit group is transmitted using a non-return to zero inverted (NRZI) signaling method.

## NRZI signaling

NRZI signaling results in a change of state used to represent a 0 bit, while no change of state represents a binary 1. NRZI is a form of differential signaling in that the polarity of different signal elements can change when their state changes. This enables the signal to be decoded by comparing the polarity of adjacent signal elements instead of the absolute value of the signal element. However, by itself NRZI signaling will not ensure a level of transitions necessary to keep a receiver in synchronization with a transmitter. This is because a long string of 0s or 1s will not have transitions. Thus, data must be encoded using the 4B/5B encoding technique which enables NRZI signaling to produce the required signal transitions.

## 4B/5B encoding

Under 4B/5B encoding, each group of four bits is encoded into a five-bit symbol. In addition to permitting signaling to be achieved at a 125-Mbps signal rate in comparison to a 200-Mbaud rate that would be required under Differential Manchester encoding, the use of 4B/5B encoding permits the design of the resulting 5B codes to ensure that a transition occurs at least twice for each five-bit code.

Table 5.1 lists the FDDI 4B/5B codes. The use of the 5B code permits patterns beyond the 16 combinations available from a four-bit code to be used to represent special network related functions. For example, the J and K bits used in Differential Manchester encoding for the Token-Ring starting delimiter are developed as special 5B codes in FDDI to prefix tokens and frames. When we examine the FDDI frame formats in Section 5.4, we will also examine the use of certain 5B code functions.

In examining Table 5.1, you will note that only twenty-four 5B codes are defined, even though 32 could be defined. The remaining eight 5B code combinations are either invalid, since under NRZI signaling no more than three zeros in a row are allowed, or represent a 'Halt' if received code.

## 5.4 FRAME FORMATS

Similar to Token-Ring networks, there are distinct frames and frame formats that are used on FDDI networks for information transfer. Figure 5.3 illustrates two FDDI frame formats used to transfer information. Like Token-Ring networks, the basic FDDI frame can convey MAC control data and LLC information. In addition, a station management frame permits management information to be transported between stations and higher-level processes. As defined by ANSI, the station management (SMT) standard is used to control the FDDI PMD, PHY, and MAC layers. Services provided by SMT include fault detection, fault isolation, and ring reconfiguration. Data carried by SMT frames can be used by such higher-level processes as Simple Network Management Protocol (SNMP) services to permit network administrators to monitor and control each FDDI

**Table 5.1** FDDI 4B/5B codes.

| Function/4-bit Group | 5B Code | Symbol |
|---|---|---|
| Starting delimiter | | |
| First symbol of sequential SD pair | 11000 | J |
| Second symbol of sequential SD pair | 10001 | K |
| Ending delimiter | 01101 | T |
| Data symbols | | |
| 0000 | 11110 | 0 |
| 0001 | 01001 | 1 |
| 0010 | 10100 | 2 |
| 0011 | 10101 | 3 |
| 0100 | 01010 | 4 |
| 0101 | 01011 | 5 |
| 0110 | 01110 | 6 |
| 0111 | 01111 | 7 |
| 1000 | 10010 | 8 |
| 1001 | 10011 | 9 |
| 1010 | 10110 | 10 |
| 1011 | 10111 | 11 |
| 1100 | 11010 | 12 |
| 1101 | 11011 | 13 |
| 1110 | 11100 | 14 |
| 1111 | 11101 | 15 |
| Control indicators | | |
| Logical ZERO (reset) | 00111 | R |
| Logical ONE (set) | 11001 | S |
| Line status symbols | | |
| Quiet | 00000 | Q |
| Idle | 11111 | I |
| Halt | 00100 | H |

network node from a central console. In addition to collecting data, SMT provides network administrators with the ability to dynamically alter the network by adding or removing predefined stations. Thus, SMT frames carry both monitoring and control information.

## FDDI token

As illustrated in the top portion of Figure 5.3, the FDDI token consists of five fields. The preamble field is variable in length

**a. FDDI Token**

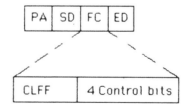

**b. FDDI Frame**

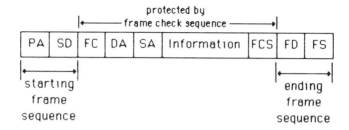

PA – Preamble
SD – Starting delimiter
FC – Frame control
ED – Ending delimiter
DA – Destination address
SA – Source address
FCS – Frame check sequence
FS – Frame status
C – Class bit
L – Length of address fields
FF – Format
Control bits – depend upon frame type

**Figure 5.3** FDDI frame formats.

and is formed by 16 or more 5B I symbols. The starting delimiter field consists of the 5B J symbol followed by the 5B K symbol. That field is followed by the frame control field which identifies the type of frame.

The frame control field is eight bits in length, with the class and length of address fields bit positions used to indicate one of two possible settings per bit position. When the class bit is set to 0, this indicates an asynchronous class of transmission, while setting the class bit to 1 indicates a synchronous class of transmission. The length of address fields bit indicates the use of 48 bit addressing fields when set to 0 and the use of 16 bit addressing fields when set to 1. The two format bits are used to indicate a MAC or SMT frame when set to 00 or an LLC frame when set to 01. A setting of 10 is implementation dependent, while a setting of 11 is currently reserved for future use. The second half of the frame control field consists of four control bits whose values are dependent upon the type of frame defined by the format bits.

There are two special values that can be assigned to the frame control field—hex 80 and hex C0. If the frame control field is set to hex 80 it indicates an unrestricted token, while a value of hex C0 in this eight-bit field indicates a restricted token. The restricted token is generated by a station on an FDDI network that wishes to communicate with another station using all of the asynchronous bandwidth available on the network. Readers are referred to Section 5.5 which discusses the allocation of bandwidth on an FDDI network and the two classes of traffic on that network—asynchronous and synchronous.

When the frame control field is directly followed by the ending delimiter an FDDI token is formed. Here the ending delimiter is the 5B T symbol.

### FDDI frame

As indicated in Figure 5.3, the first three fields of the FDDI token and frame are the same. Thereafter, the frame contains destination and source address fields which identify the frame recipient and frame originator, respectively. Each address field can be either 16 or 48 bits in length but must be of similar length.

The source address field is followed by a variable information field that can range in length from 0 to 4472 bytes. That field is followed by a frame check sequence (FCS) field 32 bits in length which protects all data from the frame control field through the information field. The ending delimiter and frame status fields function as the ending FDDI frame sequence, with the ending delimiter formed by the use of the 5B T symbol which consists of the bit pattern 01101.

## 5.5 BANDWIDTH ALLOCATION

In a Token-Ring network, access is obtained by the setting of priority and reservation bits which enables a station to acquire a token. Once a token is acquired, it is converted into a single frame to transport a unit of information. In comparison, a token flowing on an FDDI network is removed from the network by a station that has data to transmit—a process referred to as absorption. Once a token is absorbed, the absorbing station can transmit one or more frames prior to returning the token onto the network, with the number of frames that can be transmitted based upon the frame size and the setting of timers within the station. Thus, any discussion of FDDI bandwidth allocation must consider the timers supported by each station in an FDDI network. Since those timers, as well as the frame control field of an FDDI token, govern the two classes of traffic that can be carried by an FDDI network, a logical place to initiate an explanation of FDDI bandwidth allocation is by explaining the two classes of traffic supported by this network. Once we do this we will then examine the timers supported by each FDDI station and then use the preceding discussion to describe how an FDDI network allocates bandwidth capacity.

### Classes of traffic

FDDI defines two classes of traffic—asynchronous and synchronous. These classes of transmission should not be confused with an asynchronous and synchronous mode of transmission. The asynchronous class of transmission is transmission that occurs when the token-holding rules of an FDDI network permit transmission. In comparison, the synchronous class of transmission results in a guaranteed percentage of the ring's bandwidth allocated for a particular transmission. Once synchronous bandwidth is allocated, the remaining bandwidth becomes available for asynchronously transmitted frames. That bandwidth is shared by all stations in a fair and equitable manner based upon the use of timers.

### Timers

The control of the amount of asynchronous and synchronous traffic that can be transmitted by a station is governed by FDDI's timed-token access protocol. This protocol is based upon the use of timers used by each station to regulate their operation. These timers include a token rotation timer (TRT), token-holding timer (THT), and valid transmission timer (TVX).

*Token-rotation timer*

The TRT is used to time the period between the receipt of tokens. Under the timed-token access protocol, stations expect to see a token within a specified period of time, referred to as the target-token rotation time (TTRT). The value for the TTRT is set when a station initializes itself on the ring and is the same for all stations on the ring.

When a token passes a station, the station sets its TRT to the value of the TTRT and then decrements its TRT. If the TRT expires prior to the token returning to the station, a counter known as the late counter is incremented. The decision on whether a station can transmit a synchronous or asynchronous class of traffic depends upon the value of the TRT and the value of the late counter.

When a token arrives at a station three events occur which govern the allocation of bandwidth. First, upon receiving a token a station can initiate the transmission of synchronous frames. Whether or not it does so and the number of frames it can transmit depend upon several factors that will be discussed shortly.

*Token-holding timer*

If the token was received earlier than expected, the token-rotation timer (TRT) will be positive and the station will store that value in its token-holding timer (THT). Thus, the value of the THT represents the amount of time by which the token was received earlier than expected. Finally, the station resets the TRT to the value of the target-token rotation time (TTRT) and begins to decrement its TRT.

## Synchronous transmission

As previously mentioned, the receipt of a token enables a station to initiate the transmission of synchronous frames. The ability of a station to transmit synchronous frames depends upon whether or not the station was enabled by an application for synchronous transmission. If enabled, the number of synchronous frames the station can transmit is based upon the size of each frame to be transmitted and the time allocated for synchronous transmission. The frame size governs the amount of time required to place a frame on the ring, while the total time the station can transmit synchronously is based upon the value of the station's synchronous-allocation timer. That timer is set to zero when a station is not enabled by an application for synchronous transmission. When enabled for synchronous transmission, the value of the synchronous-allocation timer can be different for each station on the ring; however, the sum of all synchronous-allocation timers on the active stations on the ring must always be less than the target-token rotation time.

If enabled for synchronous transmission, a station will either transmit all the frames it has synchronously or only those frames that can be transmitted within the allocated synchronous-allocation timer value. When that timer expires or all synchronous frames are transmitted and the timer has not expired, the station may then be able to transmit asynchronous frames.

## Asynchronous transmission

The decision on whether or not a station can transmit asynchronous frames is based upon the value of the late counter. If the value of the late counter is zero, which means that the TRT did not expire, asynchronous frames can be transmitted for the length of time stored in the token holding timer (THT). When the value of that timer reaches zero the token must then be placed back onto the ring.

During both synchronous and asynchronous transmission, the token rotation timer (TRT) continues to decrement. If both synchronous and asynchronous transmissions were stopped due to the expiration of the synchronous-allocation timer and the token-holding timer and other stations have data to send the TRT can be expected to expire prior to the token reappearing at the station. When this occurs, the token will be late, the TRT will be zero, and the THT will also be set to zero. With a value of zero in the token-holding timer the station cannot transmit any asynchronous frames the next time it receives a token. Thus, the timed-token access protocol penalizes a station that transmitted its fully allocated amount of traffic; however, the penalty only applies to asynchronous traffic and a station can always transmit synchronous traffic when it receives a token.

If the station is penalized, the next token will arrive early and the station's late counter will be decremented. Once the value of the late counter reaches zero, the station can again begin to transmit asynchronous traffic.

The preceding bandwidth allocation method guarantees an amount of ring capacity to synchronous traffic. Asynchronous traffic is only transmitted when there is spare capacity on the ring and the use of the previously described counters and timers provides a level of fairness for asynchronous transmission.

In discussing the composition of the frame control field, we said that a setting of hex 80 indicates a restricted token. The use of this type of token provides another mechanism for allocating asynchronous transmission by permitting two stations to use all of the asynchronous bandwidth available on the ring. When one station wishes to communicate with another station using all of the available asynchronous bandwidth, it transmits its asynchronous frames and then releases a restricted token. Due to FDDI rules, only the last station that receives an asynchronous frame can use a restricted token for asynchronous transmission; thus, this enables two stations to continue transmitting to one another. Since the restricted token is only applicable to asynchronous transmission, any station that has synchronous traffic can use that token, ensuring that the guaranteed level of synchronous bandwidth remains available to all stations on the ring.

## Transmission example

To illustrate the FDDI capacity allocation algorithm, let us assume that the target-token rotation time was set to 100 milliseconds for all stations, while the synchronous allocation timer was set to 10 milliseconds for our station. Table 5.2 lists the settings of the different station timers and the occurrence of different events during the capacity allocation process for a station on an FDDI network based upon several predefined events occurring on the ring. By examining the entries in Table 5.2, readers will obtain an appreciation of the method by which timers and the late counter govern the ability of stations to transmit asynchronous and synchronous traffic.

**Table 5.2**   FDDI capacity allocation process example.

1. Token arrives at station.
2. TRT is set to value of TTRT (100 ms).
3. Token absorbed by station.
4. Synchronous traffic transmitted for 10 ms (synchronous allocation timer value).
5. Token released onto ring.
6. Token reappears 50 ms later.
7. Token absorbed.
8. TRT now 40 ms due to 10 ms transmission of synchronous traffic and 50 ms on ring.
9. Token holding timer set to TRT value (40 ms).
10. TRT reset to 100 and begins to decrement.
11. Synchronous traffic again sent for 10 ms.
12. Asynchronous traffic sent for 40 ms (THT value).
13. TRT now has a value of 50 (100−10−40).
14. Token released.
15. Assume other stations transmit data and token reappears after 70 ms.
16. TRT expires and late counter incremented to a value of 1.
17. THT set to a value of 0.
18. Assume no synchronous traffic to be sent. Asynchronous traffic cannot be sent since TRT expired and THT now has a value of 0.
19. TRT reset to 100.
20. Assume token reappears in 30 ms.
21. TRT now set to 70 ms. Although token is early the late counter has a value of 1. Thus, token considered to be late and the station can only transmit synchronous traffic.
22. Token absorbed.
23. Station transmits synchronous traffic for 10 ms (synchronous-allocation timer value).
24. Late counter value decremented to 0.
25. Token placed back on ring.
26. Assume token reappears 40 ms later.
27. TRT now set to 70−40, or 30 ms. Since late counter value is 0, station can transmit asynchronous traffic for up to 30 ms.

## 5.6 FDDI II AND CDDI

There are two evolving standards that have the potential to affect the utilization and adoption of timed token protocol networks. FDDI II represents an evolving standard that will enable the transmission of real-time video and audio, while CDDI represents an evolving standard that could significantly reduce the cost associated with establishing timed token protocol networks and expand their commercial use.

## FDDI II

At the time this book was written, FDDI II was a developing standard which expands upon the basic FDDI standard to include the transmission of isochronous data, where the term 'isochronous' is used to refer to a precise quantity of data delivered at a precise or standard time basis. This anticipated expansion of the FDDI standard is designed to accommodate traffic that requires a guaranteed portion of the network's bandwidth, such as real-time voice and video applications. To accomplish this, FDDI II allocates bandwidth in increments of 64 kbps for voice or data. Up to 16 separate isochronous channels can be established under FDDI II, with each channel operating at 6.144 Mbps—a rate which supports 96 64-kbps subchannels. Readers should note that 64 kbps represents a pulse code modulation (PCM) digitized voice channel operating rate. Thus, FDDI II could carry 96 simultaneous voice conversations per channel. The 16 channels use a total of 99.072 Mbps of FDDI II's 100-Mbps bandwidth. A special packet-switching channel of 768 kbps is always available on FDDI II, while the remaining 928 kbps of bandwidth is used for frame headers and other overhead.

Under FDDI, asynchronous traffic is sent whenever synchronous traffic is not sent. In comparison, under FDDI II asynchronous traffic can only be transmitted on bandwidth that is not allocated to isochronous transmission. This means that portions of each of the 16 FDDI II channels can be allocated for asynchronous or isochronous transmission.

The subdivision of the 100-Mbps FDDI II bandwidth into 16 channels is based upon a modified physical layer protocol (PHY) and media access control (MAC) standards and the introduction of a new standard. The new FDDI II standard is known as hybrid ring control (HRC) and defines the multiplexing of data which permits up to 96 groups of synchronous data to be carried by the network. This means that new adapter cards will be required to implement FDDI II, although existing FDDI cabling could be used and FDDI II is designed to be downward compatible with FDDI.

## CDDI

The development of a standard for the transmission of data at 100 Mbps using the timed-token protocol associated with FDDI over copper cable was in its final stage of development when this book was prepared. Known as the Copper Distributed Data Interface (CDDI), this evolving standard could significantly expand the use of timed-token protocol networks due to economies associated with the use of copper wiring in comparison to fiber optic cable.

One of the main hurdles of the evolving CDDI standard was overcome during 1992 with the selection of a coding scheme by the ANSI X3T9.5 subcommittee responsible for developing the standard. That committee selected the three-level multilevel transmit (MLT-3) signaling method to encode data for transmission over copper cable. This signaling method is similar to NRZI encoding, but uses three voltage levels to provide a degree of noise immunity which can be expected to enable equipment to meet US Federal Communications Commission radiated emissions requirements.

# 6

# BRIDGE ROUTING METHODS, NETWORK UTILIZATION AND PERFORMANCE ISSUES

In Chapter 3 an overview of bridge operations was presented along with information concerning the functionality of other local area network hardware and software components. That chapter deferred until now a detailed examination of bridge routing methods, their network utilization, and performance issues. In this chapter we will focus our attention upon those issues, examining different methods bridges use for routing frames, performance issues that govern their ability to examine and forward frames without introducing network bottlenecks, and their typical employment for the construction of internetworks.

## 6.1 ROUTING METHODS

Bridges operate by examining MAC layer addresses, using the destination and source addresses within a frame as a decision criteria to make their forwarding decisions. Operating at the MAC layer, bridges are not addressed and must therefore examine all frames that flow on a network.

### Address issues

Since bridges interconnect networks, it is important to ensure that duplicate MAC addresses do not occur on joined networks—a topology we will refer to as an internet. While duplicate addresses will not occur when universally administered addressing is used, when locally administered addressing is used duplicate addresses become possible. Thus, the addresses assigned to stations on separate networks joined to form an internet should be reviewed prior to using bridges to connect two or more separate networks.

Two primary routing methods are used by bridges for connecting local area networks—transparent or self-learning and source routing. Transparent bridges were originally developed to support the connection of Ethernet networks and were briefly described in Chapter 3.

## Transparent bridging

A transparent bridge examines media access control frames to learn the addresses of stations on the network, storing information in internal memory in the form of an address table. Thus, this type of bridge is also known as a self-learning bridge. To understand the operation of a transparent bridge in more detail and some of the limitations associated with the use of this device, consider the simple internet illustrated in Figure 6.1. This internet consists of one Ethernet and two Token-Ring local area networks connected through the use of two self-learning bridges. For simplicity of illustration only two workstations are shown and labeled on each local area network.

As previously mentioned, transparent bridges were originally developed to interconnect Ethernet local area networks. This type of bridge can also be used to connect Ethernet and Token-Ring networks; however, in doing so the bridge must, as a minimum, be capable of performing frame conversion.

### Frame conversion

The frame formats used by Ethernet and Token-Ring networks, while similar, are not equal to one another. For example, Ethernet frames are prefixed with a Preamble field which is followed by a Starting Delimiter field. The Ethernet Preamble field is not used in a Token-Ring frame and the Ethernet Starting Delimiter field differs in composition from its Token-Ring equivalent field. Similarly, each Token-Ring frame is prefixed with a Starting Delimiter field which is quite different

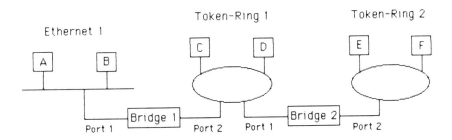

**Figure 6.1** Transparent bridge operation. A transparent or self-learning bridge examines the source and destination addresses to form address or routing tables in memory.

from the field with that name used on an Ethernet frame. Another significant difference between Ethernet and Token-Ring networks concerns the methods used for bridging. Ethernet networks use transparent bridging employing a spanning tree algorithm. IBM Token-Ring networks support an optional routing method known as source routing. If that routing method is not used, an IBM bridge can support transparent bridging. In addition, a proposed standard known as Source Routing Transparent (SRT) bridging provides the ability for bridges to support both methods in constructing Ethernet and IBM Token-Ring networks. The spanning tree algorithm used by transparent bridges, the source routing algorithm used by source routing bridges, and the operation of SRT bridges are discussed in detail later in this chapter.

*Address/routing table construction*

In examining the construction of bridge address/routing tables for the network illustrated in Figure 6.1, we will assume each bridge operates as a transparent bridge. As frames flow on the Ethernet, bridge 1 examines the source address of each frame. Eventually after both stations A and B have become active, the bridge associates their address as being on port 1 of that device. Any frames with a destination address other than stations A or B are considered to be on another network. Thus, bridge 1 would eventually associate addresses C, D, E and F with port 2 once it receives frames with those addresses in their destination address fields. Similarly, bridge 2 constructs its address/routing table. Since frames from Ethernet 1 and Token-Ring 1 can have source addresses of A, B, C or D, eventually the address/routing table of bridge 2 associates those addresses with port 1 of that device. Since frames from Ethernet 1 or Token-Ring 1 with a destination address of E or F are not on those local area networks, bridge 2 then associates those addresses with port 2 of that device.

*Advantages*

One of the key advantages of a transparent bridge is that it operates independently of the contents of the information field and is protocol independent. Since this type of bridge is self-learning, it requires no manual configuration and is essentially a 'plug and work' device. Thus, this type of bridge is attractive for connecting a few local area networks together and is commonly sufficient for most small and medium sized businesses. Unfortunately, its use limits the development of certain interconnection topologies as we will soon see.

*Disadvantages*

To illustrate the disadvantages associated with transparent bridges, consider Figure 6.2 in which the three Ethernet local area networks are interconnected through the use of three bridges. In this example the internet forms a circular or loop topology. Since a transparent bridge views stations as either being connected to port 1 or port 2, a circular or loop topology will create problems. Those problems can result in an unnecessary duplication of frames which will not only degrade the overall level of performance of the internet but quite possibly confuse end stations. For example, consider a frame whose source address is A and whose destination address is F. Both bridge 1 and bridge 2 will forward the frame.

Although bridge 1 will forward the frame to its appropriate network using the most direct route, the frame will also be forwarded by bridge 3 to Ethernet 2, resulting in a duplicate frame arriving at workstation F. At station F a mechanism would be required to reject duplicate frames. Even if such a mechanism is available, the additional traffic flowing across multiple internet paths would result in an increase in network utilization approaching 100%. This in turn would saturate some networks, while significantly reducing the level of performance of other networks. For those reasons transparent bridging is prohibited from creating a loop or circular topology. However, transparent bridging supports concurrently active multiple bridges using an algorithm known as the spanning tree to determine which bridges should forward and which bridges should only filter frames.

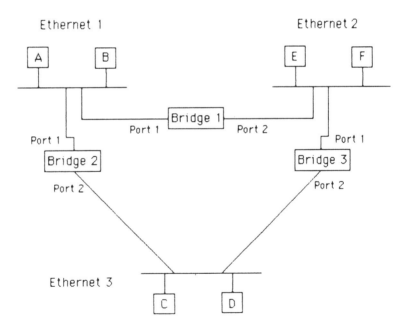

**Figure 6.2** Transparent bridges do not support network loops. The construction of a circular or loop topology through the use of transparent bridges can result in an unnecessary duplication of frames as well as confusing end stations. To avoid those problems the spanning tree protocol (STP) will open a loop by placing one bridge in a standby mode of operation.

## Spanning tree protocol

The problem of active loops was addressed by the IEEE Committee 802 in the 802.1D standard with an intelligent algorithm known as the spanning tree protocol (STP). The STP is based upon graph theory and converts a loop into a tree topology by disabling a link. This action ensures there is a unique path from any node in an internet to every other node. Disabled nodes are then kept in a standby mode of operation until a network failure occurs. At that time, the spanning tree protocol will attempt to construct a new tree using any of the previously disabled links.

*Operation*

To illustrate the operation of the spanning tree protocol, we must first become familiar with the difference between the physical and active topology of bridged networks. In addition, we should become familiar with a number of terms defined by the protocol and associated with the spanning tree algorithm. Thus, we will also review those terms prior to discussing the operation of the algorithm.

### Physical versus Active Topology

In transparent bridging, a distinction is made between the physical and active topology resulting from bridged local area networks. This distinction enables the construction of a network topology in which inactive but physically constructed routes can be placed into operation if a primary route should fail and in which the inactive and active routes would form an illegal circular path violating the spanning tree algorithm if both routes were active at the same time.

The top of Figure 6.3 illustrates one possible physical topology of bridged networks. The cost (C) assigned to each bridge will be discussed later in this chapter. The lower portion of Figure 6.3 illustrates a possible active topology for the physical configuration shown at the top of that illustration.

When a bridge is used to construct an active path, it will forward frames through those ports used to form active paths. The ports through which frames are forwarded are said to be in a forwarding state of operation. Ports that cannot forward

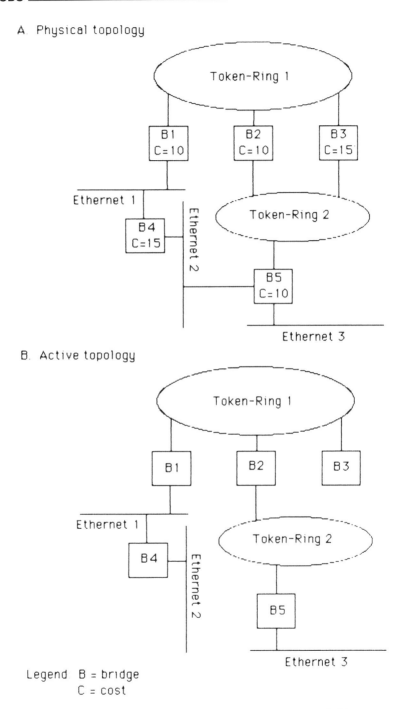

**Figure 6.3** Physical versus active topology. When transparent bridges are used, the active topology cannot form a closed loop in the internet.

frames due to their operation forming a loop are said to be in a blocking state of operation.

Under the spanning tree algorithm, a port in a blocking state can be placed into a forwarding state and provides a path that becomes part of the active network topology. This new path must not form a closed loop and usually occurs due to the failure of another path, bridge component, or the reconfiguration of interconnected networks.

### Spanning Tree Algorithm

The basis for the spanning tree algorithm is a tree structure since a tree forms a pattern of connections that has no loops. The term 'spanning' is used because the branches of a tree structure span or connect subnetworks.

### Root bridge and bridge identifiers

Similar to the root of a tree, one bridge in a spanning tree network will be assigned to a unique position in the network. Known as the root bridge, this bridge is assigned as the top of the spanning tree and has the potential to carry the largest amount of internet traffic due to its position.

Since bridges and bridge ports can be active or inactive a mechanism is required to identify bridges and bridge ports. Each bridge in a spanning tree network is assigned a unique bridge identifier. This identifier is the MAC address on the bridge's lowest port number and a two-byte bridge priority level. The priority level is defined when a bridge is installed and functions as a bridge number. Similar to the bridge priority level, each adapter on a bridge which functions as a port has a two-byte port identifier. Thus, the unique bridge identifier and port identifier enables each port on a bridge to be uniquely identified.

### Path cost

Under the spanning tree algorithm, the difference in physical routes between bridges is recognized and a mechanism is provided to indicate the preference for one route over another. That mechanism is accomplished by the ability to assign a path cost to each path. Thus, you could assign a low cost to a preferred route and a high cost to a route you only want to be used in a backup situation.

Once path costs are assigned to each path in an internet each bridge will have one or more costs associated with different paths to the root bridge. One of those costs is lower than all other path costs. That cost is known as the bridge's root path cost and the port used to provide the least path cost towards the root bridge is known as the root port.

*Designated bridge*

As previously discussed, the spanning tree algorithm does not permit active loops in an interconnected network. To prevent this situation from occurring, only one bridge linking two networks can be in a forwarding state at any particular time. That bridge is known as the designated bridge, while all other bridges linking two networks will not forward frames and will be in a blocking state of operation.

**Constructing the Spanning Tree**

The spanning tree algorithm employs a three-step process to develop an active topology. First, the root bridge is identified. In Figure 6.3b we will assume bridge 1 was selected as the root bridge. Next, the path cost from each bridge to the root bridge is determined and the minimum cost from each bridge becomes the root path cost. The port in the direction of the least path cost to the root bridge, known as the root port, is then determined for each bridge. If the root path cost is the same for two or more bridges linking LANs, then the bridge with the highest priority will be selected to furnish the minimum path cost. Once the paths are selected, the designated ports are activated.

In examining Figure 6.3a, let us now use the cost entries assigned to each bridge. Let us assume bridge 1 was selected as the root bridge as we expect a large amount of traffic to flow between Token-Ring 1 and Ethernet 1 networks. Therefore, bridge 1 will become the designated bridge between Token-Ring 1 and Ethernet 1 networks.

In examining the path costs to the root bridge, note that the path through bridge 2 was assigned a cost of 10, while the path through bridge 3 was assigned a cost of 15. Thus, the path from Token-Ring 2 via bridge 2 to Token-Ring 1 becomes the designated bridge between those two networks. Hence, Figure 6.3b shows bridge 3 inactive by the omission of a connection to the Token-Ring 2 network. Similarly, the path cost for connecting the Ethernet 3 network to the root bridge is lower by routing through the Token-Ring 2 and Token-Ring 1 networks. Thus, bridge 5 becomes the designated bridge for the Ethernet 3 and Token-Ring 2 networks.

### Bridge Protocol Data Unit

One question that is probably in readers' minds by now is how does each bridge know whether or not to participate in a spanned tree topology? Bridges obtain topology information by the use of Bridge Protocol Data Unit (BPDU) frames.

The root bridge is responsible for periodically transmitting a 'HELLO' BPDU frame to all networks to which it is connected. According to the spanning tree protocol, HELLO frames must be transmitted every 1 to 10 seconds. The BPDU has the group MAC address 800143000000 which is recognized by each bridge. A designated bridge will then update the path cost and timing information and forward the frame. A standby bridge will monitor the BPDUs but does not update nor forward them.

When a standby bridge is required to assume the role of the root or designated bridge, as the operational states of other bridges change, the HELLO BPDU will indicate that a standby bridge should become a designated bridge. The process by which bridges determine their role in a spanning tree network is an iterative process. As new bridges enter a network they assume a listening state to determine their role in the network. Similarly, when a bridge is removed, another iterative process occurs to reconfigure the remaining bridges.

Although the STP algorithm procedure eliminates duplicate frame and degraded internet performance, it can be a hindrance for situations where multiple active paths between networks are desired. Another disadvantage of the spanning tree protocol is when it is used in remote bridges connecting geographically dispersed networks. For example, returning to Figure 6.2, suppose Ethernet 1 was located in Los Angeles, Ethernet 2 in New York, and Ethernet 3 in Atlanta. If the link between Los Angeles and New York was placed in a standby mode of operation all frames from Ethernet 2 routed to Ethernet 1 would be routed through Atlanta. Depending upon the traffic between networks, this situation may require an upgrade in the bandwidth of the links connecting each network to accommodate the extra traffic flowing through Atlanta. Since the yearly cost of upgrading a 56- or 64-kbps circuit to a

128-kbps fractional T1 link can easily exceed the cost of a bridge or router, one may wish to consider the use of routers to accommodate this networking situation. In comparison, when using local bridges, their higher operating rate in interconnecting local area networks will normally allow an acceptable level of performance to occur when LAN traffic is routed through an intermediate bridge.

## Source routing

Source routing is a bridging technique developed by IBM for connecting Token-Ring networks. The key to the implementation of source routing is the use of a portion of the information field in the Token-Ring frame to carry routing information and the transmission of 'discovery' packets to determine the best route between two networks.

The presence of source routing is indicated by the setting of the first bit position in the source address field of a Token-Ring frame to a binary one. When set, this indicates that the information field is preceded by a route information field (RIF) which contains both control and routing information.

*The RIF field*

Figure 6.4 illustrates the composition of a Token-Ring (RIF). This field is variable in length and is developed during a discovery process which is described later in this section.

The control field contains information which defines how information will be transferred and interpreted as well as the size of the remainder of the RIF. The three broadcast bit positions indicate a non-broadcast, all-routes broadcast, or single-route broadcast situation. A non-broadcast designator indicates a local or specific route frame. An all-routes broadcast designator indicates that a frame will be transmitted along every route to the destination station. A single-route broadcast designator is used only by designated bridges to relay a frame from one network to another. In examining the broadcast bit settings shown in Figure 6.4, readers should note that the letter X indicates a 'don't care bit' setting that can be either a 1 or 0.

The length bits identify the length of the RIF in bytes, while the D bit indicates how the field is scanned, left to right or right to left. Since vendors have incorporated different memory

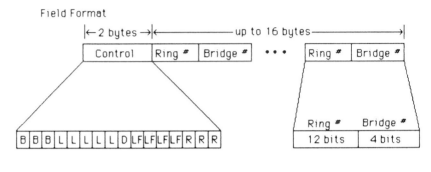

Field Format

B are broadcast bits
    bit settings    designator
        0XX        non-broadcast
        10X        all-routes broadcast
        11X        single route broadcast
L are length bits which denote length of the RIF in bytes
D is direction bit
LF identifies largest frame
    bit settings    size in bytes
        000        516
        001        1500
        010        2052
        011        4472
        100        8191
        101        reserved
        110        reserved
        111        used in all-routes broadcast frame
R are reserved bits

**Figure 6.4** Token-Ring route information field. The Token-Ring is variable in length.

in bridges which may limit frame sizes, the LF bits enable different devices to negotiate the size of the frame. Normally a default setting indicates a frame size of 512 bytes. Each bridge can select a number and, if supported by other bridges, that number is then used to represent the negotiated frame size. Otherwise, a smaller number used to represent a smaller frame size is selected and the negotiation process is repeated. Readers should note that a 1500-byte frame is the largest frame size supported by Ethernet IEEE 802.3 networks. Thus, a bridge used to connect Ethernet and Token-Ring networks cannot support the use of Token-Ring frames exceeding 1500 bytes.

Up to eight route number subfields, each consisting of a 12-bit ring number and a four-bit bridge number, can be contained in the routing information field. This permits two to eight route designators, enabling frames to traverse up to eight rings across seven bridges in a given direction. Both ring numbers and bridge numbers are expressed as hexadecimal characters, with three hex characters used to denote the ring number and one hex character used to identify the bridge number.

*Operation example*

To illustrate the concept behind source routing consider the internet illustrated in Figure 6.5. In this example let us assume two Token-Ring networks are located in Atlanta and one network is located in New York. Each Token-Ring and every bridge are assigned ring and bridge numbers. For simplicity ring numbers R1, R2, and R3 were used, although as previously explained, those numbers are actually represented in hexadecimal. Similarly, for simplicity bridge numbers are shown as B1, B2, B3, B4, and B5 instead of a hexadecimal character.

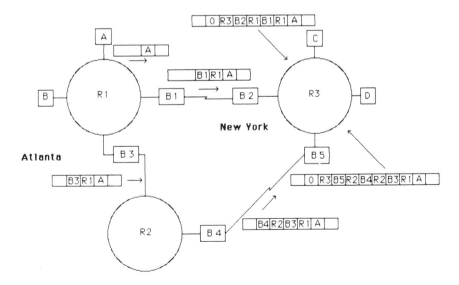

**Figure 6.5** Source routing discovery operation. The route discovery process results in each bridge entering the originating ring number and its bridge number into the route information field.

When a station wants to originate communications it is responsible for finding the destination by transmitting a discovery packet to network bridges and other network stations whenever it has a message to transmit to a new destination address. Assuming station A wishes to transmit to station C, it sends a route discovery packet which contains an empty route information field and its source address as indicated in the upper left portion of Figure 6.5. This packet is recognized by each source routing bridge in the network. When received by a source routing bridge the bridge enters the ring number from which the packet was received and its own bridge identifier in the packet's routing information field. The bridge then transmits the packet to all its connections with the exception of the connection on which the packet was received, a process known as flooding. Depending upon the topology of the interconnected networks multiple copies of the discovery packet will more than likely reach the recipient. This is illustrated in the upper right corner of Figure 6.5 in which two discovery packets reach station C. Here one packet contains the sequence R1B1R1B2R30 where the zero indicates there is no bridging in the last ring. The second packet contains the route sequence R1B3R2B4R2B5R30. Station C then picks the best route based upon either the most direct path or the earliest arriving packet and transmits a response to the discovery packet originator. The response indicates the specific route to use and station A then enters that route into memory for the duration of the transmission session.

Under source routing, bridges do not keep routing tables like transparent bridges. Instead, tables are maintained at each station throughout the network. Thus, each station must check its routing table to determine the route frames must traverse to reach their destination station. This routing method results in source routing using distributed routing tables in comparison to the centralized routing tables used by transparent bridges.

### Route discovery methods

In actuality, the preceding example represents a simplified explanation of source routing since there are two types of route discovery frames that can be used as well as two methods by which a source routing bridge can be configured. Both the type of route discovery frame and the configuration of each bridge in a source routing network will determine the flow of data through the network.

Source routing bridges can support all-routes broadcast (ARB) and single-route broadcast (SRB) route discovery operations. In addition, a source routing bridge can be configured manually as a single-route broadcast bridge, which is its default setting, or as an all-routes broadcast bridge. As an alternative to manually setting the bridge, its mode of operation can be set to automatic configuration, which enables the bridge to negotiate with other bridges to select an appropriate mode of operation.

**Types of Broadcast Frames**

An all-routes broadcast frame will traverse all possible routes between source and destination stations. This frame is indicated by the setting of the first two bits of the RI field to 10. This value tells each bridge to copy the frame onto all ports other than the port it was received on. In comparison, a single-route broadcast frame is identified by the setting of the first two bits of the RI field to a value of 11 and results in the potential for only one route being taken between source and destination stations.

Token-Ring stations can use either an all-routes or a single-route broadcast frame to determine the route to another station on the internet. When an all-routes broadcast route discovery frame is used, that frame is copied by each source routing bridge onto their adjacent rings. This occurs regardless of whether a bridge is set up as a single-route or all-routes broadcast bridge because both modes of operation forward all-routes broadcast frames. As each bridge copies the frame onto its adjoining ring, it adds the ring number the frame was copied from, the bridge number, and the ring number the frame is copied to into the frame's RIF. The destination station will then receive one frame for each path between the origination and the destination stations. Here the receipt of an all-routes broadcast frame indicates that a station is attempting to locate the destination station. The destination station can respond to the originating station in one of two ways. First, it can respond to each received all-routes broadcast frame with either a single-route or an all-routes broadcast frame. Otherwise, the destination station can reverse the order of the routes placed in each received all-routes broadcast frame and transmit specifically routed frames to the originating station. That station can then select the shortest route or the first received response.

**Bridge Mode of Operation Effect**

When a sending station transmits a single-route broadcast frame to determine the best path between that station and its destination only those bridges configured to pass single-route broadcast frames will copy those frames onto adjacent rings. Depending upon the mode of operation of the bridges one (if all bridges are set to single-route broadcast) or more frames will reach the destination station. That station can then respond with a single-route, all-routes, or a specifically routed frame.

Table 6.1 summarizes the options that control the route discovery process. The selection of options used in a network is based upon the methods vendors use to implement one or more options and the degree of control they provide to users in configuring their hardware. Once the route determination process is completed, the originating and destination stations will store a selected route in their route table. This process continues for each station requiring communication wth another station and results in a decentralized approach to routing.

**Table 6.1**  Route discovery control options.

| A. Bridge frame control Bridge mode of operation | Frames forwarded |
| --- | --- |
| Single-route broadcast | All-routes broadcast Single-route broadcast Specifically routed |
| All-routes broadcast | All-routes broadcast Specifically routed |
| B. Source and destination station route options Originating station options | Destination station options |
| Single-route broadcast All-routes broadcast Data included in route determination frame | Single-route broadcast All-routes broadcast Specifically routed |

*Traffic considerations*

In examining the route options listed in Table 6.1, we can make some general observations about the effect of different options upon internet traffic. As previously discussed, an all-routes broadcast frame will appear on the destination station ring once for each route to that ring. Although this may not appear to be significant, let us examine the flow of an all-routes broadcast frame over a network in which six rings are interconnected through the use of seven bridges. This examination will illustrate the variable effect of an all-routes broadcast frame upon the capacity of different rings formed into a network.

Figure 6.6 illustrates the worst case scenario in which a station on ring 1 needs to communicate with a station on ring 6. This is a worst case scenario since the originating and destination stations are on opposite ends of the internet. In this example, the all-routes broadcast frames would traverse four paths: R1–R2–R3–R6, R1–R2–R5–R6, R1–R4–R5–R6, and R1–R4–R5–R2–R3–R6. As indicated, a different number of all-routes broadcast frames would circulate each ring based upon the paths between ring 1 and ring 6. Since the station on ring 1 will issue one all-routes broadcast frame, that frame only flows over ring 1 once, where it is copied onto rings 2 and 4. The frame on ring 2 is copied onto ring 5, where that ring copies the frame onto rings 2 and 6. When the frame from ring 1 is copied onto frame 2, this results in two copies of the all-routes broadcast frame flowing on ring 2. Next, ring 2 copies the frame received from ring 1 onto rings 5 and 3. This results in ring 5 having two all-routes broadcast frames flowing over that ring. Similarly, the single all-routes broadcast frame occurs twice on ring 3 and four times on ring 6. Note that copies of the single all-routes broadcast frame originated on ring 1 fan out across the internet, requiring a total of 12 frames to be carried by six rings. Once the destination station on ring 6 receives the all-routes broadcast frame, if set to an all-routes broadcast mode of operation, it responds in a similar but reverse manner. That is, one all-routes broadcast frame generated by a station on ring 6 would result in four such frames being received by a station on ring 1. Thus, a total of 24 frames would be carried by six rings for one station to ascertain the location of another station at the distant end of the internet. When this is multiplied by a large number of network stations becoming active in the morning or after a power outage when stations reattach to network resources, the use of

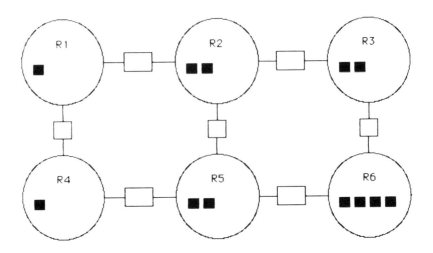

Legend  R = ring number
 = 1 copy of all-routes broadcast frame

**Figure 6.6** All-routes broadcast worst case scenario. An all-routes broadcast frame from a station on R1 to a station on R6 would follow four paths: R1–R2–R3–R6, R1–R2–R5–R6, R1–R4–R5–R6, and R1–R4–R5–R2–R3–R6.

all-routes broadcast frames by the originator and the responding destination stations can flood a network with frames that impair the capacity of rings to convey other information.

*Controlling discovery frame flow*

One technique to prevent flooding and reduce overhead traffic is obtained by using single-route broadcast frames and single-route operating bridges. A single-route broadcast frame will appear on a destination station ring only as many times as there are single-route broadcast routes to the ring. Thus, the configuration of some bridges to a single-route broadcast mode of operation can be used in conjunction with single-route broadcast frames to create preferred routes for route discovery operations.

In configuring bridges, your goal should be to create a logical network structure in which a single-route is formed to interconnect each ring. Figure 6.7 illustrates a single-route logical network structure for the six rings illustrated in Figure 6.6. This logical configuration is the spanning tree we previously examined in our discussion of transparent bridges.

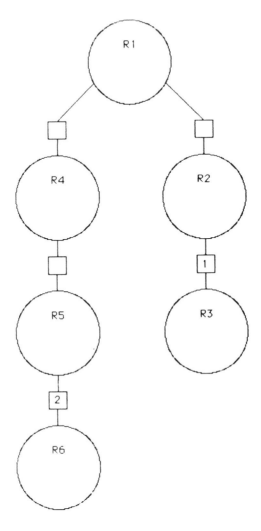

**Figure 6.7**  Single-route logical structure. By placing source routing bridges into a single-route broadcast mode of operation, a logical route structure consisting of a single route between rings can be formed. This single-route structure represents the physical topology illustrated in Figure 6.6.

You can configure bridges to form a single-route through an internet manually or you can use the automatic feature supported by Token-Ring source routing bridges. The manual method requires you to determine which bridges to set to a single-route broadcast mode of operation to create a logical single network route. In comparison, the automatic method results in bridges transmitting BPDUs to create a single-route network through the use of the spanning tree protocol.

Normally, the automatic method should be used as bridges placed in this mode will reconfigure themselves automatically when other bridges fail. In comparison, bridges set to a manual mode will require intervention to reconfigure bridges to compensate for failed components in an internet.

*Advantages*

There are several advantages associated with the use of source routing. One advantage is the ability to construct mesh networks with loops for a fault-tolerant design which cannot be accomplished with the use of transparent bridges. Another advantage is the inclusion of routing information in the information frames. Several vendors have developed network management software products which use that information to provide statistical information concerning internet activity. Those products may assist you in determining wide area network link utilization, the need to modify the capacity of those links or if one or more workstations are hogging communications between networks.

*Disadvantages*

Although the preceding advantages are considerable, they are not without a price. That price includes a requirement to specifically identify bridges and links, the presence of higher bursts of network activity, and an incompatibility between Token-Ring and Ethernet networks. In addition, due to the structure of the route information field (RIF) which supports a maximum of seven entries, routing of frames is restricted to crossing a maximum of seven bridges.

When using source routing bridges to connect Token-Ring networks you must configure each bridge with a unique bridge/ring number. In addition, unless you wish to accept the default method by which stations select a frame during the route discovery process, you will have to reconfigure your LAN software. Thus, source routing creates an administrative burden not present when using transparent bridges.

Due to the route discovery process, the flooding of discovery frames occurs in bursts when stations are powered on or after a power outage. Depending upon the complexity of an internet, the discovery process can degrade network performance.

Perhaps the biggest problem is for organizations that require the interconnection of Ethernet and Token-Ring networks.

A source routing bridge can only be used to interconnect Token-Ring networks since it operates on RIF data which is not included in an Ethernet frame. Although transparent bridges can operate in Ethernet, Token-Ring, and mixed environments, their use precludes the ability to construct loop or mesh topologies and inhibits the ability to establish operational redundant paths for load sharing. Another problem associated with bridging Ethernet and Token-Ring networks also involves the RIF in a Token-Ring frame. Unfortunately, different LAN operating systems use the RIF data in different ways. Thus, the use of a transparent bridge to interconnect Ethernet and Token-Ring networks may require the same local area network operating system on each network. To alleviate these problems, several vendors have introduced source routing transparent (SRT) bridges which function in accordance with the IEEE 802.1D standard that was approved during 1992.

## Source routing transparent bridges

A source routing transparent bridge supports both IBM's source routing and the IEEE transparent spanning tree protocol operations. This type of bridge can be regarded as two bridges in one and has been standardized by the IEEE 802.1 committee as the IEEE 802.1D standard.

*Operation*

Under source routing, the media access control packets contain a status bit in the source field which identifies whether or not source routing is to be used for a message. If source routing is indicated, the bridge forwards the frame as a source routing frame. If source routing is not indicated, the bridge determines the destination address and processes the packet using a transparent mode of operation, using routing tables generated by a spanning tree algorithm.

*Advantages*

There are several advantages associated with the use of source routing transparent bridges. First and perhaps foremost, their use enables different networks to use different local area network operating systems and protocols. This capability enables you to interconnect networks developed independently of one another and allows organization departments and branches to use LAN operating systems without restriction. Secondly and also very important, source routing transparent bridges can connect Ethernet and Token-Ring networks while preserving the ability to mesh or loop Token-Ring networks. Thus, their use provides an additional level of flexibility for network construction.

## 6.2 NETWORK UTILIZATION

In this section, we will examine the use of bridges to interconnect separate local area networks as well as to subdivide networks to improve performance. In addition, we will also focus our attention on how we can increase network availability by employing bridges to provide alternative communications paths between networks.

### Serial and sequential bridging

The top of Figure 6.8 illustrates the basic use of a bridge to interconnect two networks serially. Suppose monitoring of each network indicates a high level of intra-network utilization. One possible configuration to reduce intra-LAN traffic on each network can be obtained by moving some stations off each of the two existing networks to form a third network. The three networks would then be interconnected through the use of an additional bridge as illustrated in the middle portion of Figure 6.8. This extension results in sequential bridging and is appropriate when intra-LAN traffic is necessary but minimal. Both serial and sequential bridging are applicable to transparent, source routing, and source routing transparent bridges which do not provide redundancy nor the ability to balance traffic flowing between networks. Each of these deficiencies can be alleviated through the use of parallel bridging. However, this bridging technique creates a loop and is only applicable to source routing and source routing transparent bridges.

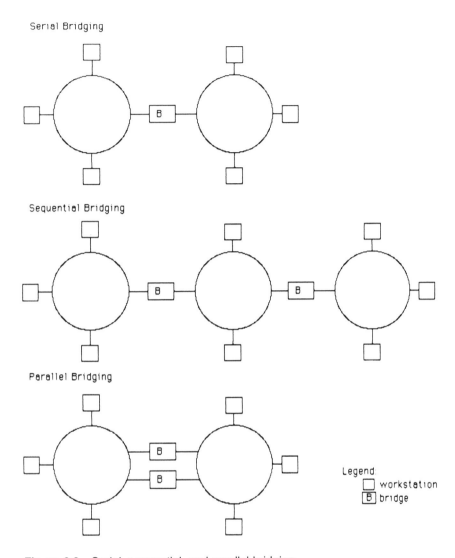

**Figure 6.8** Serial, sequential, and parallel bridging.

*Parallel bridging*

The lower portion of Figure 6.8 illustrates the use of parallel bridges to interconnect two Token-Ring networks. This bridging configuration permits one bridge to back up the other, providing a level of redundancy for linking the two networks as well as a significant increase in the availability of one network to communicate with another. For example, assume the availability of each bridge used at the top of Figure 6.8 (serial bridging) and bottom of Figure 6.8 (parallel bridging) is 90%. The availability through two serially connected bridges would be 0.9 × 0.9, or 81%. In comparison, the availability through parallel bridges would be 1−(unavailability of bridge 1 × unavailability of bridge 2), or 1−0.1 × 0.1, which is 99%.

The dual paths between networks also improve inter-LAN communications performance as communications between stations on each network can be load balanced. Thus, the use of parallel bridges can be expected to provide a higher level of inter-LAN communications than the use of serial or sequential bridges.

One of the more common uses of parallel bridging is to construct redundant backbone rings within a building. Typically, organizations will establish independent networks on each floor in a building and require a method both to interconnect those networks as well as to obtain a load sharing and redundancy capability. Figure 6.9 illustrates how those goals can be accomplished through the use of parallel bridging to connect each 'floor' network to two backbone networks routed up the vertical shafts common in most buildings. Depending upon inter-network communications requirements, the backbone networks could be a different type of network than the floor networks. For example, each floor network might be a 4-Mbps Token-Ring, while the backbone networks could be 16-Mbps Token-Ring or even a 100-Mbps FDDI networks.

From a performance perspective, a station on one network only requires, at most, the crossing of two bridges to reach any other station in the building. This provides a much lower routing delay than connecting networks sequentially. In addition, the use of one or more backbone networks simplifies the addition of more floor networks to the building internetwork at a later date. For example, if the organization expands and leases a new floor it can connect a floor network to the building internetwork by the use of one or two bridges.

When using a bridge to connect two different types of networks, such as Token-Ring to Ethernet, Token-Ring to FDDI, Ethernet to Token-Ring, or Ethernet to FDDI, it is important to note that the frame check sequence characters for each network frame are different. This means that bridges connecting dissimilar networks must recalculate the FCS as the frame is copied onto another network. This also means that there is a short delay as well as a short period of time in which the

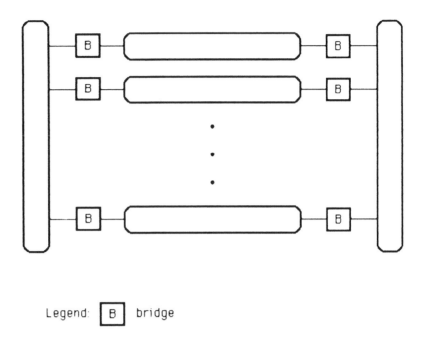

Legend: B bridge

**Figure 6.9** Constructing redundant backbone rings. Parallel bridging is often used in building to construct redundant backbone rings. Backbone rings are normally routed vertically within a building and connected via parallel bridges to 'floor' networks.

frame is not protected. Thus, a malfunctioning bridge has the potential to generate a frame in error but with a correct FCS which precludes the error from being detected. This means that a bridge self-checking mechanism is an important feature that users should consider when acquiring this device.

## 6.3 PERFORMANCE ISSUES

The key to obtaining an appropriate level of performance when interconnecting networks is planning. The actual planning process will depend upon several factors, such as whether or not separate networks are in operation, the type of networks to be connected, and the type of bridges to be used—local or remote.

## Traffic flow

If separate networks are in operation and you have appropriate monitoring equipment, you can determine the traffic flow on each of the networks to be interconnected. Once this is accomplished, you can expect an approximate 10–20% increase in network traffic. This additional traffic represents the flow of information between networks after an interconnection links previously separated local area networks. Although this traffic increase represents an average encountered by the author, your network traffic may not represent the typical average. To explore further, you can examine the potential for internet communications in the form of electronic messages that may be transmitted to users on other networks, potential file transfers of word processing files, and other types of data that would flow between networks.

## Network types

The types of networks to be connected will govern the rate at which frames are presented to bridges. This in turn will govern the filtering rate at which bridges should operate prior to their use becoming a bottleneck on a network. For example, the maximum number of frames per second will vary between different types of Ethernet and Token-Ring networks as well as between different types of the same network. Thus the operating rate of a bridge may be appropriate for connecting some networks while inappropriate for connecting other types of networks.

## Type of bridge

Last but not least, the type of bridge—local or remote—will have a considerable bearing upon performance issues. Local bridges pass data between networks at their operating rates. In comparison, remote bridges pass data between networks using wide area network transmission facilities which typically provide a transmission rate which is a fraction of a local area network operating rate. Now that we have discussed some of the aspects governing bridge and internet performance using bridges, let us probe deeper by estimating network traffic.

## Estimating network traffic

If we do not have access to monitoring equipment to analyze an existing network or are planning to install a new network, we can spend some time and develop a reasonable estimate of network traffic. To do so we should attempt to classify stations into groups based upon the type of general activity performed and then estimate the network activity for one station per group. Doing so will enable us to multiply the number of stations in the group by the station activity to determine the group network traffic. Summing up the activity of all groups will then provide us with an estimate of the traffic activity for the network.

As an example of local area network traffic estimation let us assume our network will support 20 engineers, 5 managers, and 3 secretaries. Table 6.2 shows how we would estimate the network traffic in terms of the bit rate for each station group, the total activity per group, and then sum up the network traffic for the three groups that will use the network. In this example, which for simplicity did not include the transmission of data to a workstation printer, the total network traffic was estimated to be slightly below 50 000 bps.

To plan for the interconnection of two or more networks through the use of bridges, our next step should be to perform a similar traffic analysis for each of the remaining networks. After this is accomplished, we can use the network traffic to estimate inter-LAN traffic, using 10–20% of total intra-network traffic as an estimate of the internet traffic that will result from the connection of separate networks.

*Internet traffic*

To illustrate the traffic estimation process for the interconnection of separate LANs, let us assume network A's traffic was determined to be 50 000 bps, while network B's traffic was estimated to be approximately 100 000 bps. Figure 6.10 illustrates the flow of data between networks connected via a local bridge. Note that the data flow in each direction is expressed as a range based upon the use of an industry average of 10–20% of network traffic routed between interconnected networks.

**Table 6.2**  Estimating network traffic.

Engineering workstations

| Activity | Message size (bytes) | Frequency | Bit rate* |
|---|---|---|---|
| Request program | 1500 | 1/hour | 4 |
| Load program | 480 000 | 1/hour | 1067 |
| Save files | 120 000 | 2/hour | 533 |
| Send/receive E-mail | 2 000 | 2/hour | 9 |
| | | | 1613 |

Total engineering activity = 1613 × 20 = 32 260 bps

Managerial workstations

| Activity | Message size (bytes) | Frequency | Bit rate* |
|---|---|---|---|
| Request program | 1500 | 2/hour | 7 |
| Load program | 320,000 | 2/hour | 1422 |
| Save files | 30,000 | 2/hour | 134 |
| Send/receive E-mail | 3,000 | 4/hour | 27 |
| | | | 1590 |

Total managerial activity = 1590 × 5 = 7950 bps

Secretarial workstations

| Activity | Message size (bytes) | Frequency | Bit rate* |
|---|---|---|---|
| Request program | 1500 | 4/hour | 14 |
| Load program | 640,000 | 2/hour | 2844 |
| Save files | 12,000 | 8/hour | 214 |
| Send/receive E-mail | 3,000 | 6/hour | 40 |
| | | | 3112 |

Total secretarial activity = 3112 × 3 = 9336 bps

Total estimated network activity = 45 546 bps

*Note: Bit rate computed by multiplying message rate by frequency by 8 bits/byte and dividing by 3600 seconds/hour.

*Network types*

Our next area of concern is to examine the types of networks to be interconnected. In doing so we should focus our attention upon the operating rate of each LAN. If network A's traffic was estimated to be approximately 50 000 bps, then the addition

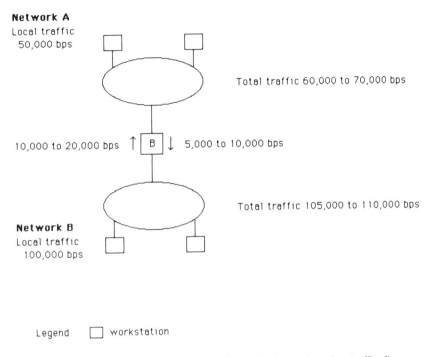

**Network A**
Local traffic
50,000 bps

Total traffic 60,000 to 70,000 bps

10,000 to 20,000 bps ↑ B ↓ 5,000 to 10,000 bps

Total traffic 105,000 to 110,000 bps

**Network B**
Local traffic
100,000 bps

Legend. ☐ workstation

**Figure 6.10** Considering internet data flow. To determine the traffic flow on separate networks after they are interconnected you must consider the flow of data onto each network from the other network.

of 10 000 to 20 000 bps from network B onto network A will raise network A's traffic level to between 60 000 and 70 000 bps. Similarly, the addition of traffic from network A onto network B will raise network B's traffic level to between 105 000 and 110 000 bps. In this example, the resulting traffic on each network is well below the operating rate of all types of local area networks and will not present a capacity problem for either network to be interconnected using local bridges.

*Bridge type*

As previously mentioned, local bridges transmit data between networks at the data rate of the destination network. This means that a local bridge will have a lower probability of being an internet bottleneck than a remote bridge, since the latter provides a connection between networks using a wide area transmission facility which typically operates at a fraction of the operating rate of a LAN.

In examining the bridge operating rate required to connect networks, we will use a bottom-up and a top-down approach. That is, we will first determine the operating rate in frames per second for the specific example previously discussed. This will be followed by computing the maximum frame rate supported by Ethernet and Token-Ring networks.

For the bridge illustrated in Figure 6.10, we previously computed its maximum transfer rate would be 20 000 bps from network B onto network A. This is equivalent to 2500 bytes per second. If we assume data is transported in 512-byte frames, this would be equivalent to 6 frames per second—a minimal transfer rate supported by every bridge manufacturer. However, when remote bridges are used, the frame forwarding rate of the bridge will more than likely be constrained by the operating rate of the wide area network transmission facility.

## Bridge operational considerations

A remote bridge wraps a LAN frame into a higher level protocol packet for transmission over a wide area network communications facility. This operation requires the addition of a header, protocol control, error detection, and trailer fields and results in a degree of overhead. Thus, a 20 000-bps data flow from network B to network A could not be accommodated by a transmission facility operating at that data rate.

In converting LAN traffic onto a wide area network transmission facility, you can expect a protocol overhead of approximately 20%. Thus, your actual operating rate must be at least 24 000 bps prior to the wide area network communications link becoming a bottleneck that would degrade internet communication. Now that we have examined the bridging performance requirements for two relatively small networks, let us focus our attention upon determining the maximum frame rates of Ethernet and Token-Ring networks. Doing so will provide us with the ability to determine the rate at which the frame processing rate of a bridge becomes irrelevant, since any processing rate above the maximum network rate will not be useful. In addition, we can use the maximum network frame rate when estimating traffic, since if we approach that rate network performance will begin to significantly degrade when utilization exceeds between 60–70% of that rate.

**Ethernet Traffic**

An Ethernet frame can vary between a minimum of 72 bytes and a maximum of 1526 bytes. Thus, the maximum frame rate on an Ethernet will vary based upon the frame size.

Ethernet operations require a 'dead' time between frames of 9.6 $\mu$s. The bit time for a 10-Mbps Ethernet is $1/10^7$ or 100 $\mu$s. Based upon the preceding, we can compute the maximum number of frames/second for 1526-byte frames. Here the time per frame becomes:

$$9.6 \mu + 1526 \text{ bytes} \times 8 \text{ bits/byte} \times 100 \text{ ns/bit} = 1.23 \text{ ms.}$$

Thus, in one second there can be a maximum of $1/(1.23 \times 10^{-3}$ ms or 812 maximum size frames. For a minimum frame size of 72 bytes, the time per frame is:

$$9.6 \mu s + 72 \text{ bytes} \times 8 \text{ bits/byte} \times 100 \text{ ns/bit} = 67.2 \mu s.$$

Thus, in one second there can be a maximum of $1/(67.2 \times 10^{-6})$ or 14 880 minimum-size 72-byte frames. Table 6.3 summarizes the frame processing requirements for a 10-Mbps Ethernet under 50% and 100% load conditions based upon minimum and maximum frame sizes. Note that those frame processing requirements define the frame examination (filtering) operating rate of a bridge connected to an Ethernet. That rate indicates the number of frames per second a bridge connected to a 10-Mbps Ethernet local area network must be capable of examining under heavy (50% load) and full (100% load) traffic conditions.

**Table 6.3** Ethernet frame processing requirements (frames per second).

| Average frame size | Frame processing requirements | |
|---|---|---|
| (bytes) | 50% load | 100% load |
| 1526 | 405 | 812 |
| 72 | 7440 | 14 880 |

We can extend our analysis of Ethernet frames by considering the frame rate supported by different link speeds. For example, let us consider a pair of remote bridges connected by a 9.6-kbps line. The time per frame for a 72-byte frame at 9.6 kbps is:

$$9.6 \ \mu s + 72 \ \text{bytes} \times 8 \ \text{bits/byte} \times 0.000 \ 1041 = 0.059 \ 9712 \ \text{s.}$$

Thus, in 1 s the number of frames is 1/0.060 0096, or 16.66 frames per second. Table 6.4 compares the frame-per-second rate supported by different link speeds for minimum and maximum size Ethernet frames. As expected, the frame transmission rate supported by a 10-Mbps link for minimum and maximum size frames is exactly the same as the frame processing requirements under 100% loading as previously indicated in Table 6.3.

**Table 6.4**   Link speed versus frame rate.

| | Frames per second | |
| --- | --- | --- |
| Link speed | Minimum | Maximum |
| 9.6 kbps | 16.66 | 0.79 |
| 19.2 kbps | 33.38 | 1.58 |
| 56.0 kbps | 97.44 | 4.60 |
| 64.0 kbps | 111.17 | 5.25 |
| 1.536 Mbps | 2815.31 | 136.34 |
| 10 Mbps | 14 880 | 812 |

In examining Table 6.4, readers should note that the entries in this table do not consider the effect of the overhead of a protocol used to transport frames between two networks. Thus, readers should decrease the frame-per-second rate by approximately 20% for all link speeds through 1.536 Mbps. The reason the 10-Mbps rate should not be adjusted is because it represents a local bridge connection that does not require the use of a wide area network protocol to transport frames. Readers should also note that the link speed of 1.536 Mbps represents a T1 transmission facility that operates at 1.544 Mbps. However, since the framing bits on a T1 circuit use 8 kbps, the effective line speed available for the transmission of data is 1.536 Mbps.

**Token-Ring Traffic**

In comparison to Ethernet, the modeling of a Token-Ring network can be much more complex. This is because the frame rate depends upon the number of nodes in a network, the token-holding time per node, the type of wire used for cabling and ring length, and the type of adapter used as a ring interface unit. In addition, such factors as the flow of discovery frames and the transmission of active monitor frames affect the flow of data on a ring. To simplify our calculations, we will ignore the latter two types of frames.

The number of nodes and their cabling govern both token propagation time and holding time as a token flows around the ring. The type of adapter used governs the maximum frame rate supported. This rate can vary between vendors as well as within a vendor's product line. For example, Texas Instruments' original MAC code permitted a maximum transmission of 2200 64-kbyte frames per second. New software from that vendor raised the frame rate to 3300 and a more recent release known as Turbo MAC 2.1 increased it to 4000 frames per second.

The type of cabling and ring length governs the propagation delay associated with the flow of tokens and frames around the ring. Although the data rate around a ring is consistent at either 4 Mbps or 16 Mbps, tokens and frames do not flow instantaneously around the ring and are delayed based upon the distance they must traverse and the type of cabling used. In addition, a slight delay is encountered at each node since the token must be examined to determine its status.

In developing a simplified model to determine Token-Ring frame rates, let us assume there are $N$ stations on the network. Then, on the average a token will travel $N/2$ stations until it is grabbed and converted into a frame. Similarly, a frame can be expected to travel $N/2$ stations until it reaches its destination and another $N/2$ stations until it returns to the origination station and is reconverted back into a token. In free space, the velocity of light is 186 000 miles per second. In a twisted-pair cable the speed of electrons is approximately 62% of the velocity of light in free space. Thus, electrons will travel at approximately $186\,000 \times 0.62$, or 115 320 miles per second. This rate is equivalent to 608 889 600 feet per second or approximately 609 feet per $\mu$s. To traverse 1000 feet of cable would then require $1.6 \times 10^{-6}$ seconds. At a Token-Ring operating rate of 4 Mbps, this is equivalent to a time delay per 1000 feet of twisted pair cable of

$(1.6 \times 10^{-6} \text{ s})/[1/(4 \times 10^6 \text{ bit/s})] = 6.4$ bits.

For the development of our Token-Ring performance model, let us start with the flow of a token as indicated by the following steps in the model development process.

1. A free token travels on the average $N/2$ stations until it is grabbed and converted into a frame.
2. Each station adds a 2.5-bit time delay to examine the token. At a 4-Mbps ring operating rate, a bit time equals $2.5 \times 10^{-7}$ s. Thus, each station induces a delay of $6.25 \times 10^{-7}$ s.
3. The token consists of 3 bytes or 24 bits. The time required for the token to be placed onto the ring is:

$24 \times 2.5 \times 10^{-7} = 60 \times 10^{-7}$ s.

4. The time for the token to be placed onto the ring and flow around half the ring until it is grabbed then becomes:

$N/2 \times 6.25 \times 10^{-7} + 60 \times 10^{-7}$ s.

5. Once a token is grabbed it is converted into a frame. On the average the frame will travel $N/2$ stations to its destination. A frame containing 64 bytes of information consists of 85 bytes, since starting and ending delimiters, source and destination addresses, and other control information must be included in the frame. Thus, the time required to place the frame on the ring becomes:

$85 \times 8 \times 2.5 \times 10^{-7} = 1.7 \times 10^{-4}$ s.

6. The frame must traverse $N/2$ stations on the average to reach its destination. Thus, the time required for the frame to be placed on the ring and traverse half the ring becomes:

$N/2 \times 6.25 \times 10^{-7} + 1.7 \times 10^{-4}$ s.

7. The total token and frame time from steps 4 and 6 above is:

$N/2 \times 6.25 \times 10^{-7} + 60 \times 10^{-7} + N/2 \times 6.25 \times 10\text{-}7 + 1.7 \times 10^{-4}$

$= N \times 6.25 \times 10^{-7} + 60 \times 10^{-7} + 1.7 \times 10^{-4}$ s.

8. To consider the effect of propagation delay time as tokens and frames flow in the cable, we must consider the sum of the ring length and twice the sum of all lobe distances. Here we must double the lobe distances since the token will flow to and from each workstation on the lobe. If we let $C$ equal the number of thousands of feet of cable, we obtain the time to traverse the ring as:

$$N \times 6.25 \times 10^{-7} + 60 \times 10^{-7} + 1.7 \times 10^{-4} + 1.6 \times 10^{-6} \times C$$

$$= N \times 6.25 \times 10^{-7} + 1.76 \times 10^{-4} + 1.6 \times 10^{-6} \times C$$

where: $N$ = number of stations, and $C$ = thousands of feet of cable.

To illustrate the use of the previously developed equation, let us assume a Token-Ring network of 50 stations has 8000 feet of cable. Then, the time for a token and frame to circulate the ring becomes:

$$50 \times 6.25 \times 10^{-7} + 1.76 \times 10^{-4} + 1.6 \times 10^{-6} \times 8$$
$$= 312.5 \times 10^{-7} + 1.76 \times 10^{-4} + 12.8 \times 10^{-6}$$
$$= 0.3125 \times 10^{-4} + 1.76 \times 10^{-4} + 0.128 \times 10^{-4}$$
$$= 2.2005 \times 10^{-4} \text{ s.}$$

Then, in one second there will be on the average: $1/(2.2005 \times 10^{-4})$, or 4544 64-byte information frames that can flow on a Token-Ring network containing 50 stations and a total of 8000 feet of cable.

To further illustrate the use of the previously developed formula, let us now consider what happens when the network is reduced in size. Suppose the number of workstations is halved to 25 and the total cable distance reduced to 4000 feet. Then, the time for a token and frame to flow around the ring becomes:

$$25 \times 6.25 \times 10^{-7} + 1.76 \times 10^{-4} + 1.6 \times 10^{-6} \times 4$$
$$= 0.156\,25 \times 10^{-4} + 1.76 \times 10^{-4} + 0.64 \times 10^{-4}$$
$$= 1.980\,25 \times 10^{-4} \text{ s.}$$

Thus, in one second there will be on the average $1/(1.980\,25 \times 10^{-4})$, or 5049 64-byte information frames. As we would intuitively expect, as the number of stations and cable distance decrease the transmission capacity of the ring increases.

**Table 6.5** Number of stations versus frame rate 64-byte information frame, 8000 feet of cable.

| Stations | Frames/second |
|----------|---------------|
| 10 | 5126 |
| 20 | 4967 |
| 30 | 4818 |
| 40 | 4677 |
| 50 | 4544 |
| 60 | 4418 |
| 70 | 4300 |
| 80 | 4187 |
| 90 | 4080 |
| 100 | 3979 |
| 110 | 3882 |
| 120 | 3790 |
| 130 | 3703 |
| 140 | 3619 |
| 150 | 3539 |
| 160 | 3462 |
| 170 | 3389 |
| 180 | 3318 |
| 190 | 3251 |
| 200 | 3186 |

Tables 6.5 and 6.6 indicate the frame rates achievable on Token-Ring networks containing 8000 and 10 000 feet of cable. Each table indicates the frame rate based upon the number of stations on the network.

Now let us examine the effect of transmitting larger information frames. Suppose we transmit a 4000-byte information frame. Here a total of 4021 bytes is required. Thus, the time required for the frame to be placed on the ring becomes:

$$4021 \times 8 \times 2.5 \times 10^{-7} = 80.42 \times 10^{-4} \text{ s.}$$

Then, the total token and frame time becomes:

$$N \times 6.25 \times 10^{-7} + 60 \times 10^{-7} + 80.42 \times 10^{-4} + 1.6 \times 10^{-6} \times C \text{ s.}$$

**Table 6.6** Number of stations versus frame rate 64-byte information frame 10 000 feet of cable.

| Stations | Frames/second |
|---|---|
| 10 | 5044 |
| 20 | 4889 |
| 30 | 4744 |
| 40 | 4608 |
| 50 | 4479 |
| 60 | 4357 |
| 70 | 4241 |
| 80 | 4132 |
| 90 | 4028 |
| 100 | 3929 |
| 110 | 3835 |
| 120 | 3745 |
| 130 | 3659 |
| 140 | 3577 |
| 150 | 3499 |
| 160 | 3424 |
| 170 | 3352 |
| 180 | 3284 |
| 190 | 3218 |
| 200 | 3154 |

Again, let us assume the number of stations, $N$, is 50, while the cabling distance is 8000 feet. Thus, we obtain the token and frame revolution time as follows:

$$50 \times 6.25 \times 10^{-7} + 60 \times 10^{-7} + 80.42 \times 10^{-4} + 1.6 \times 10^{-6} \times 8$$
$$= 0.3125 \times 10^{-4} + 0.06 \times 10^{-4} + 80.42 \times 10^{-4} + 0.128 \times 10^{-4}$$
$$= 80.9205 \times 10^{-4} \text{ s.}$$

Then, in one second there will be $1/(80.9205 \times 10^{-4})$, or 123.6 frames. Since each frame contains 4000 bytes of information, the effective operating rate becomes $123.6 \times 4000 \times 8 = 3.955$ Mbps, for a 50-station Token-Ring network with 8000 feet of cable using 4000 character frames. In comparison, a similar Token-Ring network using 64-byte information frames would have a frame rate of 4544 frames per second. However, this rate would be equivalent to an information transfer rate of 2.326 Mbps. Thus, whenever possible, larger frame sizes should be used on a Token-Ring network.

The preceding computations which represent simplified models of a 4-Mbps Token-Ring network indicate an important concept. That is, both the cabling distance and number of network stations govern the maximum frame rate that can flow on a Token-Ring network. This tells us that we should consider breaking larger networks into subnetworks interconnected by bridges to improve network performance.

One of the more interesting aspects of Token-Ring frame rates is that the majority of adapter cards from different vendors which use the Texas Instrument chip set support a maximum frame rate of 4000 frames per second. This indicates that a further constraint to the number of nodes and cable length is the adapter cards used in a network. In 1991, Madge Systems introduced an adapter card which was capable of transmitting approximately 12 000 64-byte frames per second. Thus, using that firm's adapter cards, or other higher performance adapter cards, can significantly improve the performance of a Token-Ring network. However, the use of such 'high performance' adapter cards is irrelevant when a network grows in size in terms of the number of network stations and cable distance. In such situations, the capability of high performance network adapter cards will not be effectively used.

# 7

## ROUTERS

In Chapter 3 we examined the basic operation and utilization of a variety of local area networking components, including routers. Information presented in that chapter will serve as a foundation for a more detailed discussion of the operation and utilization of routers which is presented in this chapter.

## 7.1 ROUTER OPERATION

By operating at the ISO Reference Model network layer, a router becomes capable of making intelligent decisions concerning the flow of information in a network. To accomplish this, routers perform a variety of functions that are significantly different from those performed by bridges. Unlike bridges that are not addressable, routers are. Thus, routers examine frames that are directly addressed to them by looking at the network address within each frame to make their forwarding decision.

### Basic operation and use of routing tables

To illustrate the basic operation of routers, consider the simple mesh structure formed by the use of three routers labeled R1, R2, and R3 in Figure 7.1a. In this illustration, three Token-Ring networks are interconnected through the use of three routers. The initial construction of three routing tables is shown in Figure 7.1b. Unlike bridges which learn MAC addresses, most routers are initially configured, with routing tables established at the time of equipment installation. Thereafter, periodic communications between routers dynamically updates routing tables to take into consideration changes in internet topology and traffic.

A. Simple mesh structure

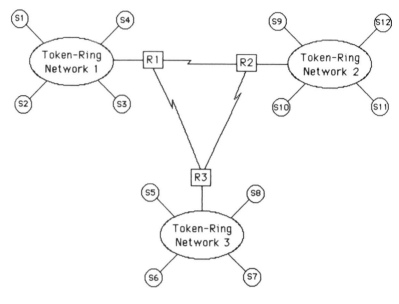

B. Routing tables

| R1 | | | R2 | | | R3 | |
|---|---|---|---|---|---|---|---|
| 1 | * | | 1 | R1 | | 1 | R1 |
| 2 | R2 | | 2 | * | | 2 | R2 |
| 3 | R3 | | 3 | R2 | | 3 | * |

C. Packet composition

| | | Destination | Source | |
|---|---|---|---|---|
| MAC | LLC | 2.S12 | 1.S2 | DATA |

Legend: [R] router    (S) network station

**Figure 7.1**  Basic router operation.

In examining Figure 7.1b, note that the routing table for router R1 indicates the routers it must communicate with to access each interconnected Token-Ring network. Hence, router R1 would communicate with router R2 to reach Token-Ring network 2 and communicate with the router R3 to reach Token-Ring network 3.

Figure 7.1c illustrates the composition of a packet originated by station S2 on Token-Ring 1 that is to be transmitted to station S12 on Token-Ring 2. Router R1 first examines the destination network address and notes it is on another network. Thus, the router searches its routing table and finds that the frame should be transmitted to router R2 to reach Token-Ring network 2. Hence, router R1 forwards the frame to router R2. Router R2 then places the frame onto Token-Ring network 2 for delivery to station S12 on that network.

Since routers use the network addresses instead of MAC addresses for making their forwarding decisions, it is possible to have duplicate locally administered MAC addresses on each network interconnected by a router. In comparison, the use of bridges would require you to first review and then eliminate any duplicate locally administered addresses common to networks to be interconnected—a process that can be time consuming when large networks are connected.

Another difference between bridges and routers is the ability of a router to support the transmission of data on multiple paths between local area networks. Although a multiport bridge with a filtering capability can be considered to perform intelligent routing decisions, the result of a bridge operation is normally valid for only one point-to-point link within a wide area network. In comparison, a router may be able to acquire information about the status of a large number of paths and select an end-to-end path consisting of a series of point-to-point links. In addition, most routers can fragment and reassemble data. This permits packets to flow over different paths and to be reassembled at their final destination. With this capability a router can route each packet to its destination over the best possible path at a particular instant in time and dynamically change paths to correspond to changes in network link status on traffic activity.

For example, each of the routing tables illustrated in Figure 7.1b can be expanded to indicate a secondary path to each network. Thus, while router R1 would continue to use the entry of R2 as its primary mechanism to reach network 2, a secondary entry of R3 could be established to provide an alternative path to network 2 via routers R3 and R2 rather than directly via router R2.

## Networking capability

To better illustrate the networking capability of routers, consider Figure 7.2 which shows three geographically dispersed

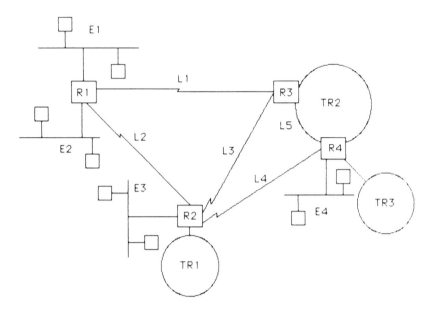

**Figure 7.2** Router operation. The use of routers enables the transmission of data over multiple paths, alternate path routing, and the use of a mesh topology which transparent bridges cannot support.

locations that have a total of four Ethernet and three Token-Ring networks interconnected through the use of four routers and four wide area network transmission circuits or links. For simplicity, the use of modems or DSUs on the wide area network is not shown. This illustration will be referenced several times in this chapter to denote different types of router operations.

In addition to supporting a mesh structure that is not obtainable from the use of transparent bridges, the use of routers offers other advantages in the form of addressing, message processing, link utilization, and priority of service. Routers are known to stations that use its service. Hence, packets can be directly addressed to a router. This eliminates the necessity for the device to examine in detail every packet flowing on a network and results in the router only having to process messages that are addressed to it by other devices. Concerning link utilization, assume a station on E1 transmits to a station on TR3. Depending upon the status and traffic on network links, packets could be routed via L1 and use TR2 to provide a transport mechanism to R4, from which the packets are delivered to TR3. Alternatively, links L2 and L4 could be used to provide a path from R1 to R4. Although link availability and link traffic usually determines routing, routers can support prioritized traffic and may store low priority traffic for a small period of time to allow higher priority traffic to gain access to the wide area transmission facility. Due to these features which are essentially unavailable from the use of bridges the router is a more complex and costlier device.

## 7.2 COMMUNICATION, TRANSPORT, AND ROUTING PROTOCOLS

For routers to be able to operate in a network they must normally be able to speak the same language at both the data link and network layers. The key to accomplishing this is the ability of routers to support common communication, transport, and routing protocols.

### Communication protocol

Communication protocols support the transfer of data from a station on one network to a station on another network and occur at the OSI network layer. In examining Figure 7.3 which illustrates several common protocol implementations with respect to the OSI Reference Model, you will note that Novell's NetWare uses IPX as their network communications protocol, while IBM LANs use the PC LAN Support Program and Microsoft's LAN Manager uses the Internet Protocol (IP). This means that a router linking networks based upon Novell, IBM, and Microsoft LAN operating systems must support those three communication protocols. Thus, router communication protocol support is a most important criteria in determining if a particular product is capable of supporting your internetworking requirements.

### Routing protocol

The routing protocol references the method used by routers to exchange routing information and forms the basis for providing a connection across an internet. In evaluating routers, it is important to determine the efficiency of the routing protocol, its effect upon the transmission of information, the method used and memory required to construct routing tables, and

OSI Layer                     Common Protocol Implementation

| Application | Application Programs | | |
| | Application Protocols | | |
| Presentation | Novell<br>Network File<br>Server Protocol<br>(NFSP) | IBM<br>Server Message<br>Block<br>(SMB) | Microsoft<br>LAN Manager |
| Session | Xerox Networking<br>System<br>(XNS) | N<br>e<br>t<br>B<br>I<br>O<br>S | NetBIOS | NetBIOS<br>Advanced Peer-to-<br>Peer Communications |
| Transport | Sequenced<br>Packet Exchange<br>(SPX) | | PC LAN<br>Support<br>Program | Transmission<br>Control Protocol (TCP)<br>Transport Protocol<br>Class 4 (TCP4) |
| Network | Internetwork<br>Packet Exchange<br>(IPX) | | | Internet<br>Protocol<br>(IP) |
| Data Link | Logical Link Control 802.2 | | |
| | Media Access Control | | |
| Physical | Transmission Media:<br>Twisted pair, coax, fiber optic | | |

**Figure 7.3** Common protocol implementations. Although Novell, IBM, and Microsoft LAN operating system software support standardized physical and data link operations, they differ considerably in their use of communication and routing protocols.

the time required to dynamically adjust those tables. Examples of router-to-router protocols include Xerox Network Systems' (XNS) Routing Information Protocol (RIP) and the Transmission Control Protocol/Internet Protocol's (TCP/IP) RIP, Open Shortest Path First (OSPF), and Hello routing protocols.

## Transport protocol

The transport protocol represents the format by which information is physically transported between two points. Here, the transport protocol represents the data link layer illustrated in Figure 7.3. Examples of transport protocols include Token-Ring and Ethernet MAC for LANs as well as such WAN protocols as X.25 and Frame Relay.

There are a wide variety of communication and transport protocols in use today. Some of these protocols were designed specifically to operate on local area networks, such as Apple Computer's AppleTalk. Other protocols, such as X.25 and Frame Relay, were developed as wide area network protocols.

**Table 7.1**  Popular communications protocols.

| | |
|---|---|
| AppleTalk | ISO CLNS |
| Applo Domain VINES | HDLC |
| Banyan | NOVELL IPX |
| CHAOSnet | SDLC |
| DECnet Phase IV | TCP/IP |
| DECnet Phase V | Xerox XNS |
| DDN X.25 | X.25 |
| Frame Relay | Ungermann-Bass Net/One |

Table 7.1 lists 16 popular communication and transport protocols. Readers are cautioned that many routers support only a subset of the protocols listed in Table 7.1.

## 7.3 ROUTER CLASSIFICATIONS

Depending upon their support of communication and transport protocols, routers can be classified into two classes—protocol dependent and protocol independent.

### Protocol dependent routers

To understand the characteristics of a protocol dependent router consider the internet previously illustrated in Figure 7.2. If a station on network E1 wishes to transmit data to a second station on network E3 router R1 must know that the second station resides on network E3 and the best path to use to reach that network. The method used to determine the network where the destination station resides determines the protocol dependency of the router.

If the station on network E1 tells router R1 the destination location it must supply a network address in every LAN packet it transmits. This means that all routers in the internet must support the protocol used on network E1. Otherwise, stations on network E1 could not communicate with stations residing on other networks and vice versa.

*NetWare IPX example*

To illustrate the operation of a protocol dependent router let us assume networks E1 and E3 use Novell's NetWare as their

LAN operating system. The routing protocol used at the network layer between a station and server on a Novell network is known as IPX. This protocol can also be used between servers as well as other protocols.

Under NetWare's IPX a packet addressed to a router will contain the destination address in the form of network and host addresses as well as the origination address in the form of the source network and source host addresses. Here the IPX term 'host' is actually the physical address of a network adapter card.

Figure 7.4a illustrates in simplified format the IPX packet composition for workstation A on network E1 transmitting data to workstation B on network E3 under Novell's NetWare IPX protocol. After router R1 receives and examines the packet it notes that the destination address E3 requires the routing of the packet to router R2. Thus, it converts the first packet into a router (R1) to router (R2) packet as illustrated in Figure 7.4b. At router R2 the packet is again examined. Router R2 notes that the destination network address (E3) is connected to that router. Thus, router R2 reconverts the packet for delivery onto network E3 by converting the destination router address to a source router address and transmitting the packet onto network E3. This is illustrated in Figure 7.4c.

### Addressing differences

In the preceding example note that each router uses the destination workstation and network addresses to transfer packets. If all protocols used the same format and addressing structure routers would be protocol insensitive at the network layer. Unfortunately this is not true. For example, under TCP/IP, addressing conventions are very different from that used by NetWare. This means that networks using different operating systems require the use of multiprotocol routers that are configured to perform address translation. To accomplish this, each multiprotocol router must maintain separate routing tables for each supported protocol, requiring additional memory and time to perform this task.

### Other problems

Two additional problems associated with protocol dependent routers are the time required for packet examination and the

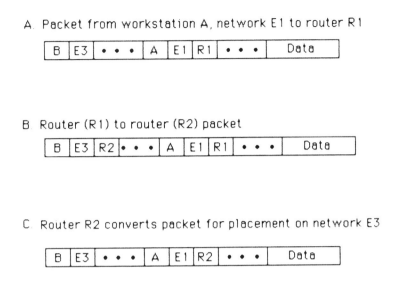

A. Packet from workstation A, network E1 to router R1

| B | E3 | • • • | A | E1 | R1 | • • • | Data |

B. Router (R1) to router (R2) packet

| B | E3 | R2 | • • • | A | E1 | R1 | • • • | Data |

C. Router R2 converts packet for placement on network E3

| B | E3 | • • • | A | E1 | R2 | • • • | Data |

**Figure 7.4** NetWare IPX routing.

fact that not all LAN protocols are routable. Concerning packet examination, if a packet must traverse a large network the time required by a series of routers to both modify the packet and assure its delivery to the next router can significantly degrade router performance. To overcome this problem, organizations should consider the use of a frame relay service.

In addition to providing an enhanced data delivery service by eliminating error detection and correction occurring within the network, the use of a frame relay service can significantly reduce the cost of routers. To illustrate this consider the network previously illustrated in Figure 7.2 in which four routers are interconnected through the use of five links. To support transmission on five links the routers require 10 ports. Normally, each router port is obtained as an adapter card installed in a high-performance computer. If a frame relay service is used the packet network providing that service also provides the routing paths to interconnect routers as illustrated in Figure 7.5. This reduces the number of required router ports to four, which can result in a considerable hardware savings.

A second problem associated with protocol dependent routers is the fact that some LAN protocols cannot be routed using that type of device. This is because some LAN protocols, such as NetBIOS and IBM's LAN Server, unlike NetWare, DECnet and TCP/IP, do not include routing information within a packet. Instead, those protocols employ a user-friendly device-naming

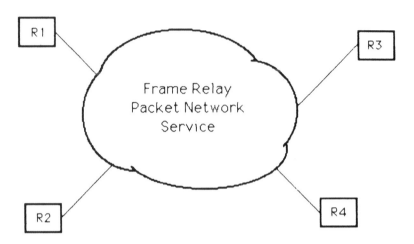

**Figure 7.5** Using a frame relay service. If a frame relay service is used, the packet network provides the capability for interconnecting each network access port to other network access ports. Thus, only one router port is required to obtain an interconnection capability to numerous routers connected to the network.

convention instead of using network and device addresses, permitting such names as 'Gil's PC', 'Accounting Printer', and other descriptors to be used. For example, IBM's Network Basic Input/Output System (NetBIOS) was designed to facilitate program-to-program communication by hiding the complexities of network addressing from the user. Thus, NetBIOS uses names that can be up to 16 alphanumeric characters in length to define clients and servers on a network. Unfortunately, NetBIOS does not include a facility to distinguish one network from another since it lacks a network addressing capability. Such protocols are restricted to using the physical addresses of adapter cards, such as Token-Ring source and destination addresses. Since a protocol dependent router must know the network on which a destination address is located it cannot route such protocols. Thus, a logical question is how does a router interconnect networks using an IBM LAN protocol? The answer to this question is bridging. That is, a protocol dependent router must operate as a bridge in the previously described situation.

## Protocol independent routers

A protocol independent router can be considered to function as a sophisticated transparent bridge. That is, it addresses the problem of network protocols that do not have network addresses, by examining the source addresses on connected networks to automatically learn what devices are on each network. The protocol independent router assigns network identifiers to each network whose operating system does not include network addresses in its network protocol. This activity enables both routable and non-routable protocols to be serviced by a protocol dependent router.

In addition to automatically building address tables like a transparent bridge a protocol independent router exchanges information concerning its routing directions with other internet routers. This enables each router to build a map of the internet. The method used to build the network map falls under the category of a link state routing protocol which is described later in this chapter.

*Advantages*

There are two key advantages associated with the use of protocol independent routers. Those advantages are the ability of routers to automatically learn network topology and to service non-routable protocols. The ability to automatically learn network topology can considerably simplify the administration of an internet. For example, in a TCP/IP network each workstation has an IP address and must know the IP addresses of other LAN devices it desires to communicate with.

IP addresses are assigned by a network administrator and must be changed if a station is moved to a different network or a network is segmented due to a high level of traffic or another reason. In such situations all LAN users must be notified about the new IP address or they will not be able to locate the moved station. Obviously, the movement of stations within a building between different LANs could become a considerable administrative burden. In comparison, the ability of a protocol independent router to automatically learn addresses removes the administrative burden of notifying users of changes in network addresses.

The ability to route non-routable protocols can be of considerable assistance in integrating IBM System Network Architecture (SNA) networks into an enterprise network. Otherwise, without the use of protocol independent routers organizations may have to maintain separate transmission facilities for SNA and LAN traffic.

*Supporting SNA traffic*

Figure 7.6 illustrates the use of protocol independent routers to support both inter-LAN and SNA traffic. In this example an IBM SNA network in which a 3174 control unit with a token-ring adapter (TRA) at a remote site provides communications connectivity to an IBM 3745 communications controller at a central site. Thus, routers must be capable of routing both SNA and LAN traffic to enable the use of a common transmission facility between the central and remote site.

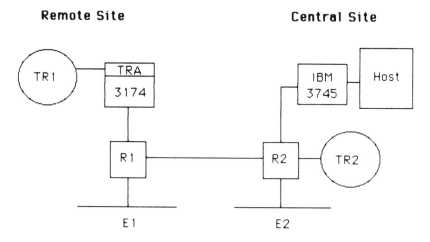

**Figure 7.6** Supporting SNA traffic. A protocol independent router can support SNA traffic as well as other LAN traffic over a common transmission facility.

**Methods to Consider**

There are essentially two methods by which SNA and LAN traffic can be combined for routing over a common network—encapsulation or through protocol independent routing. Under the encapsulation method, SNA packets are modified so that another protocol's header, addressing and trailer fields surround each SNA packet. For example, a TCP/IP protocol dependent router would encapsulate SNA into TCP/IP packets for routing through a TCP/IP network. Since a TCP/IP packet has over 60 bytes of overhead while the average SNA packet is 30 bytes in length, encapsulation can considerably reduce performance when transmission occurs over low-speed links. A second disadvantage of encapsulation is that it requires the existence of a corporate network using the encapsulation protocol. Otherwise, you would have to build this network to obtain an encapsulation capability.

The second method by which an SNA network can be integrated with LAN traffic is through protocol independent routing. Protocol independent routers would assign a LAN device address to each SNA control unit and communications controller. Then, SNA packets would be prefixed with source and destination addresses to permit their routing through the internet. At the destination router the addressing information is removed and the SNA packets are delivered to their destination in their original form. Since the addition of source and destination addresses adds a significantly smaller number of bytes than an encapsulation process, overhead is reduced in comparison to encapsulation. This in turn enables you to consider the use of lower speed circuits to interconnect locations.

Another advantage associated with the use of protocol independent routing over encapsulation relates directly to the operation of SNA networks. Although such networks are discussed in detail in Chapter 8, several SNA operational characteristics now warrant attention to appreciate the advantages of protocol independent routing and the rationale for such routers requiring a traffic-priority mechanism to efficiently support SNA traffic.

**Need for Priority Mechanism**

In its current incarnation, SNA is a hierarchical structured network as illustrated in Figure 7.7. Here, the communications controller communicates with control units which in turn communicate with attached terminal devices. The communications controller periodically polls each control unit and the control unit periodically polls each terminal device. If there is no data to transmit in response to a poll, each polled device indicates this fact to the higher-level device by negatively responding to the poll. Thus, the communications controller expects to receive a response to each poll it generates. In fact, if it does not receive a response within a predefined period of time (typically less than five seconds), the communications controller will assume that the control unit has malfunctioned, terminate any

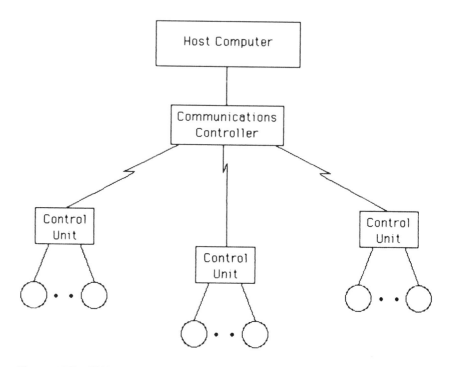

**Figure 7.7** SNA network hierarchy. In an SNA network, communications controllers poll control units which in turn poll attached devices.

active sessions to devices attached to the control unit, and then attempt to re-establish communications by sending an initialization message to the control unit.

When integrating SNA and LAN traffic onto a common router-based network, the operation of routers has the potential for adversely affecting SNA traffic due to the time delays associated with routing and encapsulation. For example, routers may dynamically alter the path used to transmit data based upon internet traffic and circuit availability. If path switching results in SNA traffic exceeding its timeout threshold, the communications controller will terminate sessions and reinitialize control units that fail to respond to its poll within the predefined time period. Similarly, delays caused by encapsulation can also result in non-intended timeouts occurring.

To prevent non-intended timeouts from occurring due to path switching, some vendors have added a traffic-priority mechanism to their protocol independent routing capability. This priority mechanism enables users to assign a higher priority to SNA traffic than to LAN traffic, which enables SNA data to be forwarded across wide area networks ahead of other inter-LAN traffic. Doing so will either considerably reduce or eliminate the potential for LAN traffic to obstruct the flow of SNA data and result in non-intended timeouts inadvertently causing session terminations.

## 7.4 ROUTING PROTOCOLS

The routing protocol is the key element which enables the transfer of information across an internet in an orderly manner. The protocol is responsible for developing paths between routers which is accomplished by a predefined mechanism by which routers exchange routing information.

## Types of routing protocols

There are two types of routing protocols—interior and exterior domain. Here, we use the term 'domain' to reference the connection of a group of networks to form a common entity, such as a corporate or university enterprise network.

An interior domain routing protocol is used to control the flow of information within a series of separate networks interconnected to form an internet. Thus, interior domain routing protocols provide a mechanism for the flow of information within a domain and are known as intra-domain routing protocols. Such protocols create routing tables for each autonomous system within the domain and use such metrics as the hop count or time delay to develop routes from one network to another within the domain. Examples of interior domain routing protocols include RIP, OSPF, and Hello.

### *Exterior domain routing protocols*

Exterior domain routing protocols are used to connect separate domains together. Thus, they are also referred to as inter-domain routing protocols. Currently, inter-domain routing protocols are only defined for OSI and TCP/IP. Example of inter-domain routing protocols include the Exterior Gateway Protocol (EGP), the Border Gateway Protocol (BGP), and the Inter-Domain Routing Protocol (IDRP). In comparison to interior domain routing protocols which are focused upon the construction of routing tables for data flow within a domain, inter-domain routing protocols specify the method by which routers exchange information concerning what networks they can reach on each domain.

Figure 7.8 illustrates the use of interior and exterior domain routing protocols. In this example, OSPF is the intra-domain protocol used in Domain A, while RIF is the intra-domain protocol used in Domain B. Routers in Domains A and B use the inter-domain routing protocols EGP and/or BGP to determine the networks on other domains they can reach.

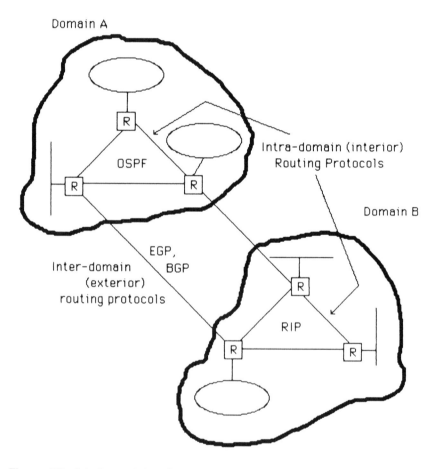

**Figure 7.8** Interior and exterior routing protocols. An interior routing protocol controls the flow of information within a collection of interconnected networks known as a domain. An exterior routing protocol provides routers with the ability to determine what networks on other domains they can reach.

**Exterior Gateway Protocol**

There are four basic functions performed by the Exterior Gateway Protocol. First, the EGP performs an acquisition function which enables a router in one domain to request a router on another domain to exchange information. Since each router serves as a gateway to the domain, they are also referred to as gateways. A second function performed by the router gateway is to periodically test whether or not its EGP neighbors are responding. The third and most important function performed by the EGP is to enable router gateways to exchange information concerning the networks in each domain by transmitting routing update messages. The fourth function involves terminating an established neighbor relationship between gateways on two domains.

To accomplish its basic functions, EGP defines nine message types. Figure 7.9 illustrates EGP message types associated with each of the three basic features performed by the protocol.

Under the EGP, once a neighbor is acquired, Hello messages must be transmitted at a minimum of 30-s intervals. In addition, routing updates must be exchanged at a minimum of two-minute intervals. This exchange of information at two-minute intervals can result in the use of a considerable amount of the bandwidth linking domains when the number of networks on each domain is large or the circuits linking domains consist of low-speed lines. To alleviate those potential problems, the Border Gateway Protocol was developed.

**Border Gateway Protocol**

The Border Gateway Protocol represents a follow-on to the EGP. Unlike the EGP in which all network information is exchanged at two-minute or less intervals, the BGP results in incremental updates being transmitted as changes occur. This can significantly reduce the quantity of data exchanged between router gateways and frees up a considerable amount of circuit bandwidth for the transmission of data. Both the EGP and the BGP run over TCP/IP and are standardized by Internet documents RFC904 and RFC1105, respectively.

*Interior domain routing protocols*

As previously discussed, interior domain routing protocols govern the flow of information between networks. Thus, this

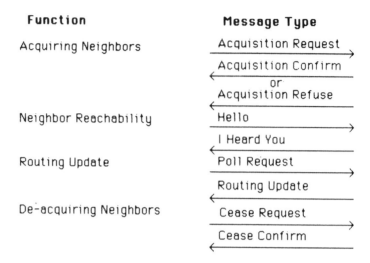

| Function | Message Type |
|---|---|
| Acquiring Neighbors | Acquisition Request → |
| | Acquisition Confirm ← |
| | or |
| | Acquisition Refuse ← |
| Neighbor Reachability | Hello → |
| | I Heard You ← |
| Routing Update | Poll Request → |
| | Routing Update ← |
| De-acquiring Neighbors | Cease Request → |
| | Cease Confirm ← |

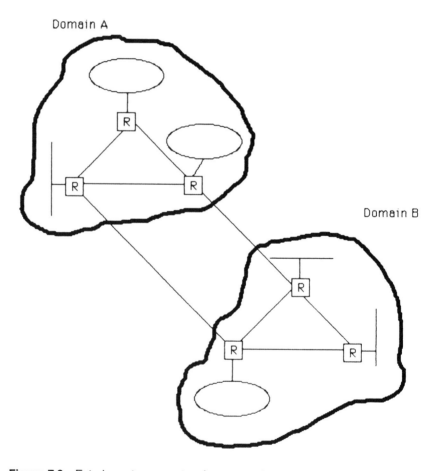

**Figure 7.9**  Exterior gateway protocol message types.

represents the type of routing protocol that is of primary interest to most organizations. Interior domain routing protocols can be further subdivided into two broad categories based upon the method they use for building and updating the contents of their routing tables—vector distance and link state.

**Vector Distance Protocol**

A vector distance protocol constructs a routing table in each router and periodically broadcasts the contents of the routing table across the internet. When the routing table is received at another router, that device examines the set of reported network destinations and the distance to each destination. The receiving router then determines whether it knows a shorter route to a network destination, or finds a destination it does not have in its routing table, or finds a route to a destination through the sending router where the distance to the destination changed. If any one of these situations occurs the receiving router will change its routing tables.

The term 'vector distance' relates to the information transmitted by routers. Each router message contains a list of pairs known as vector and distance. The vector identifies a network destination, while the distance is the distance in hops from the router to that destination.

Figure 7.10 illustrates the initial vector distance routing table for routers R1 and R2 previously illustrated in Figure 7.2. Each table contains an entry for each directly connected network and is broadcast periodically throughout the internet. Here the distance column indicates the distance to each network from the router in hops.

a. Router R1

| Destination | Distance |
|:-----------:|:--------:|
| E1 | 0 |
| E2 | 0 |

b. Router R2

| Destination | Distance |
|:-----------:|:--------:|
| E3 | 0 |
| TR1 | 0 |

**Figure 7.10** Initial vector-routing distance tables.

At the same time that router R1 is constructing its initial vector distance table other routers are performing a similar operation. The lower portion of Figure 7.10 illustrates the composition of the initial vector distance table for router R2.

As previously mentioned, under a vector distance protocol the contents of each router's routing table are periodically broadcast. Assuming routers R1 and R2 broadcast their initial vector distance routing tables, each router uses the received routing table to update its initial routing table. Figure 7.11 illustrates the result of this initial routing table update process for routers R1 and R2.

a. Router R1

| Destination | Distance | Route |
|:-----------:|:--------:|:------:|
| E1 | 0 | direct |
| E2 | 0 | direct |
| E3 | 1 | R2 |
| TR1 | 1 | R2 |

b. Router R2

| Destination | Distance | Route |
|:-----------:|:--------:|:------:|
| E1 | 1 | R1 |
| E2 | 1 | R1 |
| E3 | 0 | direct |
| TR1 | 0 | direct |

**Figure 7.11**   Initial routing table update.

As additional routing tables are exchanged the routing table in each router will converge with respect to the internet topology. However, to ensure each router knows the state of all links, routing tables are periodically broadcast by each router. Although this process has a minimal effect upon small networks, its use with large networks can significantly reduce available bandwidth for actual data transfer. This is because the transmission of lengthy router tables will require additional transmission time in which data cannot flow between routers.

Popular vector distance routing protocols include the TCP/IP Routing Information Protocol (RIP), the AppleTalk Routing Table Management Protocol (RTMP), and Cisco's Interior Gateway Routing Protocol (IGRP).

*Routing Information Protocol*

Under RIP, participants are either active or passive. Active participants are normally routers which transmit their routing tables, while passive machines listen and update their routing tables based upon information supplied by other devices. Normally host computers operate as passive participants, while routers operate as active participants.

Under RIP, an active router broadcasts its routing table every 30 seconds. Each routing table entry contains a network address and the hop count to the network. However, unlike the previous vector distance example in which a directly connected network has a hop count distance of 0, RIP uses a hop count of 1. Similarly, RIP uses a hop count of 2 for networks that are reachable through one router.

One key limitation of RIP is the maximum hop distance it supports. This distance is 16 hops, which means an alternative protocol must be used for large networks.

*Routing Table Maintenance Protocol*

The Routing Table Maintenance Protocol (RTMP) was developed by Apple Computer for use with that vendor's AppleTalk network. Under RTMP, each router transmits messages to establish and periodically update routing tables. The update process in which information on an internet is exchanged between routers also serves as a mechanism for implementing alternate routing. This is because the absence of update information for a greater than expected period of time converts the status of an entry in other router routing tables from 'good' to 'suspect' and then to 'bad'.

RTMP is delivered by AppleTalk's Data Delivery Protocol (DDP), which is a network layer connectionless service operating between two upper layer processes referred to as sockets. Four types of packets are specified by RTMP—data, request, route data request, and response. Routing updates are transmitted as data packets. Request packets are transmitted by end nodes to acquire information concerning the identity of internet routers (IRs) to which they can transmit non-local packets. IRs respond to route request packets with response packets, while end nodes that want to receive an RTMP data packet indicate this by sending a route data request packet. The latter packet type is also used by nodes which require routing information from IRs that are not directly connected to their network.

*Routing process*    In the AppleTalk routing process, the source node first examines the destination network number. If the packet has a local network address it is passed to the data link layer for delivery. Otherwise, the packet is passed to any of the IRs that may reside on a network segment. The IR will examine the destination address of the packet and then check its routing tables to determine the next hop, routing the packet on a specific port which enables it to flow towards the next hop. Thus, a packet will travel through the internet on a hop-by-hop basis. When the packet reaches an IR connected to the destination network, the data link layer is used to deliver the packet to its local destination.

Figure 7.12 illustrates a sample AppleTalk network and the routing table for one router. Each AppleTalk routing table has five entries as indicated. The network range defines the range of network numbers assigned to a particular network segment. The 'distance' entry specifies the number of routers that must be traversed prior to the destination being reached, while 'port' defines the router port used to provide access to a destination location. The 'next IR' entry indicates the identifier of the next IR on the internet, while 'entry state' defines the status of receiving routing updates. Here an entry state can go from 'good' to 'suspect' to 'bad' if routing updates have not been received within predefined time intervals.

### Interior Gateway Routing Protocol

Cisco's proprietary Interior Gateway Routing Protocol is a vector distance protocol in which updates are transmitted at 90-second intervals. Each IGRP gateway operates on a local basis to determine the best route for forwarding data packets. Unlike some protocols which require each router to have a complete routing table, each IGRP router computes only a portion of the routing table based upon its perspective of the internet. This enables the IGRP to support distributed routing without requiring each router to have a complete view of the internet.

Other features of the IGRP include the ability to automatically establish routes, dynamically perform load balancing over redundant links, and detect and remove bad circuits from the internet routing tables it develops. Routes are declared inaccessible if an update is not received within three update periods (270 s). After five update periods (450 s), the route is removed from the routing table.

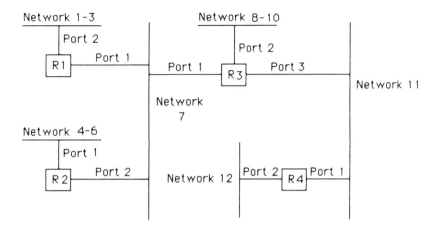

Routing table for router R1

| Network Range | Distance | Port | Next IR | Entry State |
|---|---|---|---|---|
| 1-3 | 0 | 2 | 0 | Good |
| 7-7 | 0 | 1 | 0 | Good |
| 4-6 | 1 | 1 | R2 | Good |
| 8-10 | 1 | 1 | R3 | Good |
| 11-11 | 1 | 1 | R3 | Good |
| 12-12 | 2 | 1 | R3 | Good |

**Figure 7.12** AppleTalk routing table example.

## Link State Protocols

A link state routing protocol addresses the traffic problem associated with large networks that use a vector distance routing protocol. It does this by transmitting routing information only when there is a change in one of its links. A second difference between vector distance and link state protocols concerns the manner in which a route is selected when multiple routes are available between destinations. For a vector distance protocol the best path is the one that has the fewest number of intermediate routers on hops between destinations. In comparison, a link state protocol can use multiple paths to provide traffic balancing between locations. In addition, a link state protocol permits routing to occur based upon link delay, capacity and reliability. This provides the network manager with the ability to specify a variety of route development situations.

*SPF algorithms*

Link state routing protocols are implemented through the use of a class of algorithms known as Shortest Path First (SPF). Unfortunately, the name associated with this class of algorithms is a misnomer as routing is not based upon the shortest path.

The use of SPF algorithms requires each participating router to have complete knowledge of the internet topology. Each router participating in an SPF algorithm then performs two tasks—status testing of neighboring routers and periodically transmitting link status information to other routers.

To test neighboring routers a short message is periodically transmitted. If the neighbor replies the link is considered to be up. Otherwise, the absence of a reply after a predefined period of time indicates that the link is down.

To provide link status information, each router will periodically broadcast a message which indicates the status of each of its links. Unlike the vector distance protocol in which routes are specified, an SPF link status message simply indicates whether or not communications are possible between pairs of routers. Using information in the link status message routers are able to update their network map.

In comparison to vector distance protocols in which tables are required to be exchanged, link state protocols such as SPF algorithms exchange a much lower volume of information in the form of link status queries and replies. Then, SPF participating routers simply broadcast a status of each of its links that other routers use to update their internet map. This routing technique permits each router to compute routes independently of other routers and eliminates the potential for table flooding that can occur when a vector state protocol is used to interconnect a large number of networks.

*Operation example*

To illustrate the operation of a link state routing protocol let us return to the internet configuration previously illustrated in Figure 7.2. Figure 7.13 indicates the initial network map for router R1. This map lists the destination of all networks on the internet from router R1, their distance and route. Note that, if multiple routes exist to a destination each route is listed, as doing so defines a complete network topology as well as allowing alternate routes to be selected if link status information indicates that one or more routes cannot be used.

| Destination | Distance | Route | Status |
|-------------|----------|----------|--------|
| E1 | 0 | Direct | Up |
| E2 | 0 | Direct | Up |
| E3 | 1 | R2 | Up |
| E3 | 2 | R3,R2 | Up |
| E3 | 3 | R3,R4,R2 | Up |
| E4 | 2 | R2,R4 | Up |
| E4 | 2 | R3,R4 | Up |
| E4 | 3 | R3,R2,R4 | Up |
| TR1 | 1 | R2 | Up |
| TR1 | 2 | R3,R2 | Up |
| TR1 | 3 | R3,R4,R2 | Up |
| TR2 | 1 | R3 | Up |
| TR2 | 2 | R2,R3 | Up |
| TR2 | 2 | R2,R4 | Up |
| TR3 | 2 | R3,R4 | Up |
| TR3 | 2 | R2,R4 | Up |
| TR3 | 3 | R3,R2,R4 | Up |

**Figure 7.13**   Router R1 initial network map.

Let us assume that at a particular point in time the link status messages generated by the routers in the internet are as indicated in Figure 7.14. Note that both routers R2 and R3 determined that link L3 is down. Using this information router R1 would then update the status column for its network map. Since link L3 is down, all routes that require a data flow between R2 and R3 would have their status changed to down. For example, destination E3 via route R3, R2 would have its status changed to down. Since the minimum distance to E3 is 1 hop via router R2, the failure of link L3 would not affect data flow from router R1 to network E3. Now consider the effect of link L2 becoming inoperative. That would affect route R2 which has the minimum distance to network E3. This would still leave route R3–R4–R2, although this route would have a distance of three hops. Of course, when a new link status message indicates that a previously declared down link is up, each router's network map would be updated accordingly.

Examples of link state protocols include Open Shortest Path First (OSPF), OSI Intermediate System to Intermediate System (IS-IS), DecNet Phase V, and IBM's Advanced Peer-to-Peer Networking (APPN). Due to space limitations, we will briefly

R1 link status

| Link | Status |
|------|--------|
| L1 | Up |
| L2 | Up |

R2 link status

| Link | Status |
|------|--------|
| L2 | Up |
| L3 | Down |
| L4 | Up |

R3 link status

| Link | Status |
|------|--------|
| L1 | Up |
| L3 | Down |

R4 link status

| Link | Status |
|------|--------|
| L4 | Up |
| L5 | Up |

**Figure 7.14** Link status messages.

review the operational features of only the first of these link state protocols.

*Open Shortest Path First protocol*

The OSPF protocol is an interior domain routing protocol which uses the SPF algorithm. Similar to the EGP, the OSPF protocol consists of a small core of different types of messages. Under the OSPF protocol, five message types are defined.

A Hello message is used to test the reachability of other devices. A database description message passes the topology. The remaining message types include a link status request, link status update, and a link status acknowledgement message.

Initially, OSPF generates database description messages to initialize their network topology database. These messages are flooded through the domain; however, once a topological database is formed routing table updates are then transmitted at 30-minute intervals unless there is a change in the network—a condition which results in an immediate update.

OSPF routers use a Hello message to discover their neighbors in a manner similar to how the Hello message is used by the EGP. One of the key features of the OSPF protocol is its ability to authenticate messages. This precludes the possibility of a person generating low-cost routes in an attempt to entice routers to transmit packets to a specific computer for examination or interception. Another key feature of the OSPF protocol is its ability to support multiple active paths of equal weight. When this situation occurs due to the topology of the internet, OSPF selects each path in a round robin manner. Table 7.2 provides a summary of 16 common routing protocol mnemonics, what the mnemonics represent, and a short description of the protocol.

## 7.5 PERFORMANCE CONSIDERATIONS

Regardless of the type of router, its protocol support and routing algorithm used, the processing required for its operation is considerably above that required for a bridge. This means that you can expect the packet processing capability of routers to be considerably less than the processing rate of bridges.

High-capacity bridges marketed during 1992 could be expected to provide a forwarding rate between 10 000 and 20 000 packets per second. In comparison, most routers have a forwarding capacity rated under 5000 packets per second. Although this may appear to indicate a poor level of performance in comparison to bridges, readers should note that only when functioning as a local bridge will a high-capacity bridge actually use its full capacity. Otherwise, when used to interconnect remote networks via a wide area transmission facility a remote bridge will only be able to use a fraction of its packet processing capability for the forwarding of packets over a relatively slow-speed WAN transmission facility. In comparison, when routers are connected to a T1 or E1 line or to a Frame Relay service they may be able to use their full packet forwarding capability. To illustrate this, readers are referred to Table 7.3 which indicates the maximum packets-per-second transfer capability of a router connected to five types of transmission lines based upon five packet sizes. Note that a T1 line operating at 1.544 Mbps supports a maximum transfer of 3015 64-byte packets per second. In actuality, since the wide area network transmission

**Table 7.2** Common routing protocols.

| | |
|---|---|
| AURP | AppleTalk Update Routing Protocol. This routing protocol is implemented in Apple networks and sends changes to routing tables via updates. |
| BGP | Border Gateway Protocol. This is a TCP/IP interdomain routing protocol. |
| CNLP | Connectionless Network Protocol. This is the OSI version of the IP routing protocol. |
| DDP | Datagram Delivery Protocol. This routing protocol is used in Apple's AppleTalk network. |
| EGP | Exterior Gateway Protocol. This TCP/IP protocol is used to locate networks on another domain. |
| IDRP | Inter-Domain Routing Protocol. This is the OSI interdomain routing protocol. |
| IGP | Interior Gateway Protocol. This TCP/IP protocol is used by routers to move information within a domain. |
| IGRP | Interior Gateway Routing Protocol. This is a proprietary routing protocol developed by Cisco Systems. |
| IP | Internet Protocol. The network layer protocol of the TCP/IP (Transmission Control Protocol/Internet Protocol) suite of protocols. |
| IPX | Internet Packet Exchange. This routing protocol is based on Xerox's XNS, was developed by Novell, and is implemented in Novell's NetWare. |
| IS-IS | Intermediate System to Intermediate System. This is an OSI link-state routing protocol which routes both OSI and RIP traffic. |
| NCP | NetWare Core Protocol. This is Novell's NetWare specific routing protocol. |
| OSPF | Open Shortest Path First. This is a TCP/IP link state routing protocol which can be viewed as an alternative to RIP. |
| RIP | Routing Information Protocol. This routing protocol is used in TCP/IP, XNS, and IPX. Under RIP a message is broadcast to find the shortest route to a destination based on a hop count. |
| RTMP | Routing Table Maintenance Protocol. This is Apple's distance vector protocol. |
| SPF | Shortest Path First. This link state routing protocol uses a set of user-defined parameters to find the best route between two points. |

facility results in the use of a WAN protocol to wrap LAN packets, the actual PPS rate obtainable is normally 15–20% less than that indicated in Table 7.3. Thus, the forward rate of most routers greatly exceeds the capacity of a single WAN connection. This means that only a requirement for the use of multiple router ports should make the forwarding rate of the router into a key equipment acquisition issue. Otherwise, the

**Table 7.3**  Maximum packet transfer rates (packets per second).

| Packet Size (bytes) | Wide area network transmission facility | | | | |
| --- | --- | --- | --- | --- | --- |
| | 56 kbps | 128 kbps | 256 kbps | 512 kbps | 1.544 Mbps |
| 64 | 109 | 250 | 500 | 1000 | 3015 |
| 128 | 54 | 125 | 250 | 500 | 1508 |
| 500 | 14 | 32 | 64 | 128 | 386 |
| 1000 | 7 | 16 | 32 | 64 | 193 |
| 1518 | 5 | 10 | 20 | 40 | 127 |

communication, transport, and routing protocols supported are usually more important criteria for determining if a vendor's product can support the requirements of an organization.

# 8

# GATEWAY METHODS

In Chapter 3 we discussed the basic operation of gateways and how they enable networks with different protocols to communicate. In that chapter we discussed how a gateway operates through the highest layer of the OSI Reference Model, the application layer, and how gateways essentially perform protocol conversion. In that chapter we briefly described several methods by which a Token-Ring could be connected to an IBM mainframe computer system. Although those methods involved different types of gateways our primary focus of attention until now was to simply discuss concepts and the use of different types of hardware without considering the relationship of network architecture to gateway operations.

Since the protocol conversion performed by a gateway is directly related to such architectures as IBM's SNA and Digital Equipment's DECnet, we must obtain a basic understanding of the architecture developed to support access to conventional mainframe computers. This will enable us to obtain an appreciation for the different access methods supported by gateways as well as their functions and applications which is the focus of this chapter. To accomplish this we will first discuss SNA and IBM's 3270 Information Display System to obtain an understanding of the basic functions of hardware and software used to provide a wide area networking capability that provides local and remote terminal users with access to IBM mainframe computers in an SNA environment. Using this information as a base will then provide the foundation for discussing gateways from the perspective of their use to exchange information between local area networks and mainframes connected to the dominant computer company network architecture which, with plug compatible computers, represents approximately 70% of all large computer installations.

## 8.1 NETWORK ARCHITECTURE

To satisfy the requirements of customers for remote computing capability, mainframe computer manufacturers developed a variety of network architectures. Such architectures defined the interrelationship of a particular vendor's hardware and software products necessary to permit communications to flow through a network to the manufacturer's mainframe computer.

IBM's System Network Architecture (SNA) is a very complex and sophisticated network architecture which defines the rules, procedures and structure of communications from the input/output statements of an application program to the screen display on a user's personal computer or terminal. SNA consists of protocols, formats and operational sequences which govern the flow of information within a data-communications network linking IBM mainframe computers, minicomputers, terminal controllers, communications controllers, personal computers and terminals.

Since approximately 70% of the mainframe computer market belongs to IBM and plug-compatible systems manufactured by Amdehl and other vendors, SNA can be expected to remain as a connectivity platform for the foreseeable future. This means that a large majority of the connections of local area networks to mainframe computers will require the use of gateways that support SNA operations.

### SNA concepts

An SNA network consists of one or more domains, where a domain refers to all of the logical and physical components that are connected to and controlled by one common point in the network. This common point of control is called the system services control point, which is commonly known by its abbreviation as the SSCP. The SSCP can be considered the highest location in an SNA network whose structure is based upon a rigidly defined hierarchy of devices. Within an SNA network there are three types of network-addressable units— SSCPs, physical units, and logical units.

*The SSCP*

The SSCP resides in the communications access method operating in an IBM mainframe computer, such as virtual telecommunications access method (VTAM), operating in a System/360, System/370, 4300 series or 308X, 309X or an Enterprise series computer, or in the system control program of an IBM minicomputer, such as a System/3X or AS/400. The SSCP contains the network's address tables, routing tables and translation tables which it uses to establish connections between nodes in the network as well as to control the flow of information in an SNA network.

Figure 8.1 illustrates single- and multiple-domain SNA networks. Each network domain includes one or more nodes, with an SNA network node consisting of a grouping of networking components which provides it with a unique characteristic. Examples of SNA nodes include cluster controllers which are also referred to as control units, communications controllers, and terminal devices, with the address of each device in the network providing its unique characteristic in comparison to a similar device contained in the network.

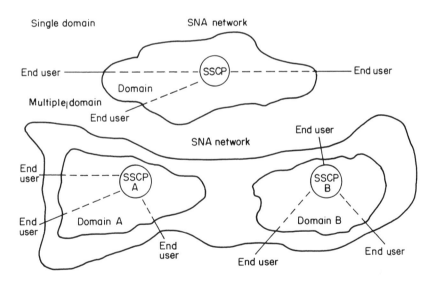

**Figure 8.1**   Single- and multiple-domain SNA networks.

*The PU*

Each node in an SNA network contains a physical unit (PU) which controls the other resources contained in the node. The

PU is not a physical device as its name appears to suggest, but rather a set of SNA components which provide services used to control terminals, controllers, processors and data links in the network. In programmable devices, such as mainframe computers and communications controllers, the PU is normally implemented in software. In less intelligent devices, such as older cluster controllers and display terminals, the PU is typically implemented in read-only memory. In an SNA network each PU operates under the control of an SSCP. The PU can be considered to function as an entry point between the network and one or more logical units.

*The LU*

The third type of network-addressable unit in an SNA network is the logical unit, known by its abbreviation as the LU. The LU is the interface or point of access between the end-user and an SNA network. Through the LU an end-user gains access to network resources and transmits and receives data over the network. Each PU can have one or more LUs, with each LU having a distinct address.

## SNA network structure

The structure of an SNA network can be considered to represent a hierarchy in which each device controls a specific part of the network and operates under the control of a device at the next higher level. The highest level in an SNA network is represented by a host or mainframe computer which executes a software module known as a communications access method. At the next lower level are one or more communications controllers—IBM's term for a front-end processor. Each communications controller executes a Network Control Program (NCP) which defines the operation of devices connected to the controllers, their PUs and LUs, operating rate, data code and other communications related functions such as the maximum packet size that can be transmitted. Connected to communications controllers are cluster controllers—IBM's term for a control unit. Thus, the third level in an SNA network can be considered to be represented by cluster controllers.

The cluster controllers support the attachment of terminals and printers which represent the lowest hierarchy of an

SNA network. Figure 8.2 illustrates the SNA hierarchy and the Network Addressable Units (NAUs) associated with each hardware component used to construct an SNA network. Readers should note that NAUs include lines connecting mainframes to communications controllers to cluster controllers and cluster controllers to terminals and printers. In addition, NAUs also define application programs that reside in the mainframe. Thus, NAUs provide the mechanism for terminals to access specific programs via a routing through hardware and transmission facilities that are explicitly identified.

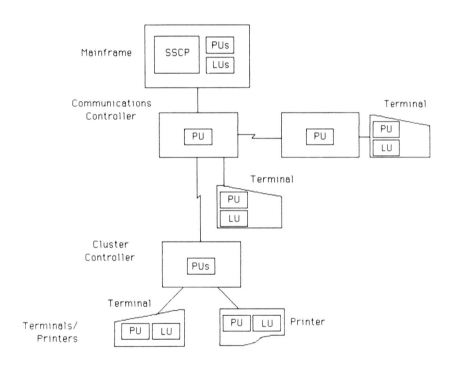

**Figure 8.2** SNA hierarchical network structure. The structure of an SNA network is built upon a hierarchy of equipment, with mainframes connected to communications controllers and communications controllers connected to cluster controllers.

An SNA network is a relatively static network in which the addition and removal of terminal devices requires specific entries in address tables. The creation and modification of macro instruction in the Network Control Program (NCP) that operates in the communications controller and VTAM which operates on the mainframe computer are required to change address table entries. Since NCP and VTAM program changes require a recompilation of each program, which temporarily places the network in never-never land when the resulting compiled programs are loaded, such program changes typically are accomplished on weekends or very early in the morning during weekdays. In addition, many organizations batch NCP and VTAM changes and only perform those changes once a week or perhaps once a month, further reducing the ability of SNA networks to be adjusted to dynamic working environments.

As an example of the communications capability of SNA, consider an end-user with an IBM PC and an SDLC communications adapter who establishes a connection to an IBM mainframe computer. The IBM PC is a PU, with its display and printer considered to be separate LUs. After communication is established, the PC user could direct a file to his or her printer by establishing an LU-to-LU session between the mainframe and printer while using the PC as an interactive terminal running an application program as a second LU-to-LU session.

### Types of PUs

In Table 8.1, the reader will find a list of the six types of physical units in an SNA network and their corresponding SNA node types. In addition, this table contains representative examples of hardware devices that can operate as a specific type of PU. As indicated in Table 8.1, the different types of PUs, with the exception of PU Type 2.1, form a hierarchy of hardware classifications. At the lowest level, PU Type 1 is a single terminal. PU Type 2 is a cluster controller which is used to connect many SNA devices into a common communications circuit. PU Type 4 is a communications controller. This device provides communications support for up to several hundred line terminations, where individual lines in turn can be connected to cluster controllers. At the top of the hardware hierarchy, PU Type 5 is a mainframe computer.

PU2.1 is a special type of node which supports IBM's Advanced Peer-to-Peer Networking (APPN). Unlike SNA which

**Table 8.1** SNA PU summary.

| PU type | Node type | Representative hardware |
|---|---|---|
| PU Type 5 | Mainframe | S/370, 43XX, 308X |
| PU Type 4 | Communications controller | 3705, 3725, 3745 |
| PU Type 3 | Not currently defined | N/A |
| PU Type 2.1 | APPN | any computer |
| PU Type 2 | Cluster controller | 3174, 3274, 3276 |
| PU Type 1 | Terminal | 3180, PC with SNA adapter |

is based upon a hierarchical, master–slave control structure, APPN permits cooperative program-to-program communications in which each computer on the network is considered as just another peer node. Thus, a session can be established between two Type 2.1 nodes without requiring a data flow through an SSCP.

*Multiple domains*

Figure 8.3 illustrates a two-domain SNA network. By establishing a physical connection between the communications controller in each domain and coding appropriate software for operation on each controller, cross-domain data flow becomes possible. When cross-domain data flow is established, terminal devices connected to one mainframe gain the capability to access applications operating on the other mainframe.

SNA was originally implemented as a networking architecture in which users establish sessions with application programs that operate on a mainframe computer within the network. Once a session is established, a network control program (NCP) operating on an IBM communications controller, which in turn is connected to the IBM mainframe, controls the information flow between the user and the applications program. With the growth in personal computing, many users no longer required access to a mainframe to obtain connectivity to another personal computer connected to the network. Thus IBM modified SNA to permit peer-to-peer communications capability in which two devices on the network with appropriate hardware and software could communicate with one another without requiring access through a mainframe computer. In doing so, IBM introduced a PU2.1 node in 1987. When used with LU6.2 described later in this chapter, communications between two PU2.1 nodes without mainframe intervention becomes possible.

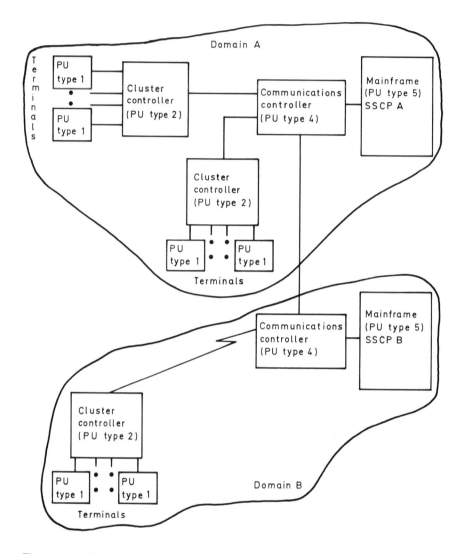

**Figure 8.3** Two–domain SNA network.

In actuality, the PU2.1 node in conjunction with LU6.2 and new releases of VTAM and associated communications products represents the evolving networking concept known as Advanced Peer-to-Peer Networking (APPN). Although the PU2.1 type node was announced in 1987, many portions of APPN were still evolving or were being developed. For example, VTAM version 4.1 which will allow IBM mainframes to actively participate within APPN as another peer-to-peer APPN node was released during the latter part of 1992. Other products, such as 3174 microcode to support an APPN network node function for both coaxial cable-connected terminals and workstations on a Token-Ring network connected via the 3174's Token-Ring adapter, were scheduled for availability in early 1993. Since many organizations have a large base of SNA communications equipment, the process to replace or upgrade that base of equipment to support APPN can be expected to be an evolutionary process. This is especially true owing to the current lack of APPN software applications. Since many organizations have invested a literal fortune in SNA applications, the expected availability of APPN applications over the next few years will not, by itself, cause a massive migration to APPN. Instead, we can expect organizations to first obtain APPN compliant equipment and gradually migrate to APPN.

*SNA layers*

IBM's SNA is a layered protocol which provides seven layers of control for every message that flows through the network. Figure 8.4 illustrates the SNA layers and provides a comparison to the seven-layer OSI Reference Model.

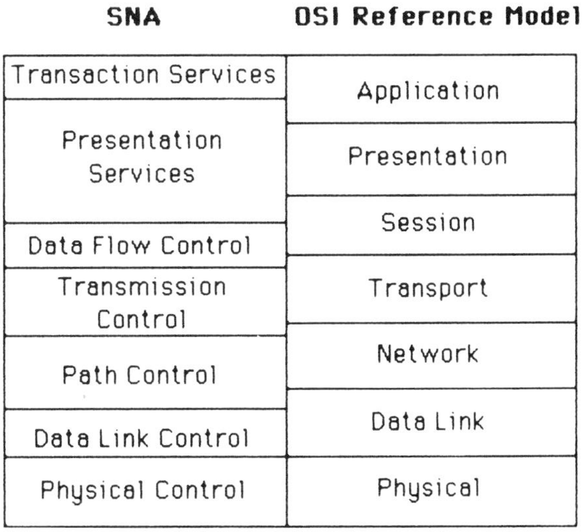

**SNA**        **OSI Reference Model**

| SNA | OSI Reference Model |
|---|---|
| Transaction Services | Application |
| Presentation Services | Presentation |
| Data Flow Control | Session |
| Transmission Control | Transport |
| Path Control | Network |
| Data Link Control | Data Link |
| Physical Control | Physical |

**Figure 8.4**  SNA and the OSI Reference Model.

Similar to the OSI physical layer, SNA's physical control layer is concerned with the electrical, mechanical and procedural characteristics of the physical media and interfaces to the physical media. SNA's data link control layer is also quite similar to OSI's data link layer. Protocols defined by SNA include SDLC, System/370 channel, Token-Ring and X.25; however, only SDLC is used on a communications link in which master or primary stations communicate with secondary or slave stations. Some implementations of SNA using special software modules can also support Bisynchronous (BSC) communications, an IBM pre-SNA protocol still widely used, as well as asynchronous communications.

Two of the major functions of the path control layer are routing and flow control. Concerning routing, since there can be many data links connected to a node, path control is responsible for ensuring that data is correctly passed through intermediate nodes as it flows from source to destination. At the beginning of an SNA session, both sending and receiving nodes, as well as all nodes between those nodes, cooperate to select the most efficient route for the session. Since this route is established only for the duration of the session, it is known as a virtual route. To increase the efficiency of transmission in an SNA network, the path control layer at each node through which the virtual route is established has the ability to divide long messages into shorter segments for transmission by the data link layer. Similarly, path control may block short messages into larger data blocks for transmission by the data link layer. This enables the efficiency of SNA's transmission facility to be independent of the length of messages flowing on the network.

The SNA transmission control layer provides a reliable end-to-end connection service, similar to the OSI Reference Model transport layer. Other transmission control layer functions include session level pacing as well as encryption and decryption of data when so requested by a session. Here, pacing ensures that a transmitting device does not send more data than a receiving device can accept during a given period of time. Pacing can be viewed as similar to the flow control of data in a network; however, unlike flow control which is essentially uncontrolled, NAUs negotiate and control pacing. To accomplish this the two NAUs at session end points negotiate the largest number of messages, known as a pacing group, that a sending NAU can transmit prior to receiving a pacing response from a receiving NAU. Here the pacing response enables the transmitting NAU to resume transmission. Session level pacing occurs in two stages along a session's route in an SNA network. One stage of pacing is between the mainframe NAU and the communications controller, while the second stage occurs between the communications controller and an attached terminal NAU.

The data flow control services layer handles the order of communications within a session for error control and flow control. Here, the order of communications is set by the layer controlling the transmission mode. Transmission modes available include full-duplex, which permits each device to transmit at any time, half-duplex flip-flop, in which devices can only transmit alternately, and half-duplex contention, in which one device is considered a master device and the slave cannot transmit until the master completes its transmission.

The SNA presentation services layer is responsible for the translation of data from one format to another. This layer also performs the connection and disconnection of sessions as well as updating the network configuration and performing network management functions. At this layer, the network addressable unit (NAU) services manager is responsible for formatting of data from an application to match the display or printer that is communicating with the application. Other functions performed at this layer include the compression and decompression of data to increase the efficiency of transmission on an SNA network.

The highest layer in SNA is the transaction services layer. This layer is responsible for application programs that implement distributed processing and management services, such as distributed databases and document interchange as well as the control of LU-to-LU session limits.

### SNA developments

The most significant development to SNA can be considered the addition of new LU and PU subtypes to support what is known as Advanced Peer-to-Peer Networking (APPN). Previously, LU types used to define an LU-to-LU session were restricted to application-to-device and program-to-program sessions. LU1–LU4 and LU7 are application-to-device sessions as indicated in Table 8.2, whereas LU4 and LU6 are program-to-program sessions.

The addition of LU6.2, which operates in conjunction with PU2.1 to support LU6.2 connections, permits devices supporting this new LU to transfer data to any other device

**Table 8.2** SNA LU session types.

| LU type | Session type |
| --- | --- |
| LU1 | Host application and a remote batch terminal |
| LU2 | Host application and a 3270 display terminal |
| LU3 | Host application and a 3270 printer |
| LU4 | Host application and SNA word processor or between two terminals via mainframe |
| LU5 | Currently undefined |
| LU6 | Between applications programs typically residing on different mainframe computers |
| LU6.2 | Peer-to-peer |
| LU7 | Host application and a 5250 terminal |

also supporting this LU without first sending the data through a mainframe computer. The introduction of new software products to support LU6.2 permits a more dynamic flow of data through SNA networks, with many data links to mainframes that were previously heavily utilized or saturated gaining capacity as sessions between devices permit data flow to bypass the mainframe.

Under APPN, multiple LU-to-LU sessions per LU6.2 become possible since LU6.2 supports parallel sessions with no restrictions on session originator. In comparison, under SNA peripheral nodes such as LUs in a control unit can only participate in one LU-to-LU session at any one time and the host resident LU must function as the master. Other differences between SNA and APPN include the maximum number of LUs supported by a peripheral node and the manner in which resources and routes are defined.

Under SNA the maximum number of LUs in a peripheral node is limited to 255. Under APPN there is a theoretical limit of 64 K LUs per link; however, in operation there will probably be only one LU6.2 per node since LU6.2 provides the ability to support multiple users. Concerning the definition of resources and routes, as previously discussed, SNA can be viewed as a relatively static networking environment in which tables must be manually coded to define resources and routes. Under APPN, most routes and resources are discovered by the equipment which minimizes the necessity for extensive manual definitions.

## SNA sessions

All communications in SNA occur within sessions between NAUs. Here a session can be defined and a logical connection established between two NAUs over a specific route for a specific period of time, with the connection and disconnection of a session controlled by the SSCP. Currently SNA defines four types of sessions: SSCP-to-PU, SSCP-to-LU, SSCP-to-SSCP, and LU-to-LU. The first two types of sessions are used to request or exchange diagnostic and status information. The third type of session enables SSCPs in the same or different domains to exchange information. The LU-to-LU session can be considered as the core type of SNA session since all end-user communications take place over LU-to-LU sessions.

### *LU-to-LU sessions*

In an LU-to-LU session one logical unit known as the primary LU (PLU) becomes responsible for error recovery. The other LU, which normally has less processing power, becomes the secondary LU (SLU).

An LU-to-LU session is initiated by the transmission of a message from the PLU to the SLU. That message is known as a bind and contains information stored in the communications access method (known as VTAM) tables on the mainframe which identifies the type of hardware devices with respect to screen size, printer type, etc., configured in the VTAM table. This information enables a session to occur with supported hardware. Otherwise, the SLU will reject the bind and the session will not start.

### *Addressing*

Previously we discussed the concept of a domain which consists of an SSCP and the network resources it controls. Within a domain there exists a set of smaller network units that are known as subareas. In SNA terminology each host is a subarea as well as each communications controller and its peripheral nodes. The identification of a NAU in an SNA network consists of a subarea address and an element address within the subarea. Here the subarea can be considered as being similar to an area code, as it identifies a portion of the network. Figure

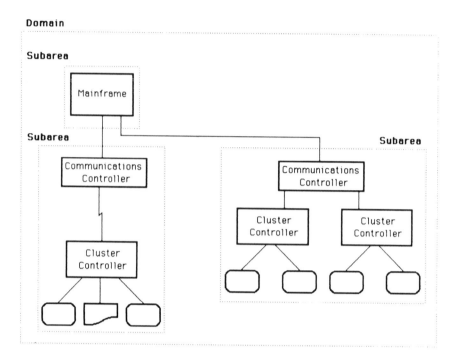

**Figure 8.5** Relationship between a domain and its subareas. A subarea is a host or a communications controller and its peripheral nodes.

8.5 illustrates the relationship between a domain and three subareas residing in that particular domain.

In SNA a subarea address is 8 bits in length, while the element address within a subarea is restricted to 15 bits. This limits the number of subareas within a domain to 256 and restricts the number of PUs and LUs within a subarea to 215.

## 8.2 THE 3270 INFORMATION DISPLAY SYSTEM

The IBM 3270 Information Display System describes a collection of products ranging from display stations with keyboards and printers that communicate with mainframe computers through several types of cluster controllers.

First introduced in 1971, the IBM 3270 Information Display System was designed to extend the processing power of the mainframe computer to locations remote from the computer room. Controllers, which are more commonly known as control units, were made available to economize on the number of lines required to link display stations to mainframe computers.

Typically, a number of display stations are connected to a control unit on individual cables and the control unit, in turn, is connected to the mainframe via a single cable. Both local and remote control units are offered, with the key differences between the two pertaining to the method of attachment to the mainframe computer and the use of intermediate devices between the control unit and the mainframe.

Local control units are usually attached to a channel on the mainframe, whereas remote control units are connected to the mainframe's communications controller. Since a local control unit is within a limited distance of the mainframe, no intermediate communications devices, such as modems, are required to connect it to the mainframe. In comparison, a remote control unit can be located in another building or in a different city which normally requires the utilization of intermediate communications devices, such as a pair of modems, for communications to occur between the control unit and the communications controller. The relationship of local and control units to display stations, mainframes and a communications controller is illustrated in Figure 8.6. Note that this hardware relationship represents the hierarchy of equipment supported by SNA.

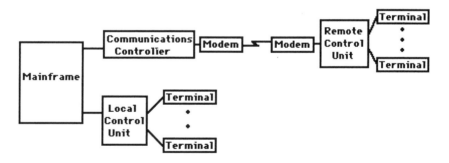

**Figure 8.6**  Relationship of 3270 Information Display products.

## Data flow

The control unit polls each connected display station to ascertain if the station has data stored in its transmit buffer. If the station has data in its buffer, it will transmit it to the control unit when it is polled. The control unit then formats the data with the display station's address, adds the control unit's address and other pertinent information and transmits it in a synchronous data format to the communications controller or to the I/O channel on the mainframe, depending upon the method used to connect the control unit to the mainframe.

Addressing information flowing to the mainframe initially begins with a terminal address. The control unit formats each data block received from a terminal device and adds its control unit identifier. If the control unit is connected to a communications controller the latter device adds a line identifier address to the data block, indicating the port on the controller where the information was received. After operating upon the data block the mainframe responds by generating a screen of data that will be routed to a specific terminal. To ensure the response is routed correctly the mainframe includes the line, control unit and terminal address. The communications controller strips off the line identifier and forwards the data onto the appropriate line. Since an SNA network supports multidrop circuits in which two or more control units can share the use of a common transmission line, the control unit address defines the control unit which will recognize the data block. That control unit removes the control unit address. Next, it examines the terminal identifier and removes it from the data block once it knows the line to transmit the block so it is received at its appropriate destination.

## 3270 protocols

Two different protocols are supported by IBM to connect 3270 devices to a mainframe. The original protocol used with 3270 devices and which is still in limited use today is the byte-oriented bisynchronous protocol, often referred to as 3270 bisyn or BSC. In the late 1970s, when IBM introduced its Systems Network Architecture, it also introduced a bit-oriented protocol for data transmission known as Synchronous Data Link Control, or SDLC. Thus, communications between an IBM mainframe and the control units attached to the communications controller are either BSC or SDLC, depending upon the type of control units obtained and the configuration of the communications controller which is controlled by software. Today almost all BSC control units have been replaced by the use of more modern SDLC devices.

## Types of control units

Control units marketed by IBM support up to 8, 16, 32 or 64 attached devices, depending upon the model. The IBM 3276 control unit supports up to eight devices while the IBM 3274 control unit can support 16 or 32 attached devices. Older control units, such as the 3271, 3272, and 3275 have essentially been replaced by the 3274 and 3276 and operate only bisynchronously, whereas certain models of the 3274 are 'soft' devices that can be programmed with a diskette to operate with the originally developed bisynchronous protocol or with the newer synchronous data link control (SDLC) protocol.

Devices to include display stations and printers are normally attached to each control unit via coaxial cable. Thus, under this design philosophy every display station must first be connected to a control unit prior to being able to access a mainframe application written for a 3270 type terminal. This method of connection excluded the utilization of dial-up terminals from accessing 3270 type applications and resulted in numerous third-party vendors marketing devices to permit lower-cost ASCII terminals to be attached to 3270 networks. In late 1986, IBM introduced a new controller known as the 3174 Subsystem Control Unit. This controller, which has now replaced older models, can be used to connect terminals via standard coaxial cable, shielded twisted-pair wire and telephone type or twisted-pair wire. Other key features of the controller include an optional protocol converter which can support up to 24 asynchronous ports and the ability of the controller to be attached to Token-Ring or Ethernet local area networks. The latter is accomplished through the use of a Token-Ring or Ethernet adapter card installed in a 3174 slot, converting the 3174 into an active participant on a Token-Ring or Ethernet network.

The 3174 can be obtained to support 8, 16, 32 or 64 ports. A 64-port 3174 supports a maximum of 254 LUs while a 32-port control unit supports a maximum of 128 LUs. All other 3174 control units normally provide an LU support capability equal to four times the number of ports on the device; however, there are some exceptions and readers should examine IBM equipment specifications to determine the LU support for different 3174 models. For example, the 64-port model slightly varies from this scheme, due to LU0 and LU1 being reserved on that device and unavailable for general use.

When used with a Token-Ring adapter (TRA), the TRA in a 3174 was originally limited to supporting up to 140 downstream PUs (DSPUs). In 1992, new microcode extended DSPU support to 250 for a local 3174. Here the term DSPU in actuality can be considered a gateway PC, with the software on each gateway determining the number of LUs supported on the Token-Ring. For example, Novell NetWare gateway software can be obtained to provide support for 16, 32 or 97 LUs. In this type of networking configuration, which is illustrated in Figure 8.7, the communications controller polls the control unit, the control unit polls individual PU gateways and each gateway is responsible for polling the LUs serviced by the gateway. In this example the gateway PC is known as a downstream PU, which polls downstream LUs.

Since SNA's architecture can be considered as a polling structure it is wise to limit the number of LUs on a gateway. Otherwise, the polling time from the gateway PC to the LUs representing different sessions on each Token-Ring station or the screen and printer of a workstation can result in excess delays. Thus, a good rule of thumb is to add another downstream PU in the form of an additional gateway for every 32 stations on a local area network.

## Terminal displays

IBM 3270 terminals fall into three display classes: monochrome, color, and gas plasma. Members of the monochrome display class include the 3278, 3178, 3180, 3191, and 3193 type terminals. The 3278 is a large, bulky terminal that covers a significant portion of one's desk and was replaced by the 3178, 3180, 3191, and 3193 display stations which are lighter, more compact and less expensive versions of the 3278. The 3279 color display station was similarly replaced by the 3179 and the 3194 which are lower cost and more compact color display terminals. The last class of display stations is the gas plasma display, consisting of the 3270 flat panel display.

The physical dimensions of a 3270 type screen may vary by class and by model within the class. As an example, the 3178 and 3278 Model 2 display stations have a screen size of 24 rows by 80 columns, while the 3278 Model 3 has a screen size of 32 rows by 80 columns and the 3278 Model 4 has a screen size of 43 rows by 80 columns.

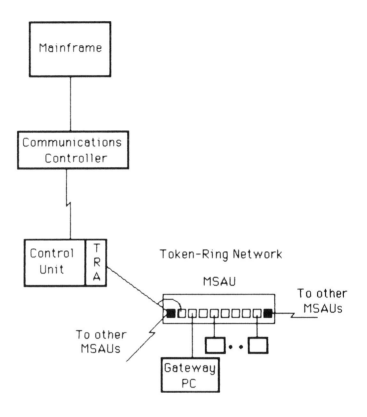

**Figure 8.7** Using a control unit TRA to interconnect a Token-Ring network. Through the installation of a TRA, both local and remote control units provide a connection capability to a Token-Ring network.

Table 8.3 lists a portion of the family of terminals marketed for use with the IBM 3270 information display system. The reader should note that the 3170 and 3180 display stations can also be used with IBM System/3X minicomputers. In addition, the 3193 and 3194 terminals can support the display of up to four host sessions when connected to the 3174 controller.

Each 3270 screen consists of fields that are defined by the application program connected to the display station. Attributes sent by the application program further define the

**Table 8.3**  IBM display stations.

| Model number | Display type | Screen (Inches) |
| --- | --- | --- |
| 3178 | Monochrome | 12 |
| 3179 | Color | 14 |
| 3180 | Monochrome | 15 |
| 3191 | Monochrome | 12 |
| 3193 | Monochrome | 15 |
| 3194 | Color | 14 |

**Table 8.4**  3270 terminal field characteristics.

| Field characteristic | Result |
| --- | --- |
| Highlighted | Field displayed at a brighter intensity than normal intensity field |
| Non-display | Field does not display any data typed into it |
| Protected | Field does not accept any input |
| Unprotected | Field accepts any data typed into it |
| Numeric-only | Field accepts only numbers as input |
| Autoskip | Field sends the cursor to the next unprotected field after it is filled with data |
| Underscoring | Causes characters to be underlined |
| Blinking | Causes characters in field to blink |

characteristics of each field as indicated in Table 8.4. As a minimum, any technique used to enable a personal computer to function as a 3270 display station requires the PC to obtain the field attributes listed in Table 8.4.

## 3270 keyboard functions

In comparison to the keyboard of most personal computers, a 3270 display station contains approximately 40 additional keys, which, when pressed, perform functions unique to the 3270 terminal environment. A list of the more common 3270 keys which differ from the keys on most personal computer keyboards is contained in Table 8.5.

**Table 8.5** Common 3270 keys differing from most personal computer keyboards.

| Key(s) | Function |
|--------|----------|
| CLEAR | Erases screen except for characters in message area, repositioning cursor to row 1, column 1. |
| PA1 | Transmits a code to the application program which is interpreted as a break signal. Thus, in TSO or CMS the PA1 key would terminate the current command. |
| PA2 | Transmits a code to the application program that is often interpreted as a request to redisplay the screen or to clear the screen and display additional information. |
| PFnn | Twenty-four program function keys on a 3270 terminal are defined by the application program in use. |
| TAB | Moves the cursor to the next unprotected field. |
| BACKTAB | Moves the cursor to the previous unprotected field. |
| RESET | Disables the insert mode. |
| ERASEEOF | Deletes everything from the cursor to the end of the input field. |
| NEWLINE | Advances the cursor to the first unprotected field on the new line. |
| FASTRIGHT | Moves the cursor to the right two characters at a time. |
| FASTLEFT | Moves the cursor to the left two characters at a time. |
| ERASE INPUT | Clears all the input fields on the screen. |
| HOME | Moves the cursor to the first unprotected field on the screen. |

Since most, if not all, of the 3270 keyboard functions may be required to successfully use a 3270 application program, the codes generated from pressing keys on a personal computer keyboard must be converted into appropriate codes that represent 3270 keyboard functions to enable a PC to be used as a 3270 terminal. Due to the lesser number of keys on a personal computer keyboard, a common approach to most emulation techniques is to use a two- or a three-key sequence on the PC keyboard to represent many of the keys unique to a 3270 keyboard.

*Emulation considerations*

In addition to converting keys on a personal computer keyboard to 3270 keyboard functions, 3270 emulation requires the PC's screen to function as a 3270 display screen. The 3270 display terminal operates by displaying an entire screen of data in one operation and then waits for the operator to signal that he or she is ready to proceed with the next screen of information. This operation mode is known as 'full-screen' operation and is exactly the opposite of TTY emulation where a terminal operates 'on a line-by-line' basis. A key advantage of full-screen editing is the ability of the operator to move the cursor to any position on the screen to edit or change data. Thus, to use a personal computer workstation located on a local area network as a 3270 display station, the transmission codes used to position the 3270 screen and effect field attributes must be converted to equivalent codes recognizable by the PC. This means that individual workstations on the local area network must operate a terminal emulation program. This program works in tandem with the application program and communications controller through the 3174 control unit and gateway to enable the workstation to be recognized as a supported 3270 type terminal. Thus, in addition to gateway software each workstation on the local area network that requires access to the mainframe must operate a terminal emulation program.

## 8.3 GATEWAY OPTIONS

Now that we have a basic understanding of the architecture of SNA and the components and operations of the 3270 information display system, let us turn our attention to linking local area networks to IBM and IBM-compatible host computers. In doing so we will first expand upon our knowledge of the operation of a 3174 control unit and the differences between its use as a gateway and the use of a gateway PC on a Token-Ring network connected to a 3174. Next, we will examine several recent enhancements to the 3174 control unit which extend the capability of this device to function as a gateway to support different organizational networking requirements.

### 3174 control unit

As previously illustrated in Figure 8.7, the IBM 3174 control unit provides a basic mechanism to connect a Token-Ring network to an SNA network. Although a gateway PC was illustrated in Figure 8.7, in actuality the gateway is optional and is primarily used for resource management and message switching. Without a gateway, all Token-Ring station definitions and definition changes must be performed on the mainframe. Thus, if a new user is added to the LAN, new definitions must be added to VTAM on the mainframe. Normally, such changes require a new compilation to source code macro changes and are typically performed late at night or on weekends. Thus, new users may experience a delay in obtaining access to a mainframe.

Through the use of a gateway PC, such changes are more readily performed since mainframe sessions can be allocated to LU and PU 'pools'. The gateway then provides a mechanism to dynamically assign new users to the pool to obtain immediate access to the mainframe. Unfortunately, there is no free lunch. Thus, the gateway adds a degree of processing delay which may be noticeable when an extended process, such as a large file transfer, occurs.

*Enhancements*

During 1992, several enhancements were introduced by IBM for their 3174 control unit which extends the capability of that device for gateway operations. Those enhancements include a multi-host support capability, extended support for up to 250 downstream physical units, Advanced Peer-to-Peer Networking (APPN) support, the ability of the 3174 to serve as an Ethernet gateway, and the introduction of a group polling feature.

**Multi-host Support**

The introduction of a concurrent communications adapter capable of supporting multiple SDLC, BSC, or X.25 protocols for the 3174 formed the basis for permitting the 3174 to serve as a multi-host Token-Ring gateway. Figure 8.8 illustrates the use of a 3174 as a multi-host Token-Ring gateway. In this example, the 3174 provides access to a local mainframe via a high-speed direct channel connection and access to a remote mainframe via a communications circuit. The multi-host Token-Ring gateway supports one direct channel and two communications circuit connections when implemented on a local control unit and up to three communications circuit connections when implemented on a remote control unit. Regardless of the control unit used, all connections are restricted to IBM SNA mainframes.

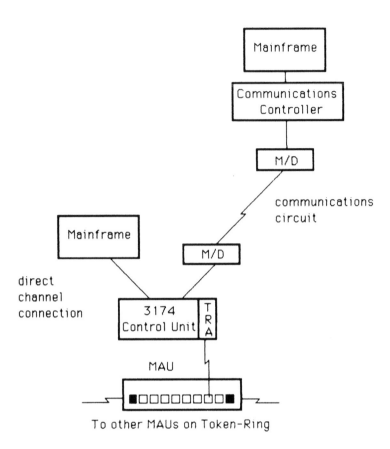

**Figure 8.8** Multi-host Token-Ring gateway. Through the use of a concurrent communications adapter, a 3174 control unit can connect LAN stations to multiple mainframe computers.

**Extended PU Support**

The first 3174 introduced with a Token-Ring adapter supported a maximum of 140 downstream physical units. Newer 3174 control units are now capable of supporting up to 250 downstream physical units; however, readers should note that not all 3174s are equal. For example, a low-cost 3174 Model 90R control unit designed to provide a remote gateway connection to a communications controller at a data rate up to 64 kbps provides a maximum support for 40 downstream physical units.

**Group Polling**

To understand the performance enhancement obtainable through the support of group polling by a 3174 Token-Ring gateway requires a review of the method by which terminals and workstations access a host via a gateway control unit. Prior to the availability of group polling, the gateway would poll each PU on the Token-Ring in response to polls generated by the communications controller. To illustrate the problem with this method of polling, assume a 3174 supported both a group of conventional 3270 display terminals and printers, as well as workstations, via a Token-Ring adapter. One PU would be assigned to the control unit to serve as a general address for the display terminals and printers cabled directly to the 3174. A second PU would be assigned to the Token-Ring adapter. Thus, the communications controller would alternately poll each PU and the control unit would alternately poll each group of LUs assigned to each PU.

Since a station on the Token-Ring can only transmit in response to a poll, a relatively large amount of time can occur until the 3174 polls the appropriate LU with data to transmit. In the interim, the 3174 may be polling many PUs with no data to send until it polls an LU with data to transmit. Figure 8.9a illustrates how the Network Control Program (NCP) operating on an IBM communications controller would poll the two PUs associated with the 3174 control unit under our scenario.

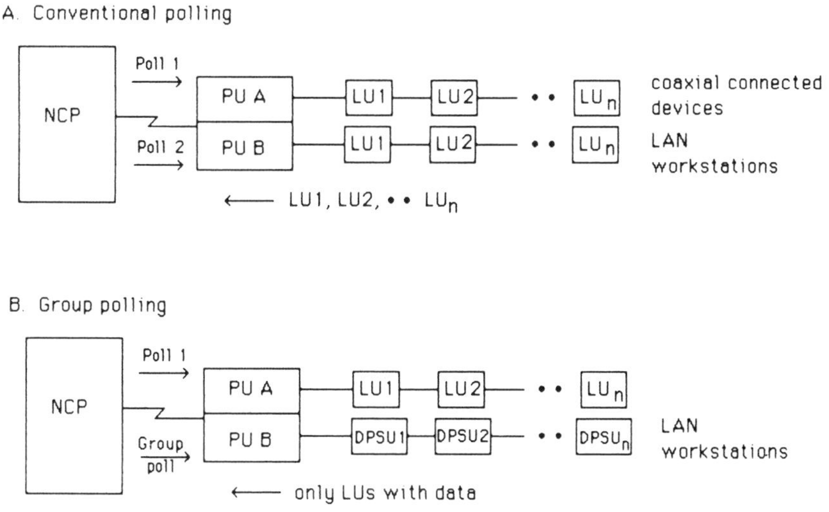

A. Conventional polling

B. Group polling

**Figure 8.9** Conventional versus group polling.

Under group polling, PU addresses are assigned to each workstation downstream from the control unit and are then referenced as downstream physical units (DSPUs). The DSPUs are defined in the NCP and the NCP will issue a group poll to the control unit's PU address. In the example illustrated in Figure 8.9b, this would be to address PU B. When the group poll to PU B occurs, the 3174 will respond by transmitting any LU data it has in storage. This enables the control unit to retrieve LU data from each DSPU and respond to the group poll by transmitting any LU data it stored rather than waiting for a specific LU poll. Thus, group polling reduces non-productive polling cycles associated with conventional LU polling. This results in an increase in the capacity of a communications line to support data transfer and typically reduces LAN workstation response times by 10–20%.

**Ethernet Connectivity**

Until 1992, 3174 control units only supported the use of Token-Ring adapter cards, limiting direct connectivity of the 3174 to a Token-Ring network. Although IBM now provides an Ethernet adapter card for its 3174 control unit, there are alternative methods to use a 3174 to provide gateway support for Ethernet networks that are worth examining since we can then note some of the numerous vendor gateway construction options available for connecting different types of LANs into an SNA network.

In Figure 8.7 we illustrated how a Token-Ring network could be connected to an SNA network through a 3174 control unit Token-Ring adapter. A similar mixture of hardware and software can be used to connect an Ethernet/IEEE 802.3 network to an SNA network.

Figure 8.10 illustrates the use of a gateway PC to connect an Ethernet 10BASE-T network to an SNA network. In this example the gateway PC contains a Token-Ring adapter card for connection to an MAU and an Ethernet card for connection to a 10BASE-T wire hub MAU. Although it may appear that the gateway functions as a bridge, it operates at a much higher level, although it does transfer information between the Token-Ring and the Ethernet network. If the Ethernet is operating Novell NetWare, the gateway PC translates LUs into IPX addresses and vice versa. This address conversion is based upon configuring the gateway PC software when the gateway is installed. Since LU assignments are defined in the NCP in the communications controller, this means that the gateway installation process must occur in close coordination with NCP programmers that encode the NCP to recognize the gateway as a downstream PU with LUs assigned to that PU. In addition, to enable stations on the Ethernet to gain full screen access to mainframe applications each station desiring such access must execute an appropriate terminal emulation program similar to that described for the previous Token-Ring network.

In the example illustrated in Figure 8.10 one vendor markets a gateway that can be configured to operate as one to eight separate PUs, with each PU capable of supporting up to 32 LUs. Since two LUs on one PU are reserved, that vendor's product provides the ability to support up to 254 LUs. This provides the servicing of up to 127 workstations that use separate LUs for screen and printer or a lesser number of workstations that require the ability to execute multiple SNA sessions in the form of additional LUs.

## 3172 InterConnect Controller

A relatively recent addition to the family of IBM networking products is that vendor's 3172 InterConnect Controller. The 3172 can be viewed as a sophisticated local 3174 control unit gateway as it provides access to a channel-attached host for workstations on Ethernet, Token-Ring, FDDI, and PC Network local area networks. The latter is a broadband LAN developed by Sitec for IBM during the mid-1980s.

Under the control of an InterConnect Control Program, LAN stations obtain access to a host subsystem operating TCP/IP. This enables the mainframe to provide TCP/IP functions to each connected LAN, including both static and RIP routing. In addition, the 3172 supports concurrent access to SNA and OSI subsystems which enables this controller to support separate local area network connections via one common direct connection to the high-speed channel of a mainframe computer, such as an Enterprise system or an older S370/390. Other differences between the 3172 and a 3174 concern the number of Token-Ring network connections and the type of networks supported as well as the number of DSPUs supported.

Table 8.6 compares the major features of a local 3174 to a 3172. In comparing the two devices it becomes apparent that the 3172 is better suited for organizations that have a number of LANs within a building where a mainframe is located. Since

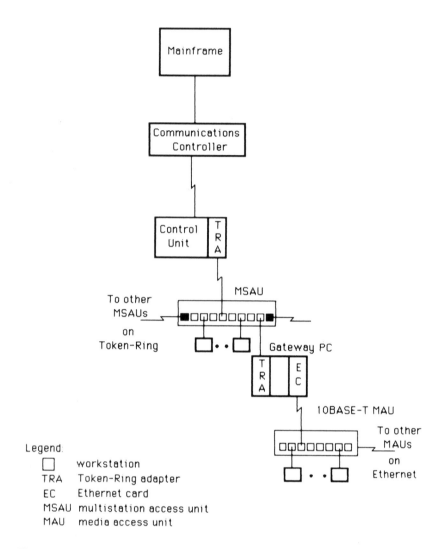

**Figure 8.10** Using a control unit TRA to interconnect an Ethernet network. Through the installation of a Token-Ring adapter and an Ethernet card and appropriate software, the gateway PC provides a connection from a 10BASE-T network to the mainframe via a Token-Ring network.

the 3172 supports a maximum of four LAN adapters, its use permits the replacement of four separate 3174 control units. In addition, by supporting four different types of local area networks the 3172 provides a considerable level of networking gateway support compared with that obtainable through the use of a 3174.

**Table 8.6**  3172 versus 3174 general feature comparison.

| Feature | 3172 | Local 3174 |
|---|---|---|
| Parallel channel support | 2 | 1 |
| Token-Ring network support | 4* | 1 |
| Ethernet support | 4* | 0 |
| FDDI | 1* | 0 |
| PC network support | 4* | 0 |
| DSPU support | 1020** | 250 |

\* Maximum total of 4 LAN adapters.
\*\* Maximum of 255 per adapter.

## Alternative gateway methods

The previous gateways used the services of a TRA on a control unit or an InterConnect Controller requiring the physical presence of a 3172 or a 3174 to interconnect to an SNA network. Recognizing that the additional hardware cost of a control unit or InterConnect Controller can limit the effectiveness of that gateway method, several vendors, including IBM and third party vendors, such as Eicon Technology of Montreal, Canada, market alternative solutions which enable different types of local area networks to access SNA networks over wide area network facilities. In the remainder of this section we will examine several of those alternative solutions.

### SDLC connectivity

An SDLC gateway consists of a pair of adapter cards installed in a personal computer and appropriate software that performs the required conversion from the packet format used on the local area network to an SNA data stream. One card is an SDLC adapter which provides the framing for the bit oriented protocol used by SNA. In actuality, most vendor SDLC gateways include SNA functions in read-only memory (ROM) on the adapter card which makes the card function as if it was a series of 3274 control units (multiple PUs) with each PU associated with a group of LUs. This second adapter is typically a Token-Ring or Ethernet adapter, used to connect the gateway to either a Token-Ring or Ethernet local area network.

Figure 8.11 illustrates the use of an SDLC gateway to obtain access to a communications controller via a wide area network

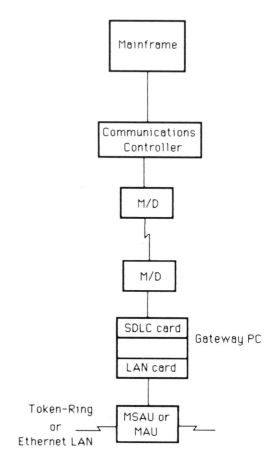

Legend
  M/D     modem or data service unit
  MSAU  multistation access unit
  MAU    media access unit

**Figure 8.11**  Using an SDLC gateway. An SDLC gateway provides access to an SNA network by providing communications between a LAN and a communications controller.

or an extended distance cable. Concerning the later, the use of an SDLC gateway may permit the connection of a LAN to a communications controller via a lengthy cable within a building. This may be more attractive than the use of the gateway via a control unit TRA whose cable distance is limited to LAN cabling restrictions.

Both RS-232 and V.35 connectors can be obtained with most SDLC adapters. The use of an RS-232 connector limits the SDLC transmission rate to 19.2 kbps while the use of a V.35 connector enables digital transmission facilities at 56 or 64 kbps to be used to connect the gateway to the communications controller.

Some SDLC gateways are limited to support of one PU and 32 LUs. Other SDLC gateways considerably expand upon that basic level of support. For example, an Eicon SNA gateway product which uses SDLC connectivity to a communications controller supports 32 PUs and up to 254 sessions. In addition, an Eicon gateway can be configured using up to four cards which results in a total of 128 PUs and 1016 sessions that can be supported by one gateway PC. Of course, limiting the transmission to either 19.2 kbps or 56/64 kbps per card may severely restrict LAN performance when accessing the mainframe.

**Gateway Software**

One of the more commonly used gateway software programs is IBM's Personal Communications/3270 (PC/3270) program which is a replacement for that vendor's earlier PC 3270 Emulation Program (EP). PC/3270 supports communications with LAN workstations that can also use PC/3270 or OS/2 Extended Edition, PC 3270 Emulation Program, or IBM's 3270 Workstation Program. The gateway can be configured to communicate with an IBM SNA host via a Token-Ring, SDLC, or as an SNA Distributed Functional Terminal (DFT). Later in this chapter we will discuss the concept behind DFT access to a mainframe.

Unlike the PC 3270 Emulation Program which limited support to 32 concurrent sessions, a gateway using IBM's PC/3270 program can support up to 253 host sessions and permits up to 256 stations to be configured per gateway although only 64 can be active at any one time. The gateway appears to the host as a single PU Type 2 node with up to 253 attached LUs. To attached stations the gateway appears as an SNA primary communications device, emulating PU and LU activation and deactivation functions that are required to establish and maintain SSCP-PU and SSCP-LU sessions between the host and the downstream workstations.

Another IBM software product worth mentioning is that firm's OS/2 Extended Edition SNA Gateway (EE gateway). Although this program is very similar in functionality to IBM's PC/3270 gateway, it added LU pooling which makes LU assignments considerably more efficient.

Under LU pooling a group of LUs is allocated on a first-come first-served basis. Since it is quite common for only a subset of users to require the simultaneous use of LU sessions, for example by directing output to a printer, the pool of LUs can be less than when LUs are assigned on an individual basis. Thus, LU pooling can reduce the number of LUs required in the network and enable those resources, such as memory buffer areas, to be used more efficiently. Doing so typically improves the response of a gateway to an LU request. In addition, to avoid any possible LU pool contention OS/2 EE permits specific sessions to be dedicated and bypass LU pool contention. Another advantage associated with LU pooling is its ability to support more than 64 concurrently active stations. This is accomplished by OS/2 EE gateway placing some or all of its available LUs into an LU pool and allocating those LUs as individual users request access to the mainframe.

### Gateway Configuration

The configuration of an SDLC gateway is similar to the process involved in configuring most gateways. That is, its configuration requires the installer to make a large number of configuration decisions as well as requiring a prior degree of knowledge concerning the SNA network the gateway will provide a connection to. Some of the configuration parameters are related to the SDLC connection to a communications controller, while other configuration parameters govern the manner in which workstation users gain access to the SNA network through the gateway.

Examples of SDLC configuration parameters include defining the type of line connection (switched or non-switched), transmission mode (full- or half-duplex), circuit type (point-to-point or multipoint), clocking provider (modem/DSU or adapter card), the maximum information frame size, number of PUs and LUs, and the maximum window size for transmission. For an SDLC leased line connection you would normally specify a non-switched, multipoint line. The maximum information frame size should be set to equal the MAXDATA macro definition defined in the Network Control Program (NCP) plus three bytes. The maximum window size references the number of frames that can be received prior to requiring an acknowledgement and to a degree governs the efficiency of the SDLC communications circuit. Conventional SDLC supports up to seven unacknowledged frames, while extended control field SDLC supports a maximum of 127 unacknowledged frames prior to requiring an acknowledgement. Normally, large window sizes are preferred for use on circuits that have a significant propagation delay, such as circuits established via satellite transmission or a relatively long international circuit. By extending the window size, delays associated with acknowledgements propagating in the reverse direction to transmission are reduced which significantly increases the transmission efficiency of the line.

A second set of configuration parameters governs the manner in which the gateway functions as a control unit. Configuration parameters include the number of PUs and LUs as well as the manner in which LUs are allocated. Under dynamic LU allocation, the SNA gateway software maintains a list of all free LUs. When a request is received from a station to function as an LU, one is assigned from the pool. In comparison, the direct allocation of LUs requires each station user to specify an LU number to be used. If the LU is not free, the user must then specify another LU.

*X.25 connectivity*

As previously mentioned in this chapter, SNA networks support the CCITT X.25 protocol. This support is not a standard part of an SNA network, requiring an IBM software program known as NCP Packet Switching Interface (NPSI) to be obtained and loaded as an NCP module in a communications controller. Through the use of NPSI an IBM communications controller, such as the 3745, can be directly connected to a packet switching network. This in turn enables any terminal device capable of supporting the X.25 protocol to communicate with the communications controller via the use of a packet network's transmission facilities.

To take advantage of NPSI and the use of a packet switching network as a data transport mechanism, several vendors have introduced X.25 gateways. This type of gateway is also constructed through the use of adapter cards installed in the system unit of a personal computer. Typically, two or three adapter cards may be required, with the actual number dependent upon a vendor's use of ROM versus loadable software. One adapter card provides the connection to the local area network while a second adapter card packetizes data for transmission on the packet network. Either a third card or perhaps loadable software makes the gateway PC function as a downstream PU with LUs, in effect functioning as a control unit. Data from the local area network is converted into a 3270 format and encapsulated into an X.25 data stream by the gateway personal computer. That data is routed through the packet network to the IBM communications controller, where the NPSI port converts the datastream back into the 3270 format created by the gateway PC. Figure 8.12 illustrates the operation of an X.25 gateway.

One of the major advantages of an X.25 gateway is the ability of the use of packet switching to inherently support multiple logical connections over a single physical connection. This means that one SNA X.25 gateway can be used to provide a connection to multiple IBM host computers connected to a packet network. Since each host computer requires a PU definition, this also means that there is a practical limit of 32 concurrent connections that are obtainable through the use of an X.25 gateway.

Figure 8.13 illustrates the use of a single SNA X.25 gateway to support multiple logical connections via a single physical link, in this example, to two SNA host computers. Software used for the support of multiple logical connections is referred to as X.25 Qualified Logical Link Control (QLLC) and must operate on the gateway as well as on each IBM communications controller.

Similar to an SDLC gateway the major constraint of an X.25 gateway concerns its operating rate, throughput, and PU and LU support. The operating rate of an X.25 card is limited to 64 kbps; however, its throughput may be considerably less than an SDLC gateway operating at the same data rate. This is because the X.25 gateway not only packetizes data adding additional overhead but, in addition, has its data checked as it flows through the packet network. The additional delays due to the error checking performed at packet switches can add between 0.25 and 0.5 seconds to the response time of network users in comparison to the use of an SDLC gateway. However, one NPSI port can provide support for more than one X.25 gateway connected via a packet network to the mainframe location. In comparison, each SDLC gateway requires the use of a separate SDLC port on the communications controller, so the decision between the use of SDLC and X.25 gateways must consider the cost of public network usage charges versus building a network as well as a trade off between performance and hardware cost in the form of additional communications controller ports. Since

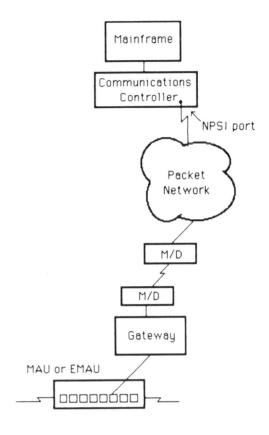

Legend
M/D    modem or data service unit
MAU    multistation access unit
EMAU   Ethernet media access unit

**Figure 8.12** X.25 gateway operation. An X.25 gateway converts LAN packets into a 3270 datastream and encapsulates the data into X.25 packets for transmission through a packet network.

an X.25 gateway can be considered to encapsulate the functions of an SDLC gateway into X.25 packets it should come as no surprise that their PU and LU support should be the same. This appears to be true for all vendor products examined by the author.

*The TIC connection*

The use of a Token Interface Coupler (TIC) installed in a communications controller provides a gateway access method

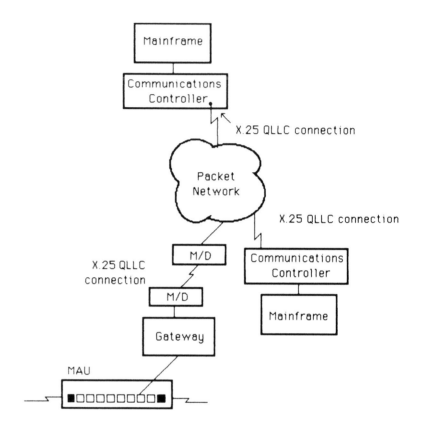

Legend
  M/D    modem or data service unit
  QLLC   qualified logical link control

**Figure 8.13**  Supporting multiple logical connections.

very similar to a control unit with a TRA. That is, the TIC is cabled to an MAU port and one or more gateway PCs are also cabled to an MAU port.

The primary differences between the use of a communications controller TIC and a control unit TRA are in the areas of cost, network interconnection distance, operating rate and PU and LU support.

A TIC can cost well over $10 000. In comparison a TRA costs under $2000. Concerning network interconnection distance, the use of a TIC restricts access to the LAN cabling distance since the communications controller must be cabled to an MAU under lobe length distance restrictions. In comparison, a local control unit can be connected via coaxial cable to a communications controller which enables the gateway distance to be extended. If a remote control unit is used that device functions similar to a remote communications controller since both the TRA and the TIC cabling distances to an MAU are governed by lobe distance restrictions.

In a local environment the communications controller and control unit are both channel attached to a host computer, and their data transfer capabilities are similar. In a remote environment the transmission rate of a control unit is restricted to a maximum of 56 kbps. In comparison, a remote communications controller can operate at T1/E1 data rates, providing over 20 times the data transfer capability of a control unit. Thus, the TIC can provide a higher level of throughput when used at a remote location.

The biggest difference between the use of a TRA and TIC is in the area of PU and LU support. The NCP on a communications controller can support up to 9999 PUs for TIC. Then, each gateway PC functioning as a PU will support a grouping of LUs based upon the gateway software used. Another key difference between the use of a TRA and a TIC concerns the method of gateway communications.

When a control unit TRA provides a connection to the Token-Ring network the communications controller polls the control unit and the control unit polls each downstream PU, with each gateway polling its LUs. When a TIC is used each downstream PU requests service from the TIC by using a 'dial-up' service when it requires service. Thus, this can considerably reduce the polls flowing on an attached local area network and can result in the TIC being able to theoretically support up to 9999 PUs.

*3278/9 coaxial connection*

A rather outdated and limited function gateway is based upon the use of a 3278/9 coaxial adapter card. Instead of emulating a 3X74 control unit like SDLC and X.25 gateways, the coaxial adapter permits a gateway PC to be connected to a port on a 3X74 control unit. That port can be configured as a distributed function terminal (DFT) port. When used in this manner the DFT port provides access to five sessions as it represents five LUs. Gateway software then divides the five SNA mainframe sessions among contending workstations on the local area network. This means that a coaxial-adapter-based gateway is limited to providing a maximum of five simultaneous host sessions. Similar to the other gateways described in this section, a Token-Ring or Ethernet adapter card would be installed in the gateway to provide a connection to the local area network. Figure 8.14 illustrates the hardware used to provide a 3278/9 coaxial cable gateway.

Although a coaxially connected gateway is limited in its session support, it operates at coaxial cable data transfer rates to the control unit. If a local control unit is used the operating rate of a coaxially connected gateway can approach 2 Mbps. In comparison, SDLC and X.25 type gateways are limited to a

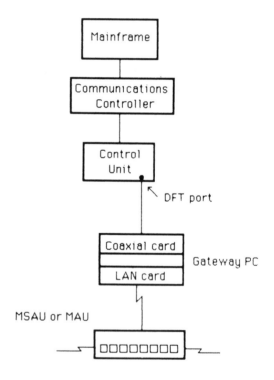

Legend:

    DFT    distributed function terminal
    MSAU multistation access unit
    MAU   media access unit

**Figure 8.14**  3278/9 coaxial connectivity. Through the use of a 3278/9 coaxial adapter card, LAN card, and a DFT port on a control unit, up to five LAN workstations can simultaneously access an SNA network.

56 kbps data transfer rate. Thus, coaxially connected gateways can provide a high level of SNA access performance for small local area networks when such networks are at the mainframe location. In addition, this method eliminates the necessity to obtain a TIC or TRA and can be used with older 3274 control units that cannot support the installation of a Token-Ring adapter. Thus, the coaxially connected gateway also represents the lowest cost gateway.

# 9

---

# MANAGING THE NETWORK

---

In this chapter we will turn our attention to the use of several products that provide us with the ability to enhance the management of local area networks. First, we will examine the use of hubs which may enhance our ability to reconfigure network topology, test selected portions of a network, as well as obtain a variety of statistics concerning the operation of our network. Next, we will turn our attention toward the use of a product that can be used both to determine the current state of your network as well as to initiate action that can alleviate potential problems from occurring.

## 9.1 INTELLIGENT HUBS

As we noted earlier in this book, every Token-Ring network contains a minimum of one hub in the form of a MAU. The MAU can be considered to operate as a multiport repeater, receiving signals from any device connected to it via a lobe and repeating the signal at its full strength.

As the number of stations on a Token-Ring expands, a hub will eventually run out of ports. To successfully expand the network requires the use of another hub or MAU, with one hub connected to another to form a ring structure. The process by which hubs or MAUs are connected to one another is commonly referred to as cascading. Figure 9.1 illustrates the cascading of three MAUs, with each capable of supporting eight devices, resulting in the support of a total of 24 devices.

Although most MAUs are capable of being rack mounted, each MAU consists of an individual chassis. In addition, the installation of two or more MAUs into a rack requires the cabling of one MAU to another in a cascading manner to form a

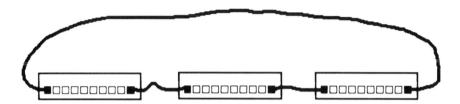

**Figure 9.1** Cascading MAUs. The process by which MAUs are connected to one another to form a ring is commonly referred to as cascading.

ring structure. To facilitate the installation of multiple MAUs, vendors have developed a device commonly referred to as a concentrator.

## Concentrators and hubs

A Token-Ring concentrator can be considered a special type of hub or MAU, as it has a built-in expansion capability which eliminates the need to install cascaded hubs as your network grows and allows such growth to be controlled from a centrally located wiring closet. A concentrator consists of a chassis to which you add module boards. Depending upon manufacturer, module boards may contain one or more ports. Some of the more common concentrators support up to 100 Token-Ring connections, with two additional connections reserved for special use. One connection is typically reserved to connect a personal computer or workstation running network management software, while the other reserved port connection allows diagnostic test equipment to be attached to the network without requiring the use of a port serving an existing device. The backplane of the concentrator serves as a cascaded cable and the insertion of module boards makes it relatively easy to expand the number of ports to accommodate a growing network.

The use of a hub or conventional concentrator treats all network devices as equals. That is, each device is cabled to a port to obtain access to the network.

## Hub cards

An alternative architecture to standalone hubs and concentrators can be obtained through the use of hub cards.

First brought to market by Novell, hub cards are designed to turn a personal computer into a network hub. Using a Novell hub, you can integrate a hub function into a NetWare server, enabling the use of Novell software operating on the server to provide a network management capability. In comparison, standalone concentrators and other types of hubs that provide network management support typically require the use of a separate personal computer to initiate network management operations.

## Advantages of use

In our introductory discussion of hubs, we alluded to a few of the advantages of their use. Now let us focus in some detail upon the advantages obtained from the use of hubs by examining the capabilities obtained through the use of different hub configurations. In our discussion of the use of different hub configurations, we will actually refer to the use of intelligent hubs. Thus, we should first differentiate between intelligent and non-intelligent hubs.

### Intelligent vs. non-intelligent hubs

An intelligent hub can be considered as a hub with a built-in microprocessor designed to perform certain predefined functions. Those functions may include recognizing commands to turn ports on and off, obtaining statistics concerning the utilization level of different ports, displaying those statistics and the status of defined ports or groups of ports, permitting network traffic to be viewed from a control console, and facilitating diagnostic testing, among other functions. In addition, certain types of intelligent hubs provide the ability to integrate different types of local area networks due to their ability to support the use of bridge and router modules. Thus, the modern intelligent hub can be considered a building block for the construction of an Enterprise network.

### Single hub/single LAN

The use of a single hub to support the connectivity requirements of users on a single LAN probably represents one of the most common types of hub applications. In using the term 'hub' readers should note that we are now excluding a passive MAU from consideration. Thus, for the remainder of this chapter, we will restrict our use of the term 'hub' to represent an intelligent device with a built-in microprocessor capable of responding to predefined commands. For simplicity, we will reference the intelligent hub as a hub; however, our discussion is also applicable to an intelligent concentrator.

The top portion of Figure 9.2 illustrates from a physical perspective the use of a 10-module hub to establish a four-station Token-Ring network. Here, the remaining six modules can be used to expand the network, provide spare connections, and connect test equipment or a network management console to the network. The lower portion of Figure 9.2 illustrates a logical view of the Token-Ring network established through the use of the hub. So far, this is no different than the results obtained from the use of a dumb MAU, so you may be inquisitive as to the advantages you can obtain through the use of intelligent hubs.

Physical view

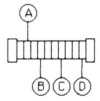

Logical view

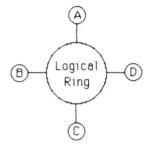

**Figure 9.2** Single hub/single LAN configuration.

With most intelligent hubs, you can turn port traffic on and off with the simple click of a mouse, drag icons representing stations to reposition devices on a ring, or remove a station from the ring for testing without disrupting traffic from stations remaining on the ring.

Figure 9.3 illustrates the physical and logical view with respect to the use of an intelligent hub to isolate station D from the Token-Ring and test the adapter board in that station without disrupting traffic on the network. Note that in comparing Figure 9.3 with Figure 9.2, the use of an intelligent hub enables test equipment to be cabled to any available port module on the hub. Then, the intelligent hub enables the user to create a test ring which is used to connect test equipment to the station to be tested. This capability to separate one network into two or more logical segments is obtained from the ability of the backplane of the hub to transfer data at a significant order

Physical view

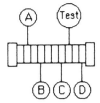

Logical view

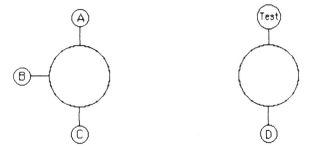

**Figure 9.3** Token-Ring testing. Many intelligent hubs permit users to logically subdivide the network, enabling test equipment to be used without adversely affecting the operation of stations not being tested.

of magnitude beyond the data rate of a LAN. This enables the creation of two or more 'separate' LANs within the hub by the multiplexing of separate LAN transmissions by time.

The ability of intelligent hubs to generate network statistics and segment a Token-Ring network into multiple rings provides LAN administrators and network managers with a powerful performance tool. When network utilization increases to the point where token rotation time becomes excessive, you will more than likely use an intelligent hub to segment an existing network. Doing so provides you with the ability to load balance traffic between workstations as well as from workstations to one or more servers.

## Multiple hubs/single LAN

Figure 9.4 illustrates how an intelligent hub can be used to segment a saturated Token-Ring network. The top portion of that illustration shows the physical view of the use of multiple hubs which may be necessary to obtain the number of ports required to construct a large Token-Ring network. In this example, it was assumed that each hub module is capable of supporting four ports. Thus, the interconnection of two 10-module hubs permits up to 40 devices to be connected to a single Token-Ring. For some hubs, the interconnection of one hub to another requires the use of a port on each hub, reducing the maximum number of devices that can be serviced by two 10-module hubs to 38.

The lower portion of Figure 9.4 illustrates the logical view of the Token-Ring network before and after the ring is segmented. In this example, it was assumed that as a result of a review of traffic statistics we decided to segment the network so that 19 stations are located on one segment and 18 stations are located on the other segment. By adding a network interface card to the server, we can connnect that device to both rings. If the server supports bridging operations, inter-ring connectivity between workstations on each ring is obtained. Otherwise, if inter-ring communications is required and the server cannot provide this capability, you can probably obtain a bridge module that can be inserted into a hub to obtain that capability.

Two additional configurations obtainable through the use of intelligent hubs that warrant discussion are single hub/multiple LAN and multiple hub/multiple LAN configurations.

Physical view

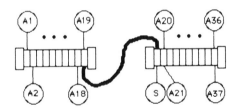

Logical view

Before segmentation          After segmentation

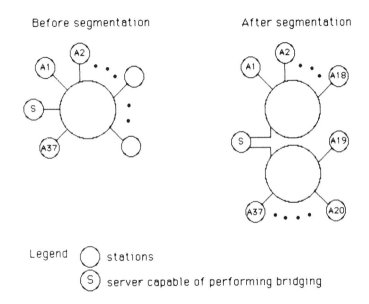

Legend ◯ stations

(S) server capable of performing bridging

**Figure 9.4** Multiple hub/multiple LAN configuration. A saturated Token-Ring LAN can be segmented into two or more networks to increase performance.

*Single hub/multiple LANs*

> Through the use of a sophisticated backplane design, most intelligent hubs support networks using different protocols, topologies, and types of wiring. When bridge and router modules are available for insertion into a hub chassis, you obtain the ability to not only support multiple LANs from a single hub, but, in addition, enable stations on one LAN to communicate with stations on another LAN that can be located hundreds or thousands of miles from the hub or within a short direct cabling distance of the hub.

The top portion of Figure 9.5 illustrates the use of a single hub to support multiple LANs from a physical perspective. The lower portion of that illustration shows the logical view in which Ethernet and Token-Ring networks are supported through a common hub. Through the use of a bridge module installed in the hub you can obtain an inter-LAN communications capability. In addition, the filtering capability built into most intelligent hubs provides you with a mechanism to control the flow of information between LANs as well as between LAN segments you may wish to create. This capability provides you with another mechanism to manage an enterprise network through the network management system of an intelligent hub.

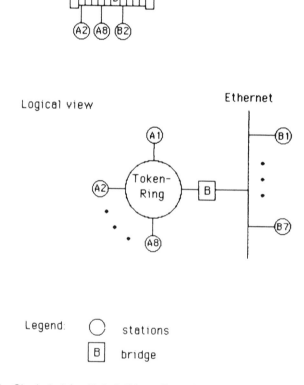

**Figure 9.5** Single hub/multiple LAN configuration.

*Multiple hubs/single LAN*

The fourth configuration obtainable through the use of intelligent hubs can be viewed as an extension of the previously discussed single hub/single LAN configuration. That is, the use of multiple hubs to construct a single LAN can provide you with alternative network testing and control locations if you locate hubs in different areas within a building or throughout a college campus. For example, you could locate an intelligent hub in the wiring closet on each floor of a building and cable each hub together to form a building-wide network. In actuality, as your network expands you will probably subdivide your network based upon the number of stations located on each floor and use bridge modules inserted in the hub to interconnect each network.

## Network management

One of the most important features of an intelligent hub is the ability of many vendor products to provide a network management capability. To obtain an appreciation for the functionality of a hub's network management capability requires us to examine the operation of a product. In doing so we can view some of the typical screens generated by a specific vendor product to obtain an appreciation for the capability and functionality of hub network management systems. In concluding this section, we will examine the Fibermux LightWatch network management system to illustrate the management capabilities of many intelligent hubs.

*Fibermux LightWatch*

The Fibermux LightWatch network management system is a window-based product which supports the point and click operations of a mouse. To illustrate its capability, let us assume our network consists of three hubs connected to one another in a triangular manner. By selecting the program's Hierarchy option, we can display our network topology as illustrated in Figure 9.6.

The Fibermux LightWatch network management system permits users to obtain a detailed physical view of each hub, including the modules installed. This is illustrated in Figure

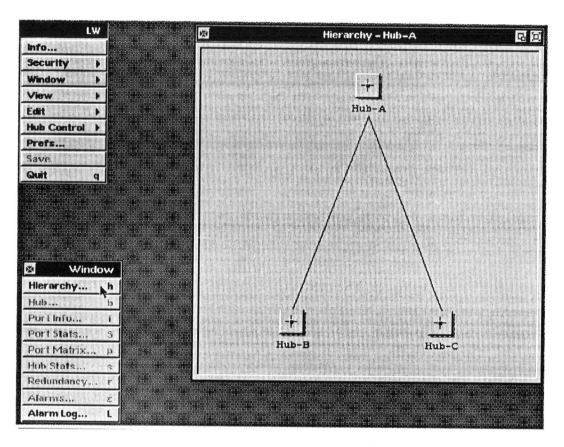

**Figure 9.6**  LightWatch network topology display obtained by selecting the hierarchy option.

9.7 which shows the physical view of hub A. Readers will note that this view immediately tells an observer that two modules are unused, represented by blank panels in the hub. Thus, a simple point and click operation can provide a wealth of information concerning the modules and capacity of each hub in our network.

**Statistics and Alarms**

One of the key features of LightWatch is its ability to generate and display a variety of statistics on both a composite hub basis as well as for individual ports on each hub. In addition, LightWatch provides users with the ability to assign thresholds to different measurements and generate alarms when those thresholds are exceeded.

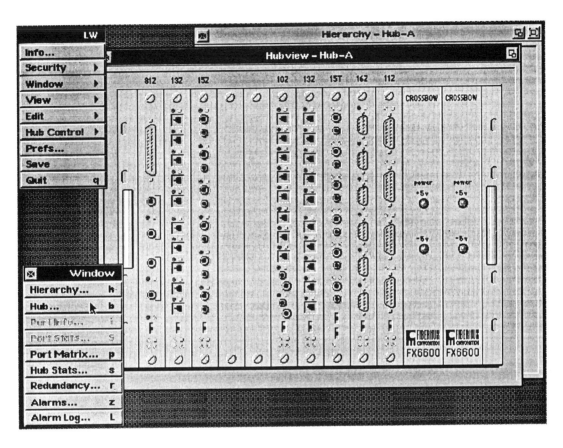

**Figure 9.7**  Viewing the physical layout of hub modules.

Figure 9.8 illustrates the port statistics display screen generated for hub A in our network. Figure 9.9 illustrates the alarm display screen for hub A. Note that the latter permits you to set the threshold values for six events as well as to assign a major or minor alarm to a threshold event when a threshold value occurs or is exceeded. By carefully monitoring the statistics generated by LightWatch, as well as by setting appropriate thresholds, you obtain the ability to enhance the control of your network to the point where you can manage the network—instead of user complaints managing your reaction to problems that can be avoided by using a network management system. Thus, intelligent hubs provide you with the ability to be proactive rather than reactive with respect to controlling your network.

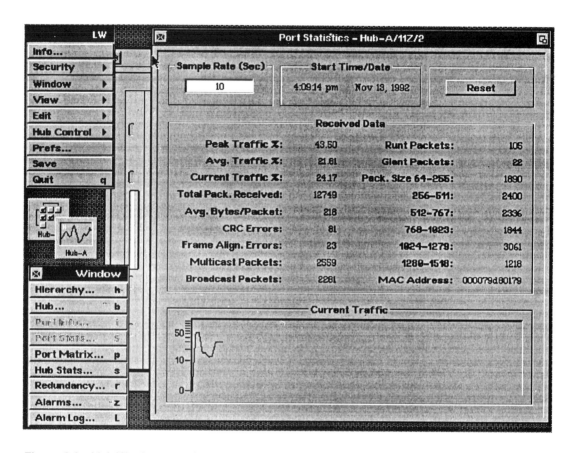

**Figure 9.8**  LightWatch port statistics screen.

## 9.2 NETWORK MANAGEMENT TOOLS

In our discussion of intelligent hubs in the first section of this chapter, we briefly examined the network management capability of a specific vendor product. In doing so our primary focus of attention was upon the use of a hub for network management and our discussion was essentially limited to the statistics and alarm generating capabilities of one product designed to work with a specific hub. In concluding this chapter, we will first expand upon our knowledge of network management by briefly examining its main functional areas and the major activities associated with each area. This will form a foundation for our examination of the use of a popular software product that can be used to perform the major activities associated with most network management functional areas.

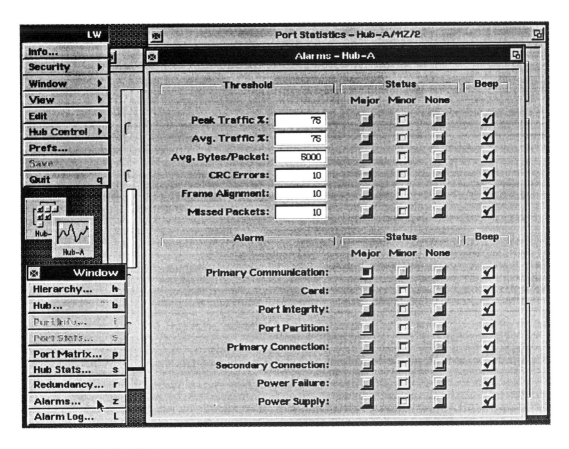

**Figure 9.9** LightWatch alarm screen.

## Network management functions

There is a core set of five functions associated with network management. Those functions include configuration, performance, fault, accounting, and security management. Within each functional area is a set of activities which each functional area manages.

Figure 9.10 illustrates the functional areas commonly associated with network management and the set of activities managed by each area.

*Configuration management*

The process of configuration management covers both the hardware and software settings required to provide an efficient and effective data transportation highway. Thus, configuration

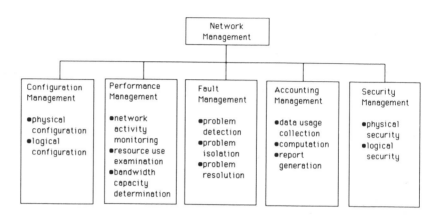

**Figure 9.10**  Network management functional areas.

management consists of managing the physical hardware, including cables, computers, and network adapters, as well as the logical network configuration governed by the installation of the network operating system, selection of a network protocol or stack of protocols, and the manner in which users can access server facilities. The last of these activities concerns the setup of the network, including permissions and routings which enable users to access different servers when a network consists of more than one server. It should be noted that this is distinct from security management, which is primarily focused upon the setting and distribution of network passwords and the assignment of file permissions. Thus, logical configuration management permits a user to reach a network facility once connected to the network, while security management involves the ability of a user to gain access to the network and into different facilities which configuration management makes reachable.

### Performance management

Performance management involves those activities required to ensure the network operates in an orderly manner, without the occurrence of unreasonable service delays. Thus, this functional area is concerned with the monitoring of network activity to ensure there are no bottlenecks that adversely affect network performance.

The monitoring of network activity can include the flow of data between stations and servers; the usage of bridges, routers, and gateways; as well as the utilization of each network segment with respect to the total capacity of each network segment. By performing these tasks, you will obtain information that will enable you to adjust the use of network hardware and software as well as consider a variety of network segmentation options that can eliminate potential network bottlenecks prior to their occurrence. Thus, performance management provides you with the ability to be proactive rather than reactive.

## Fault management

Like life, networks have their less desirable moments in which components fail, software is configured incorrectly, and other undesirable occurrences result in a variety of network associated problems. Fault management can be considered as the set of functions required to detect, isolate, and correct network problems.

Many hardware and software products are now marketed to provide a fault management capability for cables, hardware, and network software. Concerning cables, the most common type of diagnostic device is a time domain reflectometer which generates a pulse and uses its reflected time delay or absence of a reflection to isolate cable shorts and opens. LAN protocol analyzers provide you with the ability to test individual Token-Ring adapters as well as to monitor network performance and isolate certain types of network problems, such as beaconing. Both hardware-based LAN protocol analyzers as well as many software products provide a LAN frame decoding capability which enables you to obtain, via the flow of frames and frame responses, an insight into network problems, such as identifying that a station is rejecting frames due to a lack of buffer space which might easily be corrected by reconfiguring its software.

## Accounting management

Accounting management is a set of activities which enables you to determine network usage, generate usage reports, and assign costs to individuals or groups of users by organization or department within an organization. Normally, the network operating system provides a 'raw' set of network usage statistics, requiring the acquisition of one or more software packages to generate appropriate reports and assign costs to usage. While cost assignment is commonly used in wide area networks and for electronic mail usage, it is not commonly used to distribute the cost of using local area networks. Instead, accounting management is normally employed to answer such questions as 'what would be the effect upon the network if the engineering department added five new employees?' In this situation, accounting management data might provide you with network usage statistics for the engineering department, including total department usage as well as individual and average station usage data. When used in conjunction with performance monitoring, you could then determine the probable effect of the addition of new employees to the network.

## Security management

As previously discussed in our overview of configuration management, security management primarily involves the assignment of network access passwords and access permissions to applications and file storage areas on the network. Other aspects of security management can involve the physical placement of stations in areas where access to those stations is restricted as well as the selection and control of specialized hardware and software security products. Those products can range in scope from programs that can be used to encipher and decipher electronic mail messages to network modems that can be programmed to prompt users for a code when they dial into the network, disconnect the user, and then dial a number predefined as associated with the user code.

Most network management products provide excellent coverage of a subset of the five core functional areas, with few products actually covering all functional areas. Thus, most users will normally consider the use of two or more products to obtain the ability to perform all five network management functions. In the remainder of this chapter, we will examine the use of a software product marketed by Triticom of Eden Prairie, MN, which can be used to obtain the ability to manage Token-Ring networks.

## Triticom TokenVision

TokenVision is a program designed to monitor and display activity on 4- and 16-Mbps Token-Ring networks, including traffic and errors. The program has the capability to generate a number of displays while monitoring data in real time. Examples of TokenVision displays include frames transmitted by stations on the ring, network utilization, network topology, different traffic statistics, and detailed information concerning MAC frames.

*Monitoring screen display*

Figure 9.11 illustrates the TokenVision Source Address monitoring screen display which is generated by selecting the Monitoring Traffic entry from the program's main menu and then specifying whether source or destination addresses should be monitored. The top of the display screen indicates the date and time monitoring commenced. The main portion of the screen display is devoted to showing data concerning individual source or destination station addresses, according to the type of address selected. The highlighted lower area of the display shows the complete statistics for the highlighted station in the main display area, and in tandem with the movement of the highlighted bar over each station address. The lower display above the function key assignments indicates the composite monitoring results for the entire network being monitored.

By pressing the F2 key, you can toggle between the station node address being displayed in hexadecimal format, its logical name, or the vendor's ID associated with that address. For example, the addresses shown in the main portion of the screen are currently displayed based upon the hexadecimal adapter address which in most cases can be rather cryptic. The highlighted area indicates all three addresses. Pressing F5 toggles the count between frames, kbytes, percentage of all frames, average frame size, and number of frame errors. The number of frames is displayed for each station in the main portion of the screen, with the highlighted area displaying all five display options for the station highlighted in the main area.

By examining the monitoring screen, it is apparent that the station with the logical name Barney is accounting for almost 80% of monitored activity. If LAN performance was a problem (a condition we cannot directly ascertain from viewing the monitoring screen), we would obviously want to take a detailed look at the activities station Barney was performing. Perhaps that station operator continuously performed file transfers to and from the server as he did not trust having data stored

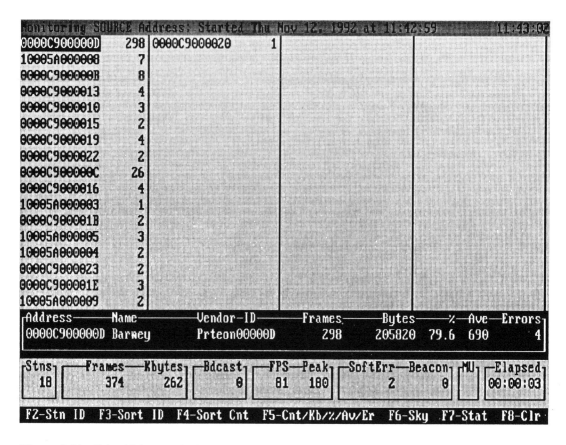

**Figure 9.11**  TokenVision monitoring screen display.

on a single device. Unknown to Barney, perhaps the LAN administrator had installed a disk server with a mirroring capability as well as performed nightly backups, reducing the probability of data storage loss below that of Harry Truman running for another term. Thus, the TokenVision display screen may provide you with the ability to note actual or potential undesirable network usage situations and initiate action to prevent such situations from adversely affecting the network.

*Skyline display screen*

We can determine network utilization by pressing the F6 key which results in a skyline display. Figure 9.12 illustrates the skyline display screen. This screen displays network utilization on a logarithmic scale by the second or minute, controlled by the

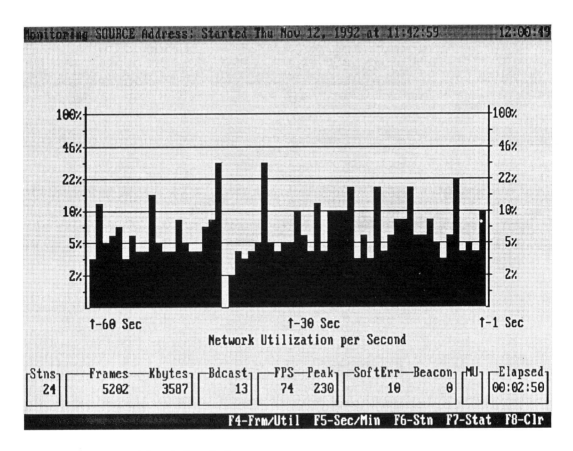

**Figure 9.12** TokenVision skyline display screen.

F5 key, for the last 60 seconds or minutes. In examining Figure 9.12, it appears that the high activity level of station Barney is not adversely affecting network performance; however, you would obviously want to monitor utilization for an extended period of time to verify this fact.

Although the TokenVision skyline display indicates network utilization as a percentage of capacity, some similar network management products developed by other vendors substitute displays on token-rotation time for network utilization. Token-rotation time is simply the time required for a token to rotate a ring and is proportional to network utilization. That is, a short token-rotation time indicates a relatively low level of LAN utilization, while a high token-rotation time indicates a relatively high level of LAN utilization. Products that use the token rotation time as a metric normally generate statistics, distributions, and graphs of this measurement metric. By providing a baseline time equated to a lack of network activity, you can use token-rotation time data to indirectly determine the load on your network. Although this is suitable for many persons, products that directly indicate network utilization are typically preferred as they eliminate end-user estimations.

*Statistics display*

By pressing the F7 key from the skyline display, you can generate a statistics display. This display, which is illustrated in Figure 9.13, provides detailed information concerning frame counts and frame size distribution, network utilization, source routing frames to include all-routes broadcast (ARB) and single-route broadcast (SRB), and the total number of hops of those frames based upon their route information field entries. The information provided by this screen can be extremely valuable in attempting to determine network performance bottlenecks due to a high level of network utilization or a large number of hops being traversed.

In the statistics display illustrated in Figure 9.13, note that the peak utilization of the network was 32% since monitoring commenced, while average utilization was computed to be 7%. Although approximately four minutes have elapsed since monitoring commenced, if those statistics remain relatively stable for a longer monitoring period, including normal peak work periods before lunch, it would indicate that your Token-Ring network has the capacity to support additional usage by existing users, additional users, or both additional usage and users prior to segmentation being required. In fact, a good rule of thumb is that little in the way of performance can be gained by subdividing a Token-Ring network unless average utilization consistently exceeds 40% and peak usage periodically exceeds 75%.

From the statistics display screen, we can select five options as indicated in the lower highlighted bar at the bottom of the display. Pressing the F4 key results in a display of the topology of our network, while pressing the F5 key results in the display of MAC statistics. Pressing the F6 key returns us to the skyline display, while pressing the F7 key returns us to the initial monitoring station display. Pressing the F8 key clears all counters, in effect, resetting the program. Due to the importance of the MAC display screen in performing fault management

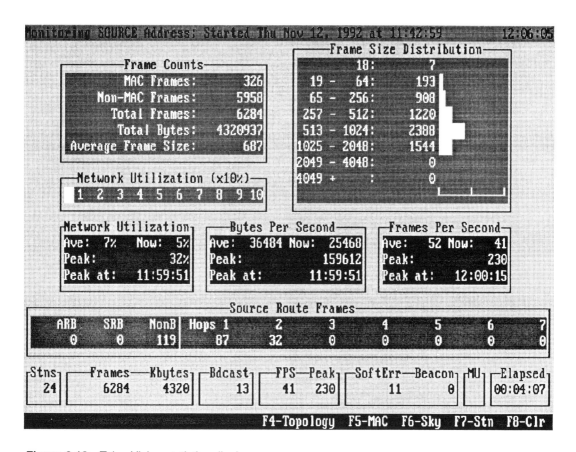

**Figure 9.13**  TokenVision statistics display.

related activities, let's press the F5 key and take a close look at the resulting screen display.

*MAC statistics display*

Figure 9.14 illustrates an example of the TokenVision MAC statistics display screen. This screen provides information concerning three categories of MAC frames—Active Monitor, Ring Recovery, and a Soft Error Report.

The active monitor frames that can be displayed include Active Monitor Present, Active Monitor Error, and Neighbor Notification Incomplete (Neighbr Ntf Inc). The Active Monitor Present frame is transmitted every seven seconds and causes each station on the network other than the active monitor to generate a Standby Monitor Present frame. Thus, every seven seconds the frame counts for all active stations should increase

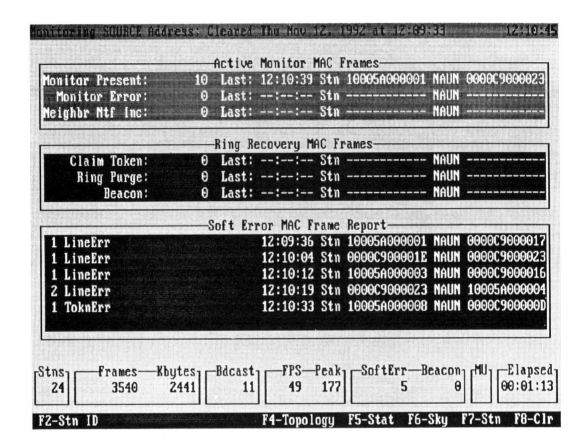

**Figure 9.14** TokenVision MAC statistics display screen.

by one if you are monitoring the source address and view TokenVision's Monitor Traffic display. The Active Monitor Error frame is transmitted by the active monitor upon receipt of a Ring Purge or a Claim Token frame, or an Active Monitor Present frame it did not generate. This error frame is also transmitted by a network station if it receives a Claim Token frame with its source address but a different nearest active upstream neighbor (NAUN) while in a claim token transmit mode. The Neighbor Notification Incomplete frame is sent by the active monitor when its neighbor notification timer expires prior to the completion of the neighbor notification process. When this frame occurs it usually indicates a problem with another adapter's ability to participate in the neighbor notification process and can be ascertained by determining which station's frame count does not increment every seven seconds.

The Soft Error MAC frame report summarizes the types of soft error. Those errors can be line errors in which a code violation in a starting or ending delimiter or FCS error was detected, an internal error in which a station recognizes a recoverable internal error, a burst error in which a station detects the absence of Differential Manchester signaling transitions for 5 half-bit time, an A/C error in which a station receives a Standby Monitor Present frame without receiving an Active Monitor Present frame, an abort delimiter in which a station transmits an abort token, as well as several additional types of errors involving receiver congestion, frame copying, and a token error. Prior to examining how we can use the soft error report, let us review what this type of error references and how such errors occur.

A soft error is an intermittent error which adversely affects network performance on a cumulative basis as those errors increase. In a Token-Ring network, we can have two types of soft errors—those that are expected to occur since they are generated by stations entering or exiting the ring and errors that occur due to abnormal conditions. The first type of soft error is known as a normal soft error, while the second type of soft error is commonly referred to as an abnormal soft error.

**Normal Soft Errors**

As previously discussed in this book, a Token-Ring adapter generates a voltage to a MAU port upon its insertion into the ring. That voltage opens a relay, which causes a momentary disruption to communications since the station lacks the ability to immediately synchronize itself to the Differential Manchester signal flowing on the network. For a period that can be up to 5 milliseconds in duration, network communications will be disrupted until the inserted adapter acquires the clocking from the signal and is then able to correctly participate on the network. A similar but not identical situation occurs when a station exits the ring, causing the lack of voltage to a port on the MAU to close the relay and cause another short break in communications to occur.

The insertion and exiting of stations can cause several types of normal soft errors. Those errors include token errors, lost or corrupted frames, and line errors.

*Token errors*

Token errors normally occur as a result of a station insertion or exit corrupting the token. Due to the difference between the operating rate of the ring and the time required for insertion or station exit you can expect up to two token errors for each occurrence of a station insertion or exit. Thus, as computers are powered on and off you can expect to periodically encounter token errors.

### Lost and corrupted frames

Based upon the duration of the insertion or exit process, it is quite possible for a frame to reach a MAU port just as the relay is being opened or closed, resulting in the frame becoming lost to the network. If the insertion or exit event occurs after the beginning of the token passed the appropriate MAU port, the frame can be expected to become corrupted as part of it may become distorted or lost. Although less common than token errors, you can expect up to one frame corruption or frame loss for the occurrence of each station insertion or exit event. Thus, you can expect to observe a small number of FCS errors due to corrupted frames resulting from station insertions and exit operations during the day.

### Line errors

The third type of a normal soft error is a line error. These errors are reported by the first station to repeat or copy a corrupted token or frame. Although a line error more than likely indicates a normal software error condition, a series of line errors generated by the same station may indicate an intermittent adapter problem.

**Abnormal Soft Errors**

Unlike normal soft errors that can be anticipated to occur based upon station insertions and exits, abnormal soft errors are random in nature. In general, an abnormal soft error is far more serious than a normal soft error due to its potential effect upon network performance. Examples of abnormal soft errors include internal, burst, A/C, frame copied, and frequency errors, as well as the occurrence of an abort delimiter and receiver congestion condition.

*Internal errors*

An internal error is generated by a station's adapter when it is in a marginal operating condition. Thus, a large number of internal errors associated with one station would indicate that the station's adapter requires replacement.

*Burst errors*

Burst errors result from electronic noise that can be generated by equipment and machinery. Since the length of a cable is proportional to its ability to serve as an antenna, burst errors often indicate an excessive main ring path or lobe connection or the routing of the cable near a source of electronic noise. By examining the station address and its NAUN you can isolate the cable in which burst errors are occurring and then investigate the movement of the cable away from machinery or its rerouting and shortening to reduce its ability to function as an antenna.

*Frame copied error*

A frame copied error occurs when a station copies a frame that was previously copied by another station. This situation will not occur if you are using IBM's LAN Manager which normally prevents duplicate locally administered network addresses. Otherwise, this situation typically indicates that two or more stations on the network have the same address. Thus, the occurrence of frame copied errors should serve as a signal to examine your locally administered address assignments.

*Frequency errors*

The frequency error results from the detection of a non J or K Differential Manchester signaling violation by a workstation. Such violations in many instances can be traced to electromagnetic interference or an excessive cable length.

*Abort delimiter*

The abort delimiter token is transmitted by a station under two conditions. If a transient error occurred within the station and the station can recover, it will generate an abort token. This informs the network to cancel the previously transmitted frame as that frame may be in error. If the station has a hard error from which it cannot recover, it will also transmit an abort token prior to disconnecting itself from the network. Thus, an abort token can indicate an intermittent or hard station failure.

*Receiver congestion errors*

One of the more interesting types of soft errors is a receiver congestion error. This error indicates that a station recognized a frame addressed to it but has no buffer space available for the frame. This condition may indicate that a station with a low-performance adapter is receiving a file transfer initiated by a station with a high-performance adapter. It may also indicate that the configuration of the Token-Ring adapter requires adjustment. For example, a station receiving a file transfer with only 8 or 16 kbytes of adapter memory reserved for memory paging would be hard pressed to keep up with a bus mastering adapter using 64 kbytes of memory to place data onto the ring. By using the entries in the MAC statistics display, you can often isolate network problems to a specific station which then permits corrective action to be initiated to resolve the problem.

**Alarms**

If you are like most persons, nothing is more boring than sitting in front of a display waiting for a condition to occur. TokenVision is similar to most hardware-based LAN analyzers in that it provides you with the ability to set a variety of alarm thresholds which will audibly alert you when a threshold is reached or an enabled condition occurs.

Figure 9.15 illustrates the TokenVision Network Alarm screen display and the default values assigned by the program to several alarms.

The network idle time alarm provides you with the ability to note the occurrence of a catastrophe since each Token-Ring should have some traffic every seven seconds. When an alarm threshold is exceeded, the program will beep and display the alarm across the top of your screen in vivid red on a color monitor.

The network utilization alarm provides you with the ability to be prompted concerning the occurrence of a predefined utilization level. When prompted, you can use the monitor display to ascertain if a user or group of users is contributing to

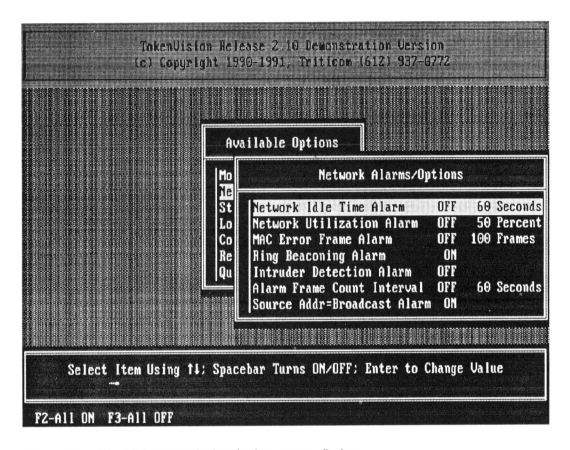

**Figure 9.15** TokenVision network alarm/options screen display.

a high level of network utilization or if the number of network users is excessive and the network requires segmentation.

The MAC error alarm can be used in conjunction with the alarm frame count interval option to trigger an alarm when the defined number of error frames occurs within the specified interval. The beaconing alarm is simply toggled between ON and OFF and when ON alerts you to the distress signal generated by a station that detects a signal loss. The last alarm TokenVision can generate is the intruder detection. This alarm is triggered in response to a new station entering the network that has not been predefined to the program. Thus, you can use this alarm to sense unauthorized addresses or address changes.

As indicated by our short review of TokenVision, its use permits you to perform most of the major functions associated with network management. Regardless of the management tool you use you should always ensure you have a management tool available for use. The periodic use of an appropriate network management tool provides you with a detailed view of network activity that can be invaluable in performing your network management functions.

# INDEX

*Index compiled by Dr. M. P. M. Merrington*

# LOCAL AREA NETWORKING

## PROTECTING LAN RESOURCES
### A Comprehensive Guide to Securing, Protecting and Rebuilding a Network

With the evolution of distributed computing, security is now a key issue for network users. This comprehensive guide will provide network managers and users with a detailed knowledge of the techniques and tools they can use to secure their data against unauthorised users. Gil Held also provides guidance on how to prevent disasters such as self-corruption of data and computer viruses.

**1995   0  471  95407  1**

## LAN PERFORMANCE
### Issues and Answers

The performance of LANs depends upon a large number of variables, including the access method, the media and cable length, the bridging and the gateway methods. This text covers all these variables to enable the reader to select and design equipment for reliability and high performance.

**1994   0  471  94223  5**

## TOKEN- RING NETWORKS
### Characteristics, Operation, Construction and Management

This timely book provides the reader with a comprehensive understanding of how Token-Ring networks operate, the constraints and performance issues that affect their implementation, and how their growth and use can be managed both locally and as part of an Enterprise network.

**1993   0  471  94041  0**

## ETHERNET NETWORKS
### Design, Implementation, Operation, and Management

**1994   0  471  59717  1**

# REFERENCE

## DICTIONARY OF COMMUNICATIONS TECHNOLOGY
### Terms, Definitions and Abbreviations

**1995   0  471  95126  9 (Paper)**
**          0  471  95542  6 (Cloth)**

## THE COMPLETE MODEM REFERENCE
### 2nd Edition

**1994   0  471  00852  4**

## THE COMPLETE PC AT AND COMPATIBLES REFERENCE MANUAL

**1991   0  471  53315  7**